The
Creative Process

The
Creative Process

Reflections on Invention in the Arts and Sciences

Edited and with an Introduction By
BREWSTER GHISELIN

TRANSFORMATIONAL BOOK CIRCLE
Studio City, California

Published by: Transformational Book Circle
12711 Ventura Blvd., Suite, 330 Studio City, CA 91604
866-288-4469 (customer service) • 866-300-4386 (orders)
www.transformationalbookcircle.com • info@transformationalbookcircle.com

ISBN 10: 1-56861-229-X

08 07 06 05 4 3 2 1
1st Printing, August 2005

To Jon and Michael
And, as an afterthought, to the man from Porlock

Prefatory Note

Some of the selections in this anthology are intact, some are excerpts drawn from contexts of less pertinent material, and some have been more or less reduced by excisions, mainly as a means of conserving space but sometimes in order to remove material not essential to the purpose of this book. Omission of material has been indicated by use of ellipsis periods in the text. In editing such passages, it has not always been possible to preserve the full esthetic integrity of the original, but utmost care has been exercised in preserving the import. B.G.

CONTENTS

Acknowledgments

My thanks are due the publishers of the following works for their courtesy in permitting me to make brief quotations in my Introduction.

The Macmillan Company, New York City, publishers of *Science and the Modern World,* by Alfred North Whitehead, 1925; and "Introduction," by T. S. Eliot in *Selected Poems,* by Marianne Moore, 1935.

Houghton Mifflin Company, Boston and New York City, publishers of *The Road to Xanadu,* by John Livingston Lowes, 1930.

Cassell & Co., Ltd., London, and Doubleday & Co., New York City, publishers of *The Life and Letters of Anton Tchekhov,* translated and edited by S. S. Koteliansky and Philip Tomlinson.

Charles Scribner's Sons, New York City, publishers of T*he Ambassadors,* by Henry James, 1922, and The American, by Henry James, 1922.

De Spieghel Ltd., Amsterdam, publishers of *Introductory Essay on van Gogh's Art,* in *Vincent van Gogh's Great Period,* by W. Scherjon and Jos. De Gruyter, 1937.

Alfred A. Knopf, Incorporated, New York City, publishers of *Joseph and His Brothers,* by Thomas Mann, copyright 1934

J. M. Dent & Sons, London, publishers of *Lord Jim,* by Joseph Conrad.

FOREWORD

When *The Creative Process* was published, in 1952, the matter it explores had excited scarcely any general interest. The book had been rejected by several publishers on the ground that a work so special in appeal could not sell enough to cover costs of production. Since then it has been continually in print. It has been a constant resource for innovative workers in the sciences and the arts, and while providing information of more general application it continues to be widely cited by specialists in research. The breadth of its relevance is suggested in a remark of Abraham H. Maslow, addressing a symposium of psychologists and other scientists in 1958, when he was Professor of Psychology and Chairman of the Department at Brandeis University: "I assure you that it was a startling thing for me to hear a woman describing her feelings as she gave birth to a child in the same words used by Bucke (1923) to describe the 'cosmic' consciousness' or by Huxley to describe the 'mystic' experience' in all cultures and eras or by Ghiselin to describe the creative process or by Suzuki to describe the Zen satori experience."

However far-reaching in some of its implications the book may be, it is severely practical in intent. The Introduction has been shaped to lead easily through concrete advances toward secure comprehension. With exact evidence and with supportive citations, it arbitrates divergent views, to provide in synthesis of insights a general perspective--not to be accepted without question but to be tested in close consideration of representations put forward by individual commentators, some of whom will be found to be more dependable than others.

One matter only, in the Introduction, calls for specific remark: the treatment there, with intimated reservations, of the idea of the unconscious mind. Long before preparing my Introduction I had welcomed C. G. Jung's admission, in his book *Psychology and Religion* (1938), that "As a matter of fact the concept of the unconscious mind is a mere assumption for the sake of convenience." In 1952 I was foreshaping demonstrations, subsequently published, of how overconfidence in theoretical assurance, such as that provided by the concept of a psychic agent elaborating insights in darkness, can preclude further discovery that might reward vigorous scrutiny of what is actually occurring, unattended and unsearched.

The possibility of revisions for this new paperback edition of *The Creative Process* was strictly considered, and rejected. The view of creativity developed in the Introduction has not been superseded. The statements constituting the body of the book remain unimpaired in pertinence, in the force with which-taken together-they illuminate the subject while qualifying one another. They sustain the idea predominant in the Introduction, that "the creative process…in the arts and in thought is a part of the invention of life…essentially a single process," understandable both in its elements and in its unity of function.

INTRODUCTION

Interest in the creative process is not exactly a new development. A story told of the working habits of Euripides may be apocryphal; but both Plato and Aristotle had something to say of the creative process, and from time to time during the next two thousand years other writers touched upon it. Early in the nineteenth century interest in it increased. Blake, Wordsworth, Coleridge, Shelley, and Keats all had their say. Poe's *Philosophy of Composition* became an incitement to further attention. Interest in the subject is still growing.

Besides a good deal of objective discussion of the creative process, chiefly by philosophers, psychologists, and other scientists, a large amount of comment and description of individual processes and insights has accumulated, most of it fragmentary, some of it not perfectly reliable. Among these materials the most illuminating and entertaining are the more full and systematic descriptions of invention and the reflections upon it made by the men and women most in position to observe and understand, the thinkers and artists themselves. Perhaps the greatest body of such writing is the monumental work of Henry James, the prefaces to the New York edition of his work.

Some of the reasons for attention to the creative process are practical. One incentive for compiling this anthology, a selection of some of the more revealing discussions of invention, is that insight into the processes of invention can increase the efficiency of almost any developed and active intelligence. Not even the most vigorously creative minds always find their way quickly to efficiency. Yet many creative workers have little knowledge of the pertinent materials and would not know where to look for them. Some of the richest and most useful are scattered and out-of-the-way. There is, moreover, no large collection of statements about the creative process that is much more than a compendium of fragments. It has therefore seemed worth while to bring together some of the longer and more complete source materials, exhibiting a fairly full range of methods in the various fields of activity. Having read through such a selection of writings one will not simply have observed the fundamentals, which are all but inescapable. one should have acquired a sense of the bearing of these fundamentals, a feeling for the whole process, and a lively sense of the divergencies of individual approach and procedure.

Today, when widespread, deep, and rapid changes are taking place in the very structure of our lives, whether we desire it or not, and when still other changes seem necessary to preserve us from disaster, understanding of the creative process is particularly important because it can assist in the control of these difficult developments. The creative process is the process of change, of development, of evolution, in the organization of subjective life. The inventive minds through whose activity that evolution has been initiated and in large part accomplished have usually been the only ones much concerned with it. Their efforts have rarely been sustained by society, and have sometimes even been hindered. There is little comfort in reflecting that vital change has gone on despite all opposition or indifference, that the work of Galileo was done and put to use in spite of obstruction and that Bartok composed a great deal of music while enduring the neglect that left him in sickening poverty. There is no way of estimating how much the development of humanity has been lamed by such delay and waste. Simply the self-interest of mankind calls for a more general effort to foster the invention of life. And that effort can be guided intelligently only by insight into the nature of the creative process. Understanding the activities of those who supply the needs of life, both their own and others', by defining some fresh organization of subjective processes, we may help them to get their work done. Opening our minds to their insights and putting them to what use they may have, we may assist in the creative process, which completes itself only as the products of invention transform the environment the inventor breathes.

The human mind is prepared to wrap the whole planet in a shroud, and the exercise of all our best effort and ingenuity has produced no assurance whatever that it will be deterred from that end. The prolonged failure of traditional means in dealing with this problem does not prove those means useless. It does strongly suggest their inadequacy. For, as knowledge of the creative process drives us to conclude, although a problem which stubbornly resists solution by traditional means may perhaps be insoluble, the probability is rather that those means are themselves inadequate: the concepts, attitudes, and procedures employed are probably at fault and in need of being transcended in a fresh approach. The only reasonable step, at this point, then, is to act upon the supposition that our problems in world crisis, as at other times, may be soluble only creatively-that is, by a profound and thorough alteration of our inner life and of the outer forms in which life finds expression and support. Certainly some changes are requisite. The necessary change, if it comes at all, may have to be so quick and sharp an evolution as to seem revolutionary. If it does not come soon, if the limiting forms of our consciousness, the sometimes too-rigid patterns of current thought and feeling, are not shaped quickly to meet the needs of life, there is grave danger that they will simply continue to possess us until too late.

One might suppose it easy to detect creative talent and to recognize creative impulse and creative work. But the difficulties are considerable. Because every creative act overpasses the established order in some way and in some degree, it is likely at first to appear eccentric to most men. An inventor ordinarily must begin in isolation and draw the group to himself only as it is discovered, sometimes very slowly, that he has invented some part of what they are in need of. At the beginning of his struggle for realization his originality may achieve no more striking manifestation than an extreme dissatisfaction with established order.

Vincent van Gogh must have felt some such dissatisfaction when in 1880 he wrote to his brother Theo about his feeling that he was one of those men who are somehow mysteriously imprisoned: "Prisoners in an I-don't-know-what-for horrible, horrible, utterly horrible cage." As we know, the trouble was not that van Gogh was incapable of action. it was rather that he had not found that expression of his impulses which would satisfy him. He writes further of "the man who is doomed to remain idle, whose heart is eaten out by an anguish for work, but who does nothing because it is impossible for him to do anything, because he is as it were imprisoned in something. Because he hasn't got just that which he needs in order to be creative. Because the fate of circumstances has reduced him to a state of nothingness. Such a man often doesn't know himself what he might do, but he feels instinctively: yet am I good for something, yet am I aware of some reason for existing! I know that I might be a totally different man! How then can I be useful, how can I be of service! Something is alive in me: What can it be!"

How are we to differentiate this expression of the artist's sense of his unrealized possibilities from the petulance of incapacity dissatisfied with its lot? There seems no immediate way to do so. The criterion is the proof of production by the artist, if he is able to find himself. But I suspect that he does not always find himself, that he may look in the end like nothing more than an ineffectual misfit.

Van Gogh's uncertainty as to what he might be is typical. The inventor, whether artist or thinker, creates the structure of his psychic life by means of his works. As C. G. Jung remarks: "The work in process becomes the poet's fate and determines his psychic development. It is not Goethe who creates Faust, but Faust which creates Goethe." Yet it is only as the work is done that the meaning of the creative effort can appear and that the development of the artist brought about by it is attained. This is why the creative urge may be at first so extremely vague as hardly to identify itself. The terms of its expression are not to be found in the world, but must be invented: The simplest terms of the new order have yet to be discovered and made explicit.

Even to the creator himself, the earliest effort may seem to involve a commerce with disorder. For the creative order, which is an extension of life, is not an elaboration of the established, but a movement beyond the established, or at the least a reorganization of it and often of elements not included in it. The first need is therefore to transcend the old order. Before any new order can be defined, the absolute power of the established, the hold upon us of what we know and are, must be broken. New life comes always from outside our world, as we commonly conceive that world. This is the reason why, in order to invent, one must yield to the indeterminate within him, or, more precisely, to certain ill-defined impulses which seem to be of the very texture of the ungoverned fullness. John Livingston Lowes calls it "the surging chaos of the unexpressed."

Chaos and disorder are perhaps the wrong terms for that indeterminate fullness and activity of the inner life. For it is organic, dynamic, full of tension and tendency. What is absent from it, except in the decisive act of creation, is determination, fixity, any commitment to one resolution or another of the whole complex of its tensions. It is a working sea of indecision, like the soul of a woman making up her mind. But if it were altogether without order of some kind it would be without life.

Creation begins typically with a vague, even a confused excitement, some sort of yearning, hunch, or other preverbal intimation of approaching or potential resolution. Stephen Spender's expression is exact: "A dim cloud of an idea which I feel must be condensed into a shower of words." Alfred North Whitehead speaks of "the state of imaginative muddled suspense which precedes successful inductive generalization," and there is much other testimony to the same effect. In some invention there is consciousness of a stage yet more primitive, a condition of complete indecision—in the words of Isadora Duncan, "a state of complete suspense"—in which nothing tends toward determination, nothing of a particular character seems to be implied, in which, therefore, all is still apparently free. It is alike for thinker and artist the offering of adventure, but adventure nameless and featureless, which shall be defined by something not even in the periphery of consciousness, but rather implicit in the whole spread of the subjective life. This state in no way involves or suggests irresolution. Paradoxically it often appears as an enhancement of certainty. It is as if the mind delivered from preoccupation with particulars were given into secure possession of its whole substance and activity. This yielding to the oceanic consciousness may be a distracting delight, which as Jacques Maritain has pointed out can divert the worker from formal achievement. In this extreme the experience verges upon the religious; but it is rarely so intense or so pure, and, when it is, it is not often so enduring a preoccupation as to constitute a real threat to performance. More often it defines itself as no more than a sense of self-surrender to an inward necessity inherent in something larger than the ego and taking precedence over the established order.

Frequently the creative worker experiences first neither this sheer readiness for the new nor that vague presentiment of some novel development felt to be specific but as yet undefined. The invention may appear spontaneously and without apparent preliminaries, sometimes in the form of a mere glimpse serving as a clue, or like a germ to be developed; sometimes a fragment of the whole, whether rudimentary and requiring to be worked into shape or already in its final form; sometimes essentially complete, though needing expansion, verification, or the like. The mathematician Jacques Hadamard records that "On being very abruptly awakened by an external noise, a solution long searched for appeared to me at once without the slightest instant of reflection on my part—the fact was remarkable enough to have struck me unforgettably—and in a quite different direction from any of those which I had previously tried to follow." Spontaneous appearance of inventions very fully formed is not extremely rare, but it is by no means ordinary. Spontaneity is common, but what is given is usually far from complete. Commonly the new element appears simultaneously with some such vague intimation of further development as I have described.

Production by a process of purely conscious calculation seems never to occur. Though Poe laid claim to it, his singular testimony is not enough to establish it as a fact. It cannot and ought not to be rejected as impossible, but it does not fit the facts reported almost universally and in every field of creative work. Not only Shelley, Blake, Ernst, Henry James and many other artists of great note or of little have described some considerable part of their invention as entirely spontaneous and involuntary-that is, as automatic. Invention automatic in this sense is claimed also by a variety of intellectual workers, such as Spencer, Nietzsche, Sir W. Rowan Hamilton, and C. F. Gauss. More or less of such automatism is reported by nearly every worker who has much to say about his processes, and no creative process has been demonstrated to be wholly free from it.

Anton Chekhov has insisted that only a lunatic would create quite automatically: "... To deny that artistic creation involves problems and purposes would be to admit that an artist creates without premeditation, without design, under a spell. Therefore if an artist boasted to me of having written a story without a previously settled design, but by inspiration, I should call him a lunatic." But this is rather a protest against the view that completely automatic production is normal than an attempt to rule out all automatism whatever in normal invention.

Automatism appears to be fundamental in the activity which Henri Poincaré observed on the notable occasion when having drunk coffee. He lay unable to sleep and became a spectator of some ordinarily hidden aspects of his own spontaneous creative activity: "Ideas rose in crowds; I felt them collide until pairs interlocked, so to speak, making a stable combination. By the next morning I had established the existence of a class of Fuchsian functions, those which come from the hypergeometric series; I had only to write out the results, which took but a few hours." Though Poincaré was conscious, he did not assume direction of his creative activity at the stage described; and as it seems to have been a sort of activity not susceptible of conscious control, apparently he could not have done so. If he is right in supposing that what he witnessed was typical of processes ordinarily subliminal, then some part of his creative process—a classical example—was automatic.

Another worker likewise of highly developed intellect, but in another field, has reported somewhat similar observations of automatic production going on under the fully wakeful eye of consciousness. In his preface to *The Ambassadors,* Henry James records some conscious production so smooth and inevitable as to suggest an unconscious, wholly automatic development if consciousness had not fully operated: "...The steps, for my fable, placed themselves with a prompt and, as it were, functional assurance—an air quite as of readiness to have dispensed with logic had I been in fact too stupid for my clue." That much did happen quite automatically, though with the assent of his judgment, becomes apparent as he continues: "Never, positively, none the less, as the links multiplied, had I felt less stupid than for the determination of poor Strether's errand and for the apprehension of his issue. These things continued to fall together, as by the neat action of their own weight and form, even while their commentator scratched his head about them; he easily sees now that they were always well in advance of him. As the case completed itself he had in fact, from a good way behind, to catch up with them, breathless and a little flurried, as he best could."

From this account of spontaneous and involuntary production in a state of heightened awareness, it would appear that automatic invention, far from being a sign of diminished, imperfectly functioning consciousness, is a healthy activity supplementary to conscious invention and in no way inconsistent with it. The automatic functioning in invention is, rather than an inferior or suspect substitute (or an exalted one), an extension of activity beyond the limited scope of that which is shaped by insight, the conscious activity, which is an observant adjustment of exactly appreciated means to known ends. Something beyond the fully observable conscious construction takes place, to the advantage of consciousness, or of the consciousness able to make use of it.

The notion that automatic and conscious production are somehow opposed is not altogether groundless, however. The constructive nature of the automatic functioning argues the existence of an activity analogous to consciousness though hidden from observation, and we have therefore termed it unconscious. The negative prefix suggests an opposition, but it is no more than verbal, not any sort of hostility or incompatibility being implied by it, but simply the absence of consciousness. Yet a real opposition between the conscious and the unconscious activity does subsist in the limitations which the former tends to impose on the latter. The established possessions of consciousness have a way of persisting, particularly when they are part of a scheme, and of determining behavior, including a large part of that which is unconscious or imperfectly conscious. If this were not so our psychic lives would of course have little stability.

But this conservative tendency hinders the introduction of anything fundamentally new. The first impulse toward new order in the psychic life is therefore, as it must be, an impulse away from the clearly determined, from all that is most easily attended to and that most forcefully imprints itself upon the attention. That is, it is an impulse away from the conscious activity already in motion or potential, which would simply reduce it to itself. In the sense of this aversion, it is an impulse toward unconsciousness. This is the real opposition to which I have referred, this reaction against one another of the old order which is more or less readily realizable in the focus of attention and the potential new order developing, and often competing against it, in obscurity. It is not the two activities which are opposed, the conscious and the unconscious, but the principles acting in them.

The opposition is often dramatized in objective situations, as when van Gogh agonizes in a morbid inactivity because none of the current ways of expression can give issue to the nameless life within him for which he has not yet found a path. As long as he tries to move in the old ways, he is frustrated. For the emphasis of desire falls upon the unrealized rather than on the explicit elements in his psychic life.

Even when an artist has found his way, the opposition between the new and the old persists, for the unrealized continues to draw him. This is true also of the scientist and creative man of action, of all inventors, who may be said to be a restless group. It has been pointed out by Jacques Hadamard that the more vigorous creative minds among the scientists are often inclined to drop a project when the less inventive begin to swarm upon it, and to go on to something fresh. Artists do this too. So Ezra Pound abandoned Imagism and other movements. Pablo Picasso creates movements but does not lead them.

The nature of this restlessness is well defined by Thomas Mann near the end of the meditations which introduce his story of Joseph: "As for me, who now draw my narrative to a close, to plunge, voluntarily, into limitless adventure (the word 'plunge' being used advisedly), I will not conceal my native and comprehensive understanding of the old man's restless unease and dislike of any fixed habitation. For do I not know the feeling? To me too has not unrest been ordained, have not I too been endowed with a heart which knoweth not repose? The story-teller's star-is it not the moon, lord of the road, the wanderer, who moves in his stations, one after another, freeing himself from each? For the storyteller makes many a station, roving and relating, but pauses only tentwise, awaiting further directions, and soon feels his heart beating high, partly with desire, partly too from fear and anguish of the flesh, but in any case as a sign that he must take the road, towards fresh adventures which are to be painstakingly lived through, down to their remotest details, according to the restless spirit's will."

The restlessness of the inventor is unending because he is adept in realization, he has an inordinate appetite for discovery and the ability to satisfy it. He is often a specialist, with less psychic inertia than the average man, and, sometimes, with less stability. But he is not inclined, as some imagine, to mere wandering, to dizzy excursions away from the determinate. He is not a tramp. He is drawn by the unrealized toward realization. His job is, as Wordsworth says, "The widening the sphere of human sensibility,...the introduction of a new element into the intellectual universe." He works toward clarification, toward consciousness.

That opposition between the conscious and the unconscious activities in creation which we have noticed is only superficial, or rather is only initial. The new order which creation is concerned with has an affinity for consciousness.

But because any new movement of the psychic life can find its freedom only outside consciousness, or at least in some degree of disassociation from consciousness, it has always at first the aspect of adventurous departure from the known, in so far as it has any aspects of which we can be aware, in so far as it is not altogether subliminal. This casting loose the ties of security requires courage and understanding. It requires some courage to move alone, often counter to popular prepossessions, and toward uncertainties. And to move free of the established requires the understanding that the established is not absolute, but is only the instrumentality of life, is justified only by the service it renders to life, and has no meaning apart from vital needs.

The faithful formalist has no chance of creating anything. Hence a certain amount of eccentricity, some excess, taint, or "tykeishness" is often prized by creative minds as a guarantee of ability to move apart or aside, outside. Drugs or alcohol are sometimes used to produce abnormal states to the same end of disrupting the habitual set of the mind, but they are of dubious value, apart from the dangers of addiction, since their action reduces judgment, and the activities they provoke are hallucinatory rather than illuminating. What is needed is control and direction.

For the desirable end is not the refreshment of escape into whatever novelty may chance to offer or impose itself, but the discovery of some novelty needed to augment or supplant the existing possessions of the mind. This is as true of invention in the arts and in pure science as it is of the so-called practical inventions the immediate use of which escapes no one. It is not always so obvious. A familiar example is furnished by the Romantic movement at about the beginning of the nineteenth century, which appeared to the unsympathetic to be something like an hysterical experiment in self-indulgence, the eccentricity of an ill-balanced, undisciplined, irresponsible crew. Some still incline to this view, but their perspective appears to be special. To others it seems clear that the movement was a vital corrective. It was a turn toward balance and wholeness, largely through resumption of interest in the particular, the individual elements of the inner and the outer life in all their variety and range. It admitted to the mind a flood of stimulating and nourishing experience that had been excluded, and it allowed a fresh examination of reality and fresh formulation of meaning and assignment of values.

In a very narrow sense, the charges brought against these initiators are valid; the Romantics were eccentric, undisciplined, and irresponsible. Certainly they were not centered upon the established order of life. They were, however, centered upon another order which they were striving to realize. Obviously they were not disciplined to sustain the established, because they would not submit to be; but they disciplined themselves to find and elaborate an order fit to supplant it. And they were not responsible to intrenched interests; yet in working and suffering to foster emergent ones, they proved their deep responsibility to life. What they achieved has been found to have, besides the novelty incidental to all invention, the specific kind of usefulness which was the consequence of their striving successfully toward a particular end.

Likewise in pure science the end is not novelty, but use. Neither in art nor in science is the use always anticipated. Application of a scientific truth to narrowly practical purposes may even never occur, and it often follows long after the discovery. But it is evident that in both art and science the inventor is to some degree incited and guided by a sense of value in the end sought, something very much like an intimation of usefulness. Jacques Hadamard has pointed out that although when the Greeks studied the ellipse they could not find any use for its properties which they discovered, their work was the necessary preliminary for some of the most important discoveries of Kepler and Newton. And he asserts on the authority of his own analogous experience that they were guided by esthetic feeling in their selection of the ellipse rather than some less fruitful matter. Other mathematicians have insisted on the importance of esthetic emotion as a guide in mathematical invention, among them Henri Poincaré, who has stated that what serves to bring certain ones (only the most useful) of all the teeming unconscious elements into the focus of the mathematician's attention is their power to affect his esthetic sensibility. In thus emphasizing the creative worker's dependence on affective guides rather than on any explicit intellectual process, the mathematicians are in essential agreement with the artists: William Butler Yeats believed that instinct led him to choose one subject rather than another; Willa Cather has said that the deeper sympathies dictate the choice. In all this it is clear that creative minds feel drawn toward specific material with which to work: the creative impulse is no mere appetite for novelty, for it is highly selective. It is so even when governed by no explicit idea of its end. The selection is evidence of an implicit end, however, to the nature of which the emotion is for a time the only clue. It is like the disturbance at the surface of the water which betokens activity beneath.

The end to be reached, then, in any creative, process, is not whatever solid or silly issue the ego or accident may decree, but some specific order urged upon the mind by something inherent in its own vital condition of being and perception, yet nowhere in view. The creative process in its unconscious action has often been compared to the growth of a child in the womb. The comparison is a good one, as it nicely communicates the important fact that the process is an organic development, and it helps to dispel the notion that creation is simply an act of canny calculation governed by wish, will, and expediency. But as the figure suggests a complete automatism, it is inapplicable to a large part of the creative process; and even in the automatic stages, those termed by Henri Poincaré "unconscious work" and "inspiration," the process is not so unconscious and sure.

The fact is that the mind in creation and in preparation for it nearly always requires some management. Most creative workers pick up what they know about this by trial and error, by casual observation of themselves and others, and from such comment as they may chance upon. The consequences of learning so haphazardly are hard to estimate, but obviously they are not always good. Joseph Conrad suffered from agonizing stoppages of work, Coleridge left masterpieces unfinished. Possibly these artists were hindered by personal defects of the sort that interfere with other activities besides invention, and they may even have been beyond help. Yet it is likely that if Coleridge had only shut the door in the face of the man "from Porlock" who interrupted the composition of "Kubla Khan," he would have been able to continue the writing. But avoiding such fatal interruptions is a minor difficulty, scarcely illustrative of the problems of management. Conrad was able to leave the matter entirely to his wife.

The larger objects of management are two: discovering the clue that suggests the development to be sought, that intimates the creative end to be reached, and assuring a certain and economical movement toward that end. The indispensable condition of success in either stage of production is that freedom from the established schemes of consciousness the importance of which I have already pointed out. It is essential to remember that the creative end is never in full sight at the beginning and that it is brought wholly into view only when the process of creation is completed. It is not to be found by scrutiny of the conscious scene, because it is never there. Yet the necessary step is not retirement altogether from the conscious scene into a meaningless blackout. Much of the meaning in that scene may survive in succeeding ones, as an essential contribution to their fresh life. What is necessary is to be able to look into the wings where the action is not yet organized, and to feel the importance of what is happening off stage. It may not seem to be much. The young artist is likely to feel that it is nothing, and to go on imitating.

Yet it is only there, behind the scenes that are so largely given over to the impressive play of traditional activity, that the new can be prepared. No matter how meager, dull, disorderly, and fragmentary the offstage action, it must be attended to. For only on the fringes of consciousness and in the deeper backgrounds into which they fade away is freedom attainable.

We are not usually much aware of this less determinate part of our psychic life, for consciousness is dominated by system, to which we cling. The schematic consciousness is safe, more or less manageable the tidy and reassuring world of our familiar psychic life. What lies outside is popularly regarded as the concern of alienists, to be noticed only as it becomes disturbing. Out of fear and misunderstanding we incline to minimize it or to disregard it altogether, when we can.

The usual response of intelligent minds confronted with it is beautifully defined in the words of Marlow, Conrad's narrator in *Lord Jim,* who is speaking of a scene of horror: "It had the power to drive me out of my conception of existence, out of that shelter each of us makes for himself to creep under in moments of danger, as a tortoise withdraws within its shell. For a moment I had a view of a world that seemed to wear a vast and dismal aspect of disorder, while, in truth, thanks to our unwearied efforts, it is as sunny an arrangement of small conveniences as the mind of man can conceive. But still—it was only a moment: I went back into my shell directly. One must—don't you know?—though I seemed to have lost all my words in the chaos of dark thoughts I had contemplated for a second or two beyond the pale. These came back, too, very soon, for words also belong to the sheltering conception of light and order which is our refuge."

That preverbal experience, in which one loses one's words, opens upon an enormous range and variety of activity. Hypnosis and other procedures such as automatic writing reveal to some degree the richness of what has been called the depths of the mind, in which apparently all the experience of the organism is in some way retained, even an incalculable multitude of experiences that never reach the threshold of awareness at all. This great psychic reservoir is not static like a letter file, or still like a pond. Certain changes evidently go on in it continually. Everyone knows from experience how a memory may alter, not merely fading but suffering distortion. Dreams are another evidence of unconscious developments.

All psychic life is activity, for even the maintenance of the established patterns is a reactivation, with inevitable variations of content and emphasis. But in the unconscious psyche and on the fringes of consciousness, change is easier because there the compulsive and inhibiting effect of system sustained by will and attention is decreased or ceases altogether. Though the system does not dissolve into nothing, it decreases in importance, becomes only an element in the unconscious psychic life, which might therefore be called the nonschematic in contrast to the conscious, which is dominated by system. The term "nonschematic" is suitable, further, for the unconscious and fringe activity, because much of it is so lacking in apparent organization that it seems altogether chaotic. A great many of the configurations that do appear in the fringes of consciousness are continually shifting because no sign has been found to impose on them the fixed status of a scheme. They slide out of consciousness like the nameless configurations of the rocking ocean. No wonder the image most often chosen for the deeper psychic life is the sea at night. The image is used among others by John Livingston Lowes in evoking for the readers of *The Road to Xanadu* his sense of the enormous activity out of which the poems of Coleridge were crystallized: "I have left two-thirds of the mass of entries in the Note Book completely untouched. But the whole could not make clearer one fact of profound significance for us. For there, in those bizarre pages, we catch glimpses of the strange and fantastic shapes which haunted the hinterland of Coleridge's brain. Most of them never escaped from their confines into the light of day. Some did, trailing clouds of glory as they came. But those which did not, like the stars of the old astrology, rained none the less their secret influence on nearly everything that Coleridge wrote in his creative prime. *The Rime of the Ancient Mariner, Christabel, Kubla Khan, The Wanderings of Cain,* are what they are because they are all subdued to the hues of that heaving and phosphorescent sea below the verge of consciousness from which they have emerged. No single fragment of concrete reality in the array before us is in itself of such far-reaching import as is the sense of that hovering cloud of shadowy presences. For what the teeming chaos of the Note Book gives us is the charged and electrical atmospheric background of a poet's mind."

Some of Lowes' terms are strikingly like those used by Dr. R. W. Gerard in describing the nervous system, which he depicts as a fluid whole, a continual alteration of flowing electrical patterns: "Now, with our discovery of a far more fluid nervous system, one unceasingly active and with neural and electrical messages rippling the whole into dynamic patterns, which flow from one contour to another as present influences play upon the condition left by past ones-with such a picture the arrival of new neural relationships is no great problem."

It is perhaps hard to see how there should be any fixity at all in so fluid a medium. Yet the fact is that there is a great deal of stability, so much that often it interferes with life. It may be that the threat of dissolution is so great that men have developed their conservatism as a necessary guard against the dispersal of the order they live by. Whatever the cause, the tendency to distrust the widest and freest ranging of the mind is so strong that the changes necessary for the development of human life could not be attained without the efforts of the more daring and ingenious of mankind.

The creative process is not only the concern of specialists, however; it is not limited to the arts and to thought, but is as wide as life. Or perhaps it would be more correct to say that invention in the arts and in thought is a part of the invention of life, and that this invention is essentially a single process. That view is made clear enough in Yeats' poem "Long Legged Fly," which appears in this volume. The minds of the artist Michelangelo, of Caesar the man of action, and of the nameless girl whose movements are only the apparently trivial motions of life at play, are seen to be all in the same condition: their minds move upon silence as the fly moves on the surface of a stream. They are brought into relation, that is to say, with the freer and more plentiful activity which transcends that of the schematic consciousness, the awareness which can be put into words or formed into other systems of signs. They are enlarged. It would not be correct to say that they have yielded to darkness or disorder so long as they remain responsive to the needs of life, to the pressures or tensions developing in the widened psychic activity in consequence of human interests and needs, including those interests and needs which are unsatisfied in the experience organized by current insight. They have yielded to a necessity inherent in their full psychic life.

This self-surrender so familiar to creative minds is nearly always hard to achieve. It calls for a purity of motive that is rarely sustained except through dedication and discipline. Subordination of everything to the whole impulse of life is easier for the innocent and ignorant because they are not so fully aware of the hazards of it or are less impressed by them, and they are not so powerfully possessed by convention. When their life is strong in them they can sometimes surrender themselves to it without effort. But shortly the girl in Yeats' poem will notice that somebody is looking, and then, unless she is very willful and full of disastrous genius, she will sink into convention.

Even when one has recognized the controlling center of life as lying outside the ego and the preoccupations of conscious life and has learned to look away from these, submitting to its guidance may be difficult. Some of the reasons why this is so need no further discussion. Much of the difficulty comes of the slightness and the often doubtful character of the means by which the guidance is asserted. The first intimations are likely to be embodied in apparently trivial things, objects or experiences that in our everyday life would seem to have little importance or none whatever. There are two clues to their real importance: first, the disproportionate or even wholly inexplicable satisfaction or excitement which they evoke in the creative worker; and secondly, their power to open his mind inward upon the stir of its own unorganized riches.

This is not to say that all that excites the mind in this way will lead directly to creation. The desired new order implicit in the stir of indeterminate activity cannot be seized in the abstract: it must crystallize in terms of some medium in which the worker is adept. Without craft it will escape. The elements that intimate the way of vital development may or may not be included or emphasized in the crystallization. Almost certainly the New Zealand landscape that evoked a world for Katherine Mansfield found a smaller place in her expression than it would have assumed if she had been a painter. The crystallization may, moreover, be delayed even for a long time, or some accident or obstacle may preclude it.

Yet though the exciting elements may not at first lead to any clear development, their whole aspect is of promise. Henry James describes the germinal trivia from which his stories developed as typically minute and superficially bare, but extraordinarily rich in their intimations of developments to be revealed. The very slightness of such elements is a guard against their taking the focus of attention or forcing a finished pattern upon the mind. On the other hand, it has the disadvantage of making them elusive. One must learn to seize and hold them without insistence, letting them agitate the mind when and as they may and make their own development, relinquishing them as they fade or fail of effect and taking up others to be cherished without attachment in the same way, shaping the expression of the growing insight critically—that is, consciously and rationally, drawing upon all resources of craft and understanding—in so far as that may be done without arresting spontaneous developments, always preserving the stir of the excited mind out of which the development issues.

The concentration of such a state may be so extreme that the worker may seem to himself or others to be in a trance or some similar hypnotic or somnambulistic state. But actually the state of so-called trance so often mentioned as characteristic of the creative process or of stages in it differs markedly from ordinary trance or hypnosis in its collectedness, its autonomy, its extreme watchfulness. And it seems never to be directly induced. It appears rather to be generated indirectly, to subsist as the characteristic of a consciousness partly unfocused, attention diverted from the too-assertive contours of any particular scheme and dispersed upon an object without complete schematic representation. In short, the creative discipline when successful may generate a trancelike state, but one does not throw oneself into a trance in order to create.

Even in those stages when willed and rational effort is dominant, the creative process is essentially the delicate action of developed life. Tricks, devices, drugs, or disciplines are useful to the inventor only in so far as they support that action or empower the organism that acts. The less the worker needs to depend on eternal things or circumstances the safer he is from disturbances and disabling accidents. The man who comes to depend on alcohol, or on paper of a specific size, or on some one favored environment in order to get his work done has narrowed his freedom of action and he may be resorting to automatic controls or to magic instead of relying on his skill, ingenuity, and sensitiveness. It is best to avoid idiosyncrasy and to cultivate the central disciplines.

Among the conditions to which every inventor must submit is the necessity for patience. The development desired may have to be waited for, even though its character has been clearly intimated. After the first suggestion which allows anticipation of anything at all, a long gestation may be required. The need for such hidden organic development at some stage of the creative process appears to be universal. It may be completed before the first flash of suggestion that brings the creative development to attention, and the worker may then be able to go on without interruption to the conclusion of his work. William Blake claimed that some of his poetry came without any apparent premeditation, as if dictated to him. But often some period of gestation must follow the first flash of insight. With A. E. Housman it was usually short: a poem ordinarily completed itself by stages within a few hours or days. But long or short, the gestation has to be endured. Bertrand Russell has remarked upon the fruitless effort he used to expend in trying to push his creative work to completion by sheer force of will before he discovered the necessity of waiting for it to find its own subconscious development. The reasonable attitude toward this sometimes embarrassing necessity is illustrated by a famous passage in Henry James' preface to his novel *The American:* "I was charmed with my idea, which would take, however, much working out; and precisely because it had so much to give, I think, must I have dropped it for the time into the deep well of unconscious cerebration: not without the hope, doubtless, that it might eventually emerge from that reservoir, as one had already known the buried treasure to come to light, with a firm iridescent surface and a notable increase of weight."

Invention is easier when we learn willingly to submit to necessity, or even, like James, to find real advantage in it. One can save oneself much trouble by recognizing the limitations of the will in creation. It is interesting to see how often it is repudiated as a primary instrument in much of the creative process by all kinds of artists and thinkers, from Picasso to John Dewey, a group so large and representative as to leave no doubt that agreement is general. Will belongs to the conscious life only. It is effective in attaining objects in view, but it cannot enable us to move in directions that have not yet been discovered. Will rather tends to arrest the undetermined development, by laying the emphasis of a heightened tension upon whatever is already in mind. When what is required is work to be done on something already defined, such an emphasis is useful. And will is helpful therefore in many matters assisting the creative process. It may help the worker to stick to his discipline. It may sustain his effort to stay at his desk—or to leave it, for the relief of too concentrated attention or for the pursuit of incitements to further spontaneous developments. Or it may make firm his purpose to dismiss the man "from Porlock."

But even in such apparently conscious matters as organizing a novel or choosing a subject for research or for a poem, the will may do vital damage. In the introduction to her novel *Mrs. Dalloway*, Virginia Woolf describes how she was forced to abandon her attempts at a plan for the book and to go forward without method or theory. Her difficulty arose from the fact that the form or plan of the novel as she knew it, was unsuitable for the expression of her impulse, which therefore was bound to be suppressed by the imposition upon its movements of the known, conventional order, the only one that could be produced by willful labor. This is not to be taken as evidence that planning is detrimental, but only that plan must not be enforced by will. Plan must come as a part of the organic development of a project, either before the details are determined, which is more convenient, or in the midst of their production, which is sometimes confusing.

It is organic need, too, rather than will, that must determine the choice of a subject. Often in this matter will and need do not come into conflict. When they do there should be no question about submitting to the vital necessity. To select a subject against inclination and force the mind to elaborate it is damaging and diminishing. The crux of the problem particularly as it exists in the arts is indicated by T. S. Eliot in his introduction to *The Selected Poems of Marianne Moore:* "For a mind of such agility, and for a sensibility so reticent, the minor subject, such as a pleasant little sand-coloured skipping animal, may be the best release for the major emotions. Only the pedantic literalist could consider the subject matter to be trivial; the triviality is in himself. We all have to choose whatever subject-matter allows us the most powerful and most secret release; and that is a personal affair."

But by no means all the creative process is primarily a spontaneous development. Two important stages in it are predominantly conscious and critical, and in these the will properly functions. It is of use in that preliminary labor, or sometimes less burdensome preparation, without which there can be no significant creative activity, and in the work of verification, correction, or revision that ordinarily follows the more radical inventive activity and completes or refines its product.

A great deal of the work necessary to equip and activate the mind for the spontaneous part of invention must be done consciously and with an effort of will. Mastering accumulated knowledge, gathering new facts, observing, exploring, experimenting, developing technique and skill, sensibility, and discrimination, are all more or less conscious and voluntary activities. The sheer labor of preparing technically for creative work, consciously acquiring the requisite knowledge of a medium and skill in its use, is extensive and arduous enough to repel many from achievement.

Creative workers reporting their processes of production often inadvertently conceal the amount of conscious and voluntary work by their failure to stress it or to consider it in much detail, probably because so much of it belongs primarily or even entirely to the special disciplines of the worker's field and is thought of as wholly a matter of craft or technique. It is true that some technical operations are nothing more than that, since they are determined purely by the intrinsic nature of the medium. An example is the rejection of the words "orange" or "month" as rime words in a strictly conventional sonnet because there are no exact rhymes for them in English. But if, on the other hand, these words were rejected because as approximate or slant rhymes, paired, say, with "forage" and "thump," they would form dissonances destructive of some creative end in view, the process would not be merely technical, though technique would be largely involved. Management of the medium becomes more complex, and the technical processes merge indissolubly with the creative process, as soon as the use of substances and forms begins to be guided by a sense of their sufficiency or insufficiency in formulating insights and attitudes. Though the technical component of such work remains ponderable in itself, it is not completely understandable except as a part of the creative process. And all of it that is not spontaneous, ordinarily a great deal, is part of the conscious and voluntary labor of the creative process.

In a different way, we are led to underestimate the labor of invention by the appearance of the finished product. Freed of every irrelevance, especially the sweat and litter of the workroom, the work of thought or art or ritual stands as the simple formula of a subjective action. The impression it gives of unlabored force is not to be trusted. There are no certain grounds for disbelieving in the difficulty of any process of invention. Every genuinely creative worker must attain in one way or another such full understanding of his medium and such skill, ingenuity, and flexibility in handling it that he can make fresh use of it to construct a device which, when used skillfully by others, will organize their experience in the way that his own experience was organized in the moment of expanded insight. Among the users of his device may be the inventor himself, who may recover the configurations of his insight in this way, though not the full activity out of which they were crystallized. His device may even fail to remind him of his labor. All finished productions have the simplicity of order, which reveals itself rather than its origins.

Even the most energetic and original mind, in order to reorganize or extend human insight in any valuable way, must have attained more than ordinary mastery of the field in which it is to act, a strong sense of what needs to be done, and skill in the appropriate means of expression. It seems certain that no significant expansion of insight can be produced otherwise, whether the activity is thought of as work or not. Often an untutored beauty appears in the drawings of children, and we rightly prize the best of them because they have wholeness of motive, but they have scarcely the power to open the future to us. For that, the artist must labor to the limit of human development and then take a step beyond. The same is true for every sort of creative worker.

That step beyond is stimulated by labor upon the limits of attainment. The secret developments that we call unconscious because they complete themselves without our knowledge and the other spontaneous activities that go forward without foresight yet in full consciousness are induced and focused by intense conscious effort spent upon the material to be developed or in the area to be illuminated. Though the tension of conscious striving tends to overdetermine psychic activity, to narrow and fix it, such tension gives stimulation and direction to the unconscious activity which goes on after the tension is released. The desired developments are usually delayed for some time, during which presumably something like incubation is going on and attention may be profitably turned to something else. Then without warning the solution or the germinal insight may appear. This was the usual experience of Henri Poincaré and of many others. But though "inspiration" may be produced by such conscious labors, by what Katherine Mansfield called "terrific hard gardening," the procedure is not always successful; problems may remain unsolved, insights undeveloped, no matter how much effort is given to them. Nor is there always even when the procedure is successful a notable amount of unconscious development. Long periods of alternating conscious and unconscious activity may be required. When the process is an agonizing, fumbling search, as it was for Thomas Wolfe, some morbid condition may be suspected, such as the hyperamnesia which seems to have afflicted him with an assaulting torrent of recalled detail.

The unsearchable insight which we call inspiration is sometimes given wholly at one stroke. Poincaré indicates that for him it was. Henry James reports a somewhat similar experience in writing *The Ambassadors*. Others, like Stephen Spender, begin in considerable uncertainty and find successive clarifications in a sort of continuing inspiration as they go on with their conscious work. This happens with many workers in the arts. Van Gogh and Kuniyoshi tell of making many paintings of the same object in order to develop and refine the insight expressed in representing it. D. H. Lawrence is reported to have written *Lady Chatterley's Lover* three times. This process of reworking is very close to revision, but since it involves repeating virtually the whole process of production it appears more likely to preserve the spontaneous character of the initial attempt. Revision need not lack spontaneity, however, and there would be little use in it if it did. It is hard to say whether when Allen Tate added his "wind-leaves refrain" to his "Ode to the Confederate Dead" nearly five years after the first draft of the poem was made, he was continuing the composition of the poem or revising it. Under such circumstances the distinction becomes unreal; the two processes merge.

Although the work that tests, refines, and consolidates what is attained in moments of inspiration is not likely to be, in the arts at least, all conscious calculation, it is largely so. Its object, both in art and in intellectual invention, is to make sure that the product is really serviceable. A work may seem valuable to its creator because of his sense of stirring life and fresh significance while he was producing it. After that excitement is dissipated, its intrinsic value is its only relevant one even to himself. He must find out if it will serve to organize experience in a fresh and full and useful way. To that end he tests it critically. If he finds it is not sound and complete, he may be able to make it so, either by conscious craft or consciously directed research or by a fresh exercise of his whole power to which he has been urged by a critical consciousness of his need. Or he may have to reject the work because he finds it fundamentally wrong or hopelessly vapid, or simply because he is unable to bring to it the necessary spontaneous work to complete it. Shelley, who found his inspiration declining as soon as he began to compose, and who considered the products of revision lifeless stopgaps, left many fragments.

There is much lore about the creative process that I have not discussed. Some of it is useful, some not. Whether found gathered into books, as much of it is, or as scattered items, this material should not be approached as a body of fragments to be tested experimentally for their value in practical guidance and accepted or rejected as they are found useful or not. The caution holds even for the more highly organized material of the following essays, letters, and poems. Some of this material is conflicting. Part of it may have been shaped by individual limitations of the writers. Its authority cannot be regarded as absolute. It is more manageable and meaningful when understood in terms of the general principles by which it should also be tested, and which in turn it should test and illustrate.

Practical guidance can often be deduced from the general principles alone. Most writers find it easier to work in the morning-as one should expect, since then the mind has not been so much incited from without, focused, and fixed. John Peale Bishop recommended going as soon as possible from sleep to the writing desk. On the other hand, A. E. Housman wrote his poems mostly in the afternoon. Others have preferred to do their work at night. How shall we turn such information to guidance unless we understand that the time for work should be that time when the excited mind moves most free of the encumbrance of its consciously supported order? If we cannot because of circumstances choose the best time, we may be able to help ourselves through reducing the schematic fixation that interferes with production. Similar considerations govern our treatment of the problem of inciting unconscious work, or any other problem. I have emphasized the value of understanding, discipline, and hard work in the creative process. High and sustained achievement demands even more, the concentration of a life. And even that is not all. In the absence of fresh insight, devotion is powerless, and the best technique is meaningless, since it can only repeat mechanically. Invention may be precluded by a distrust of deviation. Every new and good thing is liable to seem eccentric and perhaps dangerous at first glimpse, perhaps more than what is really eccentric, really irrelevant to life. And therefore we must always listen to the voice of eccentricity, within ourselves and in the world. The alien, the dangerous, like the negligible near thing, may seem irrelevant to purpose and yet be the call to our own fruitful development. This does not mean that we should surrender to whatever novelty is brought to attention. It does mean that we must practice to some extent an imaginative surrender to every novelty that has even the most tenuous credentials. Because life is larger than any of its expressions, it must sometimes do violence to the forms it has created. We must expect to live the orderly ways we have invented continually conscious of the imminence of change.

MATHEMATICAL CREATION

Henri Poincaré

The genesis of mathematical creation is a problem which should intensely interest the psychologist. It is the activity in which the human mind seems to take least from the outside world, in which it acts or seems to act only of itself and on itself, so that in studying the procedure of geometric thought we may hope to reach what is most essential in man's mind.

This has long been appreciated, and some time back the journal called *L'Enseignement Mathématique,* edited by Laisant and Fehr, began an investigation of the mental habits and methods of work of different mathematicians. I had finished the main outlines of this article when the results of that inquiry were published, so I have hardly been able to utilize them and shall confine myself to saying that the majority of witnesses confirm my conclusions; I do not say all, for when the appeal is to universal suffrage unanimity is not to be hoped.

A first fact should surprise us, or rather would surprise us if we were not so used to it. How does it happen there are people who do not understand mathematics? If mathematics invokes only the rules of logic, such as are accepted by all normal minds; if its evidence is based on principles common to all men, and that none could deny without being mad, how does it come about that so many persons are here refractory?

That not every one can invent is in no ways mysterious. That not every one can retain a demonstration once learned may also pass. But that not every one can understand mathematical reasoning when explained appears very surprising when we think of it. And yet those who can follow this reasoning only with difficulty are in the majority: that is undeniable, and will surely not be gainsaid by the experience of secondary-school teachers.

And further: how is error possible in mathematics? A sane mind should not be guilty of a logical fallacy, and yet there are very fine minds who do not trip in brief reasoning such as occurs in the ordinary doings of life, and who are incapable of following or repeating without error the mathematical demonstrations which are longer, but which after all are only an accumulation of brief reasonings wholly analogous to those they make so easily. Need we add that mathematicians themselves are not infallible?

The answer seems to me evident. Imagine a long series of syllogisms, and that the conclusions of the first serve as premises of the following: we shall be able to catch each of these syllogisms, and it is not in passing from premises to conclusion that we are in danger of deceiving ourselves. But between the moment in which we first meet a proposition as conclusion of one syllogism, and that in which we reencounter it as premise of another syllogism occasionally some time will elapse, several links of the chain will have unrolled; so it may happen that we have forgotten it, or worse, that we have forgotten its meaning. So it may happen that we replace it by a slightly different proposition, or that, while retaining the same enunciation, we attribute to it a slightly different meaning, and thus it is that we are exposed to error.

Often the mathematician uses a rule. Naturally he begins by demonstrating this rule; and at the time when this proof is fresh in his memory he understands perfectly its meaning and its bearing, and he is in no danger of changing it. But subsequently he trusts his memory and afterward only applies it in a mechanical way; and then if his memory fails him, he may apply it all wrong. Thus it is, to take a simple example, that we sometimes make slips in calculation because we have forgotten our multiplication table.

According to this, the special aptitude for mathematics would be due only to a very sure memory or to a prodigious force of attention. It would be a power like that of the whist-player who remembers the cards played; or, to go up a step, like that of the chess-player who can visualize a great number of combinations and hold them in his memory. Every good mathematician ought to be a good chess-player, and inversely; likewise he should be a good computer. Of course that sometimes happens; thus Gauss was at the same time a geometer of genius and a very precocious and accurate computer.

But there are exceptions; or rather I err; I can not call them exceptions without the exceptions being more than the rule. Gauss it is, on the contrary, who was an exception. As for myself, I must confess, I am absolutely incapable even of adding without mistakes. In the same way I should be but a poor chess-player; I would perceive that by a certain play I should expose myself to a certain danger; I would pass in review several other plays, rejecting them for other reasons, and then finally I should make the move first examined, having meantime forgotten the danger I had foreseen.

In a word, my memory is not bad, but it would be insufficient to make me a good chess-player. Why then does it not fail me in a difficult piece of mathematical reasoning where most chess-players would lose themselves? Evidently because it is guided by the general march of the reasoning. A mathematical demonstration is not a simple juxtaposition of syllogisms, it is syllogisms *placed in a certain order,* and the order in which these elements are placed is much more important than the elements themselves. If I have the feeling, the intuition, so to speak, of this order, so as to perceive at a glance the reasoning as a whole, I need no longer fear lest I forget one of the elements, for each of them will take its allotted place in the array, and that without any effort of memory on my part.

It seems to me then, in repeating a reasoning learned, that I could have invented it. This is often only an illusion; but even then, even if I am not so gifted as to create it by myself, I myself re-invent it in so far as I repeat it.

We know that this feeling, this intuition of mathematical order, that makes us divine hidden harmonies and relations, can not be possessed by every one. Some will not have either this delicate feeling so difficult to define, or a strength of memory and attention beyond the ordinary, and then they will be absolutely incapable of understanding higher mathematics. Such are the majority. Others will have this feeling only in a slight degree, but they will be gifted with an uncommon memory and a great power of attention. They will learn by heart the details one after another; they can understand mathematics and sometimes make applications, but they cannot create. Others, finally, will possess in a less or greater degree the special intuition referred to, and then not only can they understand mathematics even if their memory is nothing extraordinary, but they may become creators and try to invent with more or less success according as this intuition is more or less developed in them.

In fact, what is mathematical creation? It does not consist in making new combinations with mathematical entities already known. Any one could do that, but the combinations so made would be infinite in number and most of them absolutely without interest. To create consists precisely in not making useless combinations and in making those which are useful and which are only a small minority. Invention is discernment, choice.

How to make this choice I have before explained; the mathematical facts worthy of being studied are those which, by their analogy with other facts, are capable of leading us to the knowledge of a mathematical law just as experimental facts lead us to the knowledge of a physical law. They are those which reveal to us unsuspected kinship between other facts, long known, but wrongly believed to be strangers to one another.

Among chosen combinations the most fertile will often be those formed of elements drawn from domains which are far apart. Not that I mean as sufficing for invention the bringing together of objects as disparate as possible; most combinations so formed would be entirely sterile. But certain among them, very rare, are the most fruitful of all.

To invent, I have said, is to choose; but the word is perhaps not wholly exact. It makes one think of a purchaser before whom are displayed a large number of samples, and who examines them, one after the other, to make a choice. Here the samples would be so numerous that a whole lifetime would not suffice to examine them. This is not the actual state of things. The sterile combinations do not even present themselves to the mind of the inventor. Never in the field of his consciousness do combinations appear that are not really useful, except some that he rejects but which have to some extent the characteristics of useful combinations. All goes on as if the inventor were an examiner for the second degree who would only have to question the candidates who had passed a previous examination. But what I have hitherto said is what may be observed or inferred in reading the writings of the geometers, reading reflectively.

It is time to penetrate deeper and to see what goes on in the very soul of the mathematician. For this, I believe, I can do best by recalling memories of my own. But I shall limit myself to telling how I wrote my first memoir on Fuchsian functions. I beg the reader's pardon; I am about to use some technical expressions, but they need not frighten him, for he is not obliged to understand them. I shall say, for example, that I have found the demonstration of such a theorem under such circumstances. This theorem will have a barbarous name, unfamiliar to many, but that is unimportant; what is of interest for the psychologist is not the theorem but the circumstances.

For fifteen days I strove to prove that there could not be any functions like those I have since called Fuchsian functions. I was then very ignorant; every day I seated myself at my work table, stayed an hour or two, tried a great number of combinations and reached no results. One evening, contrary to my custom, I drank black coffee and could not sleep. Ideas rose in crowds; I felt them collide until pairs interlocked, so to speak, making a stable combination. By the next morning I had established the existence of a class of Fuchsian functions, those which come from the hypergeometric series; I had only to write out the results, which took but a few hours.

Then I wanted to represent these functions by the quotient of two series; this idea was perfectly conscious and deliberate, the analogy with elliptic functions guided me. I asked myself what properties these series must have if they existed, and I succeeded without difficulty in forming the series I have called theta-Fuchsian.

Just at this time I left Caen, where I was then living, to go on a geologic excursion under the auspices of the school of mines. The changes of travel made me forget my mathematical work. Having reached Coutances, we entered an omnibus to go some place or other. At the moment when I put my foot on the step the idea came to me, without anything in my former thoughts seeming to have paved the way for it, that the transformations I had used to define the Fuchsian functions were identical with those of non-Euclidean geometry. I did not verify the idea; I should not have had time, as, upon taking my seat in the omnibus, I went on with a conversation already commenced but I felt a perfect certainty. On my return to Caen, for conscience' sake I verified the result at my leisure.

Then I turned my attention to the study of some arithmetical questions apparently without much success and without a suspicion of any connection with my preceding researches. Disgusted with my failure, I went to spend a few days at the seaside, and thought of something else. One morning, walking on the bluff, the idea came to me, with just the same characteristics of brevity, suddenness and immediate certainty, that the arithmetic transformations of indeterminate ternary quadratic forms were identical with those of non-Euclidean geometry.

Returned to Caen, I meditated on this result and deduced the consequences. The example of quadratic forms showed me that there were Fuchsian groups other than those corresponding to the hypergeometric series; I saw that I could apply to them the theory of theta-Fuchsian series and that consequently there existed Fuchsian functions other than those from the hypergeometric series, the ones I then knew. Naturally I set myself to form all these functions. I made a systematic attack upon them and carried all the outworks, one after another. There was one however that still held out, whose fall would involve that of the whole place. But all my efforts only served at first the better to show me the difficulty, which indeed was something. All this work was perfectly conscious.

Thereupon I left for Mont-Valérien, where I was to go through my military service; so I was very differently occupied. One day, going along the street, the solution of the difficulty which had stopped me suddenly appeared to me. I did not try to go deep into it immediately, and only after my service did I again take up the question. I had all the elements and had only to arrange them and put them together. So I wrote out my final memoir at a single stroke and without difficulty.

I shall limit myself to this single example; it is useless to multiply them. In regard to my other researches I would have to say analogous things, and the observations of other mathematicians given in *L'Enseignement Mathématique* would only confirm them.

Most striking at first is this appearance of sudden illumination, a manifest sign of long, unconscious prior work. The role of this unconscious work in mathematical invention appears to me incontestable, and traces of it would be found in other cases where it is less evident. Often when one works at a hard question, nothing good is accomplished at the first attack. Then one takes a rest, longer or shorter, and sits down anew to the work. During the first half-hour, as before, nothing is found, and then all of a sudden the decisive idea presents itself to the mind. It might be said that the conscious work has been more fruitful because it has been interrupted and the rest has given back to the mind its force and freshness. But it is more probable that this rest has been filled out with unconscious work and that the result of this work has afterward revealed itself to the geometer just as in the cases I have cited; only the revelation, instead of coming during a walk or a journey, has happened during a period of conscious work, but independently of this work which plays at most a role of excitant, as if it were the goad stimulating the results already reached during rest, but remaining unconscious, to assume the conscious form.

There is another remark to be made about the conditions of this unconscious work: it is possible, and of a certainty it is only fruitful, if it is on the one hand preceded and on the other hand followed by a period of conscious work. These sudden inspirations (and the examples already cited sufficiently prove this) never happen except after some days of voluntary effort which has appeared absolutely fruitless and whence nothing good seems to have come, where the way taken seems totally astray. These efforts then have not been as sterile as one thinks; they have set agoing the unconscious machine and without them it would not have moved and would have produced nothing.

The need for the second period of conscious work, after the inspiration, is still easier to understand. It is necessary to put in shape the results of this inspiration, to deduce from them the immediate consequences, to arrange them, to word the demonstrations, but above all is verification necessary. I have spoken of the feeling of absolute certitude accompanying the inspiration; in the cases cited this feeling was no deceiver, nor is it usually. But do not think this is a rule without exception; often this feeling deceives us without being any the less vivid, and we only find it out when we seek to put on foot the demonstration. I have especially noticed this fact in regard to ideas coming to me in the morning or evening in bed while in a semi-hypnagogic state.

Such are the realities; now for the thoughts they force upon us. The unconscious, or, as we say, the subliminal self plays an important role in mathematical creation; this follows from what we have said. But usually the subliminal self is considered as purely automatic. Now we have seen that mathematical work is not simply mechanical, that it could not be done by a machine, however perfect. It is not merely a question of applying rules, of making the most combinations possible according to certain fixed laws. The combinations so obtained would be exceedingly numerous, useless and cumbersome. The true work of the inventor consists in choosing among these combinations so as to eliminate the useless ones or rather to avoid the trouble of making them, and the rules which must guide this choice are extremely fine and delicate. It is almost impossible to state them precisely; they are felt rather than formulated. Under these conditions, how imagine a sieve capable of applying them mechanically?

A first hypothesis now presents itself: the subliminal self is in no way inferior to the conscious self; it is not purely automatic; it is capable of discernment; it has tact, delicacy; it knows how to choose, to divine. What do I say? It knows better how to divine than the conscious self, since it succeeds where that has failed. In a word, is not the subliminal self superior to the conscious self? You recognize the full importance of this question. Boutroux in a recent lecture has shown how it came up on a very different occasion, and what consequences would follow an affirmative answer.

Is this affirmative answer forced upon us by the facts I have just given? I confess that, for my part, I should hate to accept it. Reexamine the facts then and see if they are not compatible with another explanation.

It is certain that the combinations which present themselves to the mind in a sort of sudden illumination, after an unconscious working somewhat prolonged, are generally useful and fertile combinations, which seem the result of a first impression. Does it follow that the subliminal self, having divined by a delicate intuition that these combinations would be useful, has formed only these, or has it rather formed many others which were lacking in interest and have remained unconscious?

In this second way of looking at it, all the combinations would be formed in consequence of the automatism of the subliminal self, but only the interesting ones would break into the domain of consciousness. And this is still very mysterious. What is the cause that, among the thousand products of our unconscious activity, some are called to pass the threshold, while others remain below? Is it a simple chance which confers this privilege? Evidently not; among all the stimuli of our senses, for example, only the most intense fix our attention, unless it has been drawn to them by other causes. More generally the privileged unconscious phenomena, those susceptible of becoming conscious, are those which, directly or indirectly, affect most profoundly our emotional sensibility.

It may be surprising to see emotional sensibility invoked à propos of mathematical demonstrations which, it would seem, can interest only the intellect. This would be to forget the feeling of mathematical beauty, of the harmony of numbers and forms, of geometric elegance. This is a true esthetic feeling that all real mathematicians know, and surely it belongs to emotional sensibility.

Now, what are the mathematic entities to which we attribute this character of beauty and elegance, and which are capable of developing in us a sort of esthetic emotion? They are those whose elements are harmoniously disposed so that the mind without effort can embrace their totality while realizing the details. This harmony is at once a satisfaction of our esthetic needs and an aid to the mind, sustaining and guiding. And at the same time, in putting under our eyes a well-ordered whole, it makes us foresee a mathematical law. Now, as we have said above, the only mathematical facts worthy of fixing our attention and capable of being useful are those which can teach us a mathematical law. So that we reach the following conclusion: The useful combinations are precisely the most beautiful, I mean those best able to charm this special sensibility that all mathematicians know, but of which the profane are so ignorant as often to be tempted to smile at it.

What happens then? Among the great numbers of combinations blindly formed by the subliminal self, almost all are without interest and without utility; but just for that reason they are also without effect upon the esthetic sensibility. Consciousness will never know them; only certain ones are harmonious, and, consequently, at once useful and beautiful. They will be capable of touching this special sensibility of the geometer of which I have just spoken, and which, once aroused, will call our attention to them, and thus give them occasion to become conscious.

This is only a hypothesis, and yet here is an observation which may confirm it: when a sudden illumination seizes upon the mind of the mathematician, it usually happens that it does not deceive him, but it also sometimes happens, as I have said, that it does not stand the test of verification; well, we almost always notice that this false idea, had it been true, would have gratified our natural feeling for mathematical elegance.

Thus it is this special esthetic sensibility which plays the role of the delicate sieve of which I spoke, and that sufficiently explains why the one lacking it will never be a real creator.

Yet all the difficulties have not disappeared. The conscious self is narrowly limited, and as for the subliminal self we know not its limitations, and this is why we are not too reluctant in supposing that it has been able in a short time to make more different combinations than the whole life of a conscious being could encompass. Yet these limitations exist. Is it likely that it is able to form all the possible combinations, whose number would frighten the imagination? Nevertheless that would seem necessary, because if it produces only a small part of these combinations, and if it makes them at random, there would be small chance that the *good,* the one we should choose, would be found among them.

Perhaps we ought to seek the explanation in that preliminary period of conscious work which always precedes all fruitful unconscious labor. Permit me a rough comparison. Figure the future elements of our combinations as something like the hooked atoms of Epicurus.

During the complete repose of the mind, these atoms are motionless, they are, so to speak, hooked to the wall; so this complete rest may be indefinitely prolonged without the atoms meeting, and consequently without any combination between them.

On the other hand, during a period of apparent rest and unconscious work, certain of them are detached from the wall and put in motion. They flash in every direction through the space (I was about to say the room) where they are enclosed, as would, for example, a swarm of gnats or, if you prefer a more learned comparison, like the molecules of gas in the kinematic theory of gases. Then their mutual impacts may produce new combinations.

What is the role of the preliminary conscious work? It is evidently to mobilize certain of these atoms, to unhook them from the wall and put them in swing. We think we have done no good, because we have moved these elements a thousand different ways in seeking to assemble them, and have found no satisfactory aggregate. But, after this shaking up imposed upon them by our will, these atoms do not return to their primitive rest. They freely continue their dance.

Now, our will did not choose them at random; it pursued a perfectly determined aim. The mobilized atoms are therefore not any atoms whatsoever; they are those from which we might reasonably expect the desired solution. Then the mobilized atoms undergo impacts which make them enter into combinations among themselves or with other atoms at rest which they struck against in their course.

Again I beg pardon, my comparison is very rough, but I scarcely know how otherwise to make my thought understood.

However it may be, the only combinations that have a chance of forming are those where at least one of the elements is one of those atoms freely chosen by our will. Now, it is evidently among these that is found what I called the *good combination.* Perhaps this is a way of lessening the paradoxical in the original hypothesis.

Another observation. It never happens that the unconscious work gives us the result of a somewhat long calculation *all made,* where we have only to apply fixed rules. We might think the wholly automatic subliminal self particularly apt for this sort of work, which is in a way exclusively mechanical. It seems that thinking in the evening upon the factors of a multiplication we might hope to find the product ready made upon our awakening, or again that an algebraic calculation, for example a verification, would be made unconsciously. Nothing of the sort, as observation proves. All one may hope from these inspirations, fruits of unconscious work, is a point of departure for such calculations. As for the calculations themselves, they must be made in the second period of conscious work, that which follows the inspiration, that in which one verifies the results of this inspiration and deduces their consequences. The rules of these calculations are strict and complicated. They require discipline, attention, will, and therefore consciousness. In the subliminal self, on the contrary, reigns what I should call liberty, if we might give this name to the simple absence of discipline and to the disorder born of chance. Only, this disorder itself permits unexpected combinations.

I shall make a last remark: when above I made certain personal observations, I spoke of a night of excitement when I worked in spite of myself. Such cases are frequent, and it is not necessary that the abnormal cerebral activity be caused by a physical excitant as in that I mentioned. It seems, in such cases, that one is present at his own unconscious work, made partially perceptible to the over-excited consciousness, yet without having changed its nature. Then we vaguely comprehend what distinguishes the two mechanisms or, if you wish, the working methods of the two egos. And the psychologic observations I have been able thus to make seem to me to confirm in their general outlines the views I have given.

Surely they have need of it, for they are and remain in spite of all very hypothetical: the interest of the questions is so great that I do not repent of having submitted them to the reader.

Translated by George Bruce Halsted

From "Mathematical Creation," by Henri Poincaré in *The Foundations of Science,* translated by George Bruce Halsted. By permission of the publishers: The Science Press, Lancaster, Pennsylvania, copyright 1915, reprinted 1921. First printed as "Le Raisonnement Mathématique" in *Science et méthode.* By permission of the French publishers: Ernest Flammarion, 1908, Paris.

LETTER TO
JACQUES HADAMARD

Albert Einstein

My dear colleague:
In the following, I am trying to answer in brief your questions as well as I am able. I am not satisfied myself with those answers and I am willing to answer more questions if you believe this could be of any advantage for the very interesting and difficult work you have undertaken.

(A) The words or the language, as they are written or spoken, do not seem to play any role in my mechanism of thought. The psychical entities which seem to serve as elements in thought are certain signs and more or less clear images which can be "voluntarily" reproduced and combined.

There is, of course, a certain connection between those elements and relevant logical concepts. It is also clear that the desire to arrive finally at logically connected concepts is the emotional basis of this rather vague play with the above mentioned elements. But taken from a psychological viewpoint, this combinatory play seems to be the essential feature in productive thought-before there is any connection with logical construction in words or other kinds of signs which can be communicated to others.

(B) The above mentioned elements are, in my case, of visual and some of muscular type. Conventional words or other signs have to be sought for laboriously only in a secondary stage, when the mentioned associative play is sufficiently established and can be reproduced at will.

(C) According to what has been said, the play with the mentioned elements is aimed to be analogous to certain logical connections one is searching for.

(D) Visual and motor. In a stage when words intervene at all, they are, in my case, purely auditive, but they interfere only in a secondary stage as already mentioned.

(E) It seems to me that what you call full consciousness is a limit case which can never be fully accomplished. This seems to me connected with the fact called the narrowness of consciousness (Enge des Bewusstseins).

Remark: Professor Max Wertheimer has tried to investigate the distinction between mere associating or combining of reproducible elements and between understanding (organisches Begreifen); I cannot judge how far his psychological analysis catches the essential point.

With kind regards...
Albert Einstein

[Note by Jacques Hadamard] Questions (A), (B), (C) correspond to number 30 of the questionnaire issued by *L'Enseignement Mathématique:* It would be very helpful for the purpose of psychological investigation to know what internal or mental images, what kind of "internal word" mathematicians make use of; whether they are motor, auditory, visual, or mixed, depending on the subject which they are studying.

I have asked question (D) on the psychological type, not in research but in usual thought.

Question (E) corresponds to our number 31: a. Especially in research thought, do the mental pictures or internal words present themselves in the full consciousness or in the fringe-consciousness (such as defined in Wallas's *Art of Thought,* pp. 51, 95 or under the name "antechamber of consciousness" in Galton's *Inquiries into Human Faculty,* p. 203 of the edition of 1883; p.146 of the edition of 1910) ? b. The same question is asked concerning the arguments which these mental pictures or words may symbolize.

From "The Letter of Albert Einstein to M. Hadamard," in T*he Psychology of Invention in the Mathematical Field,* by Jacques Hadamard. By permission of the publishers: Princeton University Press, Princeton, New Jersey.

A LETTER

Wolfgang Amadeus Mozart

W hen I am, as it were, completely myself, entirely alone, and of good cheer—say, travelling in a carriage, or walking after a good meal, or during the night when I cannot sleep; it is on such occasions that my ideas flow best and most abundantly. *Whence* and *how* they come, I know not; nor can I force them. Those ideas that please me I retain in memory, and am accustomed, as I have been told, to hum them to myself. If I continue in this way, it soon occurs to me how I may turn this or that morsel to account, so as to make a good dish of, it, that is to say, agreeably to the rules of counterpoint, to the peculiarities of the various instruments, etc.

All this fires my soul, and, provided I am not disturbed, my subject enlarges itself, becomes methodised and defined, and the whole, though it be long, stands almost complete and finished in my mind, so that I can survey it, like a fine picture or a beautiful statue, at a glance. Nor do I hear in my imagination the parts successively, but I hear them, as it were, all at once *(gleich alles zusammen)*. What a delight this is I cannot tell! All this inventing, this producing, takes place in a pleasing lively dream. Still the actual hearing of the *tout ensemble* is after all the best. What has been thus produced I do not easily forget, and this is perhaps the best gift I have my Divine Maker to thank for.

When I proceed to write down my ideas, I take out of the bag of my memory, if I may use that phrase, what has been previously collected into it in the way I have mentioned. For this reason the committing to paper is done quickly enough, for everything is, as I said before, already finished; and it rarely differs on paper from what it was in my imagination. At this occupation I can therefore suffer myself to be disturbed; for whatever may be going on around me, I write, and even talk, but only of fowls and geese, or of Gretel or Barbel, or some such matters. But why my productions take from my hand that particular form and style that makes them Mozartish, and different from the works of other composers, is probably owing to the same cause which renders my nose so large or so aquiline, or, in short, makes it Mozart's, and different from those of other people. For I really do not study or aim at any originality.

From *Life of Mozart,* by Edward Holmes (Everyman's Library). By permission of the publishers: J. M. Dent & Sons, Ltd., London, and E. P. Dutton & Co., Inc., 1912, New York City.

THE COMPOSER AND
HIS MESSAGE
Roger Sessions

I have tried to point out how intimately our musical impulses are connected with those primitive movements which are among the very conditions of our existence. I have tried to show, too, how vivid is our response to the primitive elements of musical movement.

Is not this the key both to the content of music and to its extraordinary power? These bars from the prelude to Tristan do not express for us love or frustration or even longing: but they reproduce for us, both qualitatively and dynamically, certain gestures of the spirit which are to be sure less specifically definable than any of these emotions, but which energize them and make them vital to us.

So it seems to me that this is the essence of musical expression. "Emotion" is specific, individual and conscious; music goes deeper than this, to the energies which animate our psychic life, and out of these creates a pattern which has an existence, laws, and human significance of its own. It reproduces for us the most intimate essence, the tempo and the energy, of our spiritual being; our tranquility and our restlessness, our animation and our discouragement, our vitality and our weakness—all, in fact, of the fine shades of dynamic variation of our inner life. It reproduces these far more directly and more specifically than is possible through any other medium of human communication.

In saying this I do not wish to deny that there is also an associative element in musical expression, or that this has its very definite place in certain types of music. It must be remembered that the emergence of music as an entirely separate art has been, as I have pointed out, of very recent origin; that until the last three hundred years it was always connected with more concrete symbols, whether of the word or the dance. It is but natural, therefore, that this associative element should form a part of the composer's medium. It is, however, I believe, not an essential part, especially since it consists so largely in associations which have their basis in movement. Quiet, lightly contrasted movement, for instance, may be associated with outer as well as inner tranquility—the light rustling of leaves in the wind, or the movement of a tranquil sea-just as agitated movement may be employed to suggest the storms in nature, as well as the perturbations of the spirit. On the other hand, we meet with associations of a far less essential nature-the tone of the trumpet, for instance, suggesting martial ideas, or certain localisms-folk songs, exotic scales, bizarre instrumental combinations, etc., which are used for the purposes of specific and literal coloring. But one would hardly attach more than a very superficial musical significance to associations of this type. They belong definitely in the sphere of applied art, and when they occur in works of serious import they serve, in conformity with an expressed intention of the composer, in a decidedly subordinate capacity, to direct the listener to more concrete associations than the music, in its essential content, can convey.

The above considerations indicate why a certain type of literary rhapsody seems to the musician quite amateurish and beside the point, in spite of the fact that musicians themselves-even great ones-have occasionally indulged in it. At best it is a literary production, bearing no real relationship to the music and throwing no real light on its content, but expressing the literary impulses of the author with more or less significance, according to his personality. Thus it is that of three distinguished commentators on Beethoven's *Seventh Symphony*—all three of them composers, and two of them composers of genius—one finds it a second *Eroica,* another a second *Pastorale,* and the third "the apotheosis of the dance." It must not be forgotten that, for the composer, notes, chords, melodic intervals-all the musical materials-are far more real, far more expressive, than words; that, let us say, a "leading tone" or a chord of the subdominant are for him not only notes, but sensations, full of meaning and capable of infinite nuances of modification; and that when he speaks or thinks in terms of them he is using words which, however obscure and dry they may sound to the uninitiated, are for him fraught with dynamic sense.

So, in trying to understand the work of the composer, one must first think of him as living in a world of sounds, which in response to his creative impulse become animated with movement. The first stage in his work is that of what is generally known by the somewhat shopworn and certainly unscientific term "inspiration." The composer, to use popular language again, "has an idea"—an idea, let me make clear, consisting of definite musical notes and rhythms, which will engender for him the momentum with which his musical thought proceeds. The inspiration may come in a flash, or as sometimes happens, it may grow and develop gradually. I have in my possession photostatic copies of several pages of Beethoven's sketches for the last movement of his "Hammerklavier Sonata;" the sketches show him carefully modelling, then testing in systematic and apparently cold-blooded fashion, the theme of the fugue. Where, one might ask, is the inspiration here? Yet if the word has any meaning at all, it is certainly appropriate to this movement, with its irresistible and titanic energy of expression, already present in the theme. The inspiration takes the form, however, not of a sudden flash of music, but a clearly envisaged impulse toward a certain goal for which the composer was obliged to strive. When this perfect realization was attained, however, there could have been no hesitation-rather a flash of recognition that this was exactly what he wanted.

Inspiration, then, is the impulse which sets creation in movement: it is also the energy which keeps it going. The composer's principal problem is that of recapturing it in every phase of his work; of bringing, in other words, the requisite amount of energy to bear on every detail, as well as, constantly, on his vision of the whole.

This vision of the whole I should call the conception. For the musician this too takes the form of concrete musical materials-perceived, however, not in detail but in foreshortened form. The experience, I believe, is quite different for the mature and experienced composer from what it is for the young beginner. As he grows in practice and imagination it assumes an ever more preponderant role, and appears more and more to be the essential act of creation. It differs from what I have described as "inspiration" only in works of large dimensions which cannot be realized in a short space of time. It arises out of the original inspiration, and is, so to speak, an extension of its logic.

What I have described as inspiration, embodies itself in what is the only true sense of the word "style;" conception, in the only true sense of the word "form." Neither style nor form, in their essence, are derived from convention; they always must be, and are, created anew, and establish and follow their own laws. It is undeniable that certain periods—and the most fortunate ones—have established clearly defined patterns or standards which give the artist a basis on which to create freely. Our own is not one of these; today the individual is obliged to discover his own language before he has completed the mastery of it. Where such standards exist, however, they retain their vitality only as long as they are in the process of development. After this process has stopped, they wither and die, and can be re-created

only by a conscious and essentially artificial effort, since they are produced by a unique and unrecoverable impulse, and are suited only to
the content which has grown with them.

After inspiration and conception comes execution. The process of
execution is first of all that of listening inwardly to the music as it
shapes itself; of allowing the music to grow; of following both inspiration and conception wherever they may lead. A phrase, a motif, a
rhythm, even a chord, may contain within itself, in the composer's
imagination, the energy which produces movement. It will lead the
composer on, through the force of its own momentum or tension, to
other phrases, other motifs, other chords.

...Composition is a *deed,* an action, and a genuine action of any
kind is, psychologically speaking, the simplest thing in the world. Is
not its subjective essence intentness on the deed? The climber in the
high mountains is intent on the steps he is taking, on the practical
realization of those steps; if he allows his consciousness to dwell even
on their implications, his foot may move the fatal half inch too far
in the direction of the abyss at his side. The composer working at his
music is faced with no such tragic alternatives; but his psychology is
not dissimilar. He is not so much conscious of his ideas as possessed
by them. Very often he is unaware of his exact processes of thought
till he is through with them; extremely often the completed work is
incomprehensible to him immediately after it is finished.

Why? Because his experience in creating the work is incalculably more intense than any later experience he can have from it; because the finished product is, so to speak, the goal of that experience and not in any sense a repetition of it. He cannot relive the experience without effort which seems quite irrelevant. And yet he is too close to it to detach himself to the extent necessary to see his work objectively, and to allow it to exert its inherent power over him.

For this reason I have always profoundly disagreed with the definition made by one of my most distinguished living colleagues who, elaborating Aristotle's famous definition of art, wrote that art on the highest level is concerned with *"der Wiedergabe der inneren Natur"*—literally translated, "the reproduction of inner nature." It seems to me on the contrary, that art is a function, an activity of the inner nature—that the artist's effort is, using the raw and undisciplined materials with which his inner nature provides him, to endow them with a meaning which they do not of themselves possess—to transcend them by giving them artistic form. Is not this what a far greater musician, Beethoven, meant, in the words quoted by Bettina Brentano: *"Ruhrung passt nur an Frauenzimmer (verzeih 'mir); dem Manne muss Musik Feuer aus dem Geiste schlagen"*—"Emotion is fit only for women—for man, music must strike fire from his mind."

From "The Composer and His Message," by Roger Sessions in *The Intent of the Artist,* edited by Augusto Centeno. By permission of the publishers: Princeton University Press, Princeton, New Jersey.

THE MUSICAL MIND

Harold Shapero

The musical mind is concerned predominantly with the mechanism of tonal memory. Before it has absorbed a considerable variety of tonal experiences it cannot begin to function in a creative way complex enough to be considered as art. Though the tonal experiences offered to it at any given period of musical history are subject to change—for example, Bach could not hear the timbre of the saxophone, or the pan-diatonic chordal arrangements of Stravinsky; nor could a modern musician hear the sonorities of the baroque trumpets, or the exact nature of the improvised accompaniments derived from the thorough-bass—the mnemonic methods by which these experiences are retained and later exploited creatively remain the same.

The musical memory, where its physiological functions are intact, functions indiscriminately: a great percentage of what is heard becomes submerged in the unconscious, and is subject to literal recall. The creative portion of the musical mind, however, operates selectively, and the tonal material which it offers up has been metamorphosed, and has become unidentifiable from the material which was originally absorbed. In the metamorphosis which has taken place the original tonal material has become compounded with remembered emotional experiences, and it is this action of the creative unconscious which renders music more than an acoustical series of tones, which gives to music its humanistic aspect.

In our time the musical mind is confronted with a great variety of tonal experiences: an immense historical literature has been accumulated and is constantly performed. It is, then, more difficult than ever before for the creative musician to absorb, select and integrate the materials which will make up his art. How then can he make his task easier? If he re-examines the fundamental nature of musical syntax, which actually involves the effort of understanding in the most profound way the manner in which the creative mind works, he cannot fail to gain a true insight into his artistic powers. There is prevalent the superstition that if the composer devotes too much attention to the analysis of the creative process, a catastrophe results in which his inspiration is destroyed and his art rendered meaningless, and that this meddling with a natural function is a result of over-rationalistic thinking stemming from the modern emphasis on scientific method. It is supposed that in earlier periods artists less preoccupied with this problem of understanding found it easier to produce satisfactory works of art. But there is evidence that the earlier composers were concerned to a greater extent with the mechanisms of the creative mind than are the composers of today. The well-known letter of Mozart in which he describes the methods by which a composition takes shape in his mind demonstrates clearly the degree of his interest in the matter. It is known that one of the few books which he owned was Hume's *Treatise on Human Understanding,* and that Mesmer, the discoverer of hypnotism, was one of his close friends. The following letter by Beethoven shows that he as well possessed a remarkable insight into the structure of his creative mind:

Baden, Sept. 10, 1821
To Tobias von Haslinger
My very dear friend,
On my way to Vienna yesterday, sleep overtook me in my carriage....While thus slumbering I dreamt that I had gone on a far journey, to no less a place than Syria, on to Judea and back, and then all the way to Arabia, when at length I actually arrived at Jerusalem. The Holy City gave rise to thoughts of the Holy Books. No wonder then if the man Tobias occurred to me, which led me to think of our own little Tobias and our great Tobias.

But scarcely did I awake when away flew the canon, and I could not recall any part of it. On returning here however, next day, in the same carriage...I resumed my dream-jour ney, being on this occasion wide awake, when lo and behold! in accordance with the laws of association of ideas *[The use of this phrase is indeed striking.-H.S.],* the same canon flashed across me; so being now awake I held it as fast as Menelaus did Proteus, only permitting it to be changed into three parts....

If the modern composer, in the effort to understand better his creative mind, attempts to re-examine the elements of musical syntax, he must immediately find himself occupied with the nature of melody, for it is the melodic phrase, exactly equivalent to the sentence in the syntax of language, which serves as the primary element in almost any musical structure. By investigating the possibilities of phrase construction and discovering for himself what can be done within a small formal frame the composer not only disciplines his creative unconscious so that the melodic fragments which it offers up possess increased sharpness of contour, but develops at the same time the architectural faculty which will enable him to calculate correctly the time-spaces involved in the manipulation of larger musical forms. Haydn, Mozart and Beethoven possessed the greatest mastery of musical phraseology, and it was at that historical period that such a mastery was stylistically most welcome, for the composers who followed soon became interested in subjectifying the tonal material, with the result that continuity established by means of small connected phrase groups broke down and was replaced by the concept of organic form.

If a composer finds himself sympathetic to the classical quality of expression, he can derive immense benefit from a detailed examination of the melodic procedures of the three great Viennese masters. He will find it logical to begin his studies with the trio forms, such as the minuet and scherzo, for these do not demand the complexities of episodic treatment, and present the clearest examples of the simple musical sentence. As a technical exercise he may copy down the soprano line of one of these sentences and attempt to supply the accompanying parts, comparing his result with that of the master. He will find that with practice he is able to duplicate the original accompaniments or supply alternatives which are equally proficient technically. As a further step he may begin writing accompanying parts to soprano lines which he has himself composed in imitation of his models. Gradually his mind will acquire the ability to direct a phrase which starts in the tonic to the dominant, mediant, submediant, or other destinations, as well as to extend it to any desired length. It is then that he will understand that if he focuses his attention on a definite key and beats mentally in a chosen meter, musical images will be set in motion in his mind, and the entire musical texture generated in this way. It is extremely important to practice these exercises in all keys and all rhythms so that the greatest degree of fluency may be attained. The importance of daily practice also cannot be overemphasized, for without it the bridge established between the conscious and the creative unconscious by technical exercise is soon blocked by non-musical associations. Just as the function of daily ritual and prayer, as related to the intuitive realization of deity, is that of preserving the thread of connected thoughts which lead to the intuition itself, so the function of daily technical practice, as related to musical composition, is that of maintaining free the inroad to that corner of the mind from which the music comes.

As the composer continues to work exercises in imitation of his models he will be surprised to find that along with the thousand subtleties of technique he will absorb from his masters, he will discover the personal materials of his own art. These will often be presented to him in dreams, or in the half-waking state of consciousness, before the inner critical faculty has had the opportunity to act in selecting and repressing the given material. From these experiences he will gradually accumulate the technical stuffs of a private creative world, possessing capabilities of change and expansion according to his expressive needs.

It is not only in our time that composers have been compelled to build this inner world, though the breakdown of the old tonal system and the great diversity of contemporary styles have created this illusion among us. Bach copied zealously the manuscripts of Buxtehude in which he found a point of departure. Beethoven as a young man spoke of the excitement with which he discovered for himself a certain modulatory sequence (I-V of II—II-V of III—III-V of IV—IV, etc.) especially suited for climaxes. It seems to us, as we survey the music of these earlier composers with the comfortable assurance given us by centuries of musical analysis, that they faced problems which were negligible compared with those facing the composers of today, yet each of them discovered technical devices in advance of the theoretical understanding of his time, musical uses which could not be analyzed by his contemporaries.

We are familiar with the efforts of the great modern composers to create technical systems which will provide them with the tools of expression. Schonberg and Hindemith, not satisfied with pointing out the esthetic inevitability of the paths they have chosen, have taken great pains to establish their systems on a- scientific basis. They have encountered so many difficulties in reconciling their systems with those of the past that we may assume that they have come into conflict with the natural functions of the musical mind. Though it is true, as they contend, that the creative mentality can be forced to function within an atonal frame (Hindemith's system is less atonal than Schonberg's in its implications, for though it endeavors to support a free chromatic scheme, it is concerned with the binding qualities of intervals and polar tones), it undergoes a considerable warping in the process. It is as if a man were taught to walk with bent knees because of the inordinate lowness of the ceiling. Many of us feel that it is Stravinsky, in the works of his late period, who has best succeeded in organizing the elements of his musical speech, and that the direction he has indicated offers a most important road for future development. It is interesting that he has not felt it necessary to attempt a scientific justification for his diatonic methods, but has relied on the intelligence of his inner ear.

If the composer is to reject systems such as those of Hindemith and Schonberg on the grounds that they conflict with the natural functions of the musical mind, he must be prepared to stand ground as to what can be considered natural functioning. It is evident that inspiration is a most vital component of art. It is through inspired thematic and structural materials that the composer most surely communicates to his listeners the force of his creations, through them that his works possess their greatest chance for survival. In this sense it is possible to consider inspiration the creative absolute. It is certain that inspiration occurs only when the artist is compelled to give something of himself, and when his creative imagination is unhampered by technical procedures unsuited to it. Thus a system of musical materials which fails to lead to inspiration can be considered unnatural, and a system which leads to inspiration can be considered one which insures the natural functioning of the creative mind. The composer can be certain that something has gone wrong with his musical thinking when he loses his inspiration. The composer to whom inspiration is granted can be assured that he is drawing on the most significant creative forces which are available to him. He is in a position to perceive the musical mind in its permanent aspects.

From "The Musical Mind," by Harold Shapero, in *Modern Music,* Winter, 1946. By permission of the author and the publishers of *Modern Music:* The League of Composers, New York City.

LETTER TO ANTON RITTER VAN RAPPARD

Vincent van Gogh

I have been working very hard. I had not made many compositions or studies for a long time, so when I once got started, I became so eager that many a morning I got up at four o'clock....
It must not surprise you that some of my figures are so entirely different from those I make at times when I use models.

I seldom work from memory—I do not practice that kind of thing very much. Besides, I am so used to work with the natural form now and can keep my personal feeling out of it much better than I could at first. I waver less—and just because I am sitting opposite the model, SOMETIMES I FEEL MORE LIKE MYSELF. When I have a model who is quiet and steady and with whom I am acquainted, then I draw repeatedly till there is one drawing that is different from the rest, which does not look like an ordinary study, but more typical and with more feeling. All the same it was made under circumstances similar to those of the others, yet the latter are just studies with less feeling and life in them. This manner of working is like another one, just as plausible. As to *The Little Winter Gardens,* for example, you said yourself they had so much feeling; all right, but that was not accidental—I drew them several times and there was no feeling in them. Then afterwards—after I had done the ones that were so stiff—came the others. It is the same with the clumsy and awkward things. HOW IT HAPPENS THAT I CAN EXPRESS SOMETHING OF THAT KIND? Because the thing has already taken form in my mind before I start on it. The first attempts are absolutely unbearable. I say this because I want you to know that if you see something worth while in what I am doing, it is not by accident but because of real intention and purpose.

I am very much pleased to have you notice that of late I have been trying to express the values of crowds, and that I try to separate things in the dizzy whirl and chaos one can see in each little corner of Nature.

Formerly the light and shade in my studies were mostly arbitrary, at least they were not put down logically, and so they were colder and flatter. When I once get the *feeling of my subject,* and get to know it, I usually draw it in three or more variations—be it a figure or landscape—only I always refer to Nature for every one of them and then I do my best not to put in *any detail,* as the dream quality would then be lost. When Tersteeg or my brother then says to me: "What is that, grass or coal?" I answer: "Glad to hear that you cannot see what it is."

Still it is enough like Nature for the simple peasants of this part of the country. They say: "Yes, that's the hedge of Juffrouw Renese," and: "There are the beanpoles of van der Louw."

Translated by Rela van Messel

From *Letters to an Artist: Vincent van Gogh to Anton Ridder van Rappard,* translated by Rela van Messel. By permission of the publishers: The Viking Press, Inc., copyright 1936, New York City.

CONVERSATION WITH PICASSO

Christian Zervos

L ast winter, I was with Picasso at his estate of Boisgeloup, for the purpose of choosing the works reproduced in this number [of Cahiers d'Art]. At the moment I had already in mind the examination of art, published in the first number of this year, and I focused my conversation on this subject. Picasso spoke to me simply, but with the emotion which he knows how to put into his words, when he speaks-of art (he speaks about it rarely), and which gives to each word a direct sense that transcription cannot preserve.

"I report his ideas here as accurately as my memory made possible on the very evening of my visit to Boisgeloup. They have not been read over by Picasso. To my proposal to show my notes to him, he answered: 'You need not show them to me. The essential, in these times of moral misery, is to create enthusiasm. How many people have read Homer? Nevertheless everyone speaks of him. Thus the Homeric myth has been created. A myth of this kind creates a precious excitation. It is enthusiasm of which we have the most need, we and the young.'

"This conversation by fits and starts is then reproduced here without order or sequence, for fear of involuntarily distorting the sense." Christian Zervos.

We can make over to fit the artist the quip of the man who said there is nothing more dangerous than instruments of war in the hands of generals. In the same way there is nothing more dangerous than justice in the hands of judges and paint brushes in the hands of the painter! Imagine the danger for a society! But today we haven't the spirit to banish the poets and painters, for we no longer have any idea of the danger of keeping them in the city.

To my distress and perhaps to my delight, I order things in accordance with my passions. What a sad thing for a painter who loves blondes but denies himself the pleasure of putting them in his picture because they don't go well with the basket of fruit! What misery for a painter who detests apples to have to use them all the time because they harmonize with the table cloth! I put in my pictures everything I like. So much the worse for the things—they have to get along with one another.

Heretofore pictures moved toward their completion by progression. Each day brought something new. A picture was a sum of additions. With me, a picture is a sum of destructions. I make a picture, and proceed to destroy it. But in the end nothing is lost; the red I have removed from one part shows up in another.

It would be very interesting to record photographically, not the stages of a painting, but its metamorphoses. One would see perhaps by what course a mind finds its way towards the crystallization of its dream. But what is really very curious is to see that the picture does not change basically, that the initial vision remains almost intact in spite of appearances. I see often a light and a dark, when I have put them in my picture, I do everything I can to 'break them up,' in adding a color that creates a counter effect. I perceive, when this work is photographed, that what I have introduced to correct my first vision has disappeared, and that after all the photographic image corresponds to my first vision, before the occurrence of the transformations brought about by my will.

The picture is not thought out and determined beforehand, rather while it is being made it follows the mobility of thought. Finished, it changes further, according to the condition of him who looks at it. A picture lives its life like a living creature, undergoing the changes that daily life imposes upon us. That is natural, since a picture lives only through him who looks at it.

When I am working on a picture, I think of a white and apply a white. But I cannot continue to work, think and apply a white; colors, like lineaments, follow the changes of emotion. You have seen the sketch I made of a picture with all the colors indicated. What is left? Still, the white I thought of, the green I thought of are in the picture; but not in the place foreseen, nor in the expected quantity. Naturally pictures can be made out of harmonizing patches, but they will have no dramatic quality.

I want to develop the ability to do a picture in such a way that no one can ever see how it has been done. To what end? What I want is that my picture should evoke nothing but emotion.

Work is a necessity for man.

A horse does not go by itself between the shafts.

Man invented the alarm clock.

At the beginning of each picture there is someone who works with me. Toward the end I have the impression of having worked without a collaborator.

When one begins a picture one often discovers fine things. One ought to beware of these, destroy one's picture, recreate it many times. On each destruction of a beautiful find, the artist does not suppress it, to tell the truth; rather he transforms it, condenses it, makes it more substantial. The issue is the result of rejected discoveries. Otherwise one becomes one's own admirer. I sell myself nothing!

In reality one works with few colors. What gives the illusion of many is that they have been put in the right place.

Abstract art is only painting. And drama?

There is no abstract art. One always has to begin with something. One can then remove all appearance of reality; one runs no risk, for the idea of the object has left an ineffaceable imprint. It is the thing that aroused the artist, stimulated his ideas, stirred his emotions. Ideas and emotions will ultimately be prisoners of his work; whatever they do, they can't escape from the picture; they form an integral part of it, even when their presence is no longer discernible. Whether he likes it or not, man is the instrument of nature; it imposes its character, its appearance, upon him. In my Dinard pictures, as in those of Pourville, I expressed almost the same vision. But you have seen yourself how different is the atmosphere of the pictures made in Brittany and in Normandy, since you have recognized the light of the cliffs of Dieppe. I did not copy this light, I didn't pay particular attention to it. I was simply bathed by it; my eyes saw and my subconscious registered their vision; my hand recorded my sensations. One cannot oppose nature. It is stronger than the strongest of men! We have all an interest in being on good terms with her. We can permit ourselves some liberties, but only in detail.

There is not, moreover, a figurative and a nonfigurative art. Everything appears to us in the form of figures. Even in metaphysics ideas are expressed by figures; thus you can understand how absurd it would be to think of painting without images of figures. A person, an object, a circle, are figures; they act upon us more or less intensely. Some are nearer to our sensations, produce emotions which concern our affective faculties; others appeal more especially to the intellect. They must all be accepted, for my spirit has as much need of emotion as my senses. Do you think it interests me that this picture represents two people? These two people once existed, but they exist no longer. The vision of them gave me an initial emotion, little by little their real presence became obscured, they became for me a fiction, then they disappeared, or rather were transformed into problems of all sorts. For me they aren't two people any more, but forms and colors, understand, forms and colors which sum up, however, the idea of the two people and conserve the vibration of their life.

I behave with my painting as I behave with things. I paint a window, just as I look through a window. If this window when open doesn't look good in my picture, I draw a curtain and close it as I would have done in my room. One must act in painting, as in life, directly. Admittedly painting has its conventions, of which it is necessary to take account, since one can't do otherwise. For this reason one must have constantly before one's eyes the very presence of life.

The artist is a receptacle of emotions come from no matter where: from the sky, the earth, a piece of paper, a passing figure, a cobweb. This is why one must not discriminate between things. There is no rank among them. One must take one's good where one finds it, except in one's own works. I have a horror of copying myself, but I have no hesitation, when I am shown for example a portfolio of old drawings, in taking from them whatever I want.

When we invented Cubism, we had no intention of inventing cubism, but simply of expressing what was in us. Nobody drew up a program of action, and though our friends the poets followed our efforts attentively, they never dictated to us. The young painters of today often outline a program for themselves to follow and try to do their assignments correctly like well-behaved schoolboys.

The painter passes through states of fullness and of emptying. That is the whole secret of art. I take a walk in the forest of Fontainebleau.

There I get an indigestion of greenness. I must empty this sensation into a picture. Green dominates in it. The painter paints as if in urgent need to discharge himself of his sensations and his visions. Men take possession of it as a means of covering their nakedness a little. They take what they can and as they can. I believe that finally they take nothing, they quite simply cut out a coat to the measure of their own incomprehension. They make in their own image everything from God to the picture. That is why the nail is the undoer of painting. Painting has always some importance, at least that of the man who made it. The day it is bought and hung on the wall it takes on an importance of another kind, and the painting is done for.

The academic teaching about beauty is false. We are deceived, but so well deceived that it is impossible to recover even the shadow of a truth. The beauties of the Parthenon, the Venuses, the Nymphs, the Narcissuses, are so many lies. Art is not the application of a canon of beauty, but what instinct and intellect can conceive independently of the canon. When one loves a woman one doesn't take instruments and measure her, one loves her with desire, and nevertheless everything has been done to introduce the canon even into love. To tell the truth the Parthenon is nothing but a farmhouse with a roof; colonnades and sculptures were added because in Athens there were people who worked and who wanted to express themselves. It is not what the artist does that counts, but what he is. Cézanne would never have interested me if he had lived and thought like Jacques-Emile

Blanche, even if the apple he painted had been ten times as beautiful. What interests us is the uneasiness of Cézanne, the real teaching of Cézanne, the torments of van Gogh, that is to say the drama of the man. The rest is false.

Everybody wants to understand painting. Why is there no attempt to understand the song of birds? Why does one love a night, a flower, everything that surrounds a man, without trying to understand it all? While as for painting, one wants to understand. Let it be understood above all that the artist works by necessity, that he is, he too, a least element of the world, to which no more importance should be attached than to so many natural things which charm us but which we do not explain to ourselves. Those who try to explain a picture are most of the time on the wrong track. Gertrude Stein announced to me joyously some time ago that she had at last understood what my picture represented: three musicians. It was a still life!

How would you have a spectator live my picture as I have lived it? A picture comes to me from far off, who knows how far, I divined it, I saw it, I made it, and yet next day I myself don't see what I have done. How can one penetrate my dreams, my instincts, my desires, my thoughts, which have taken a long time to elaborate themselves and bring themselves to the light, above all seize in them what I brought about, perhaps, against my will?

With the exception of some painters who are opening new horizons to painting, the youth of today do not know any more where to go. Instead of taking up our researches in order to react sharply against us, they apply themselves to reanimating the past. Yet the world is open before us, everything is still to be done, and not to be done over again. Why hang on hopelessly to everything that has fulfilled its promise? There are kilometers of painting in the manner of; but it is rare to see a young man working in his own way.

Is there some notion abroad that man can't repeat himself? To repeat is to go against the laws of the spirit, its forward motion.

I am no pessimist, I do not dislike art, for I could not live without devoting all my hours to it. I love it as the whole end of my life. Everything I do in connection with art gives me a tremendous joy. Nevertheless I don't see why everybody busies himself about art, calls it to account, and on the subject gives vent freely to his own folly. The museums are so many lies, the people who occupy themselves with art are for the most part imposters. I don't understand why there should be more prejudices about art in the revolutionary countries than in the backward ones! We have imposed upon the pictures in the museums all our stupidities, our errors, the pretenses of our spirit. We have made poor ridiculous things of them. We cling to myths instead of sensing the inner life of the men who painted them. There ought to be an absolute dictatorship...a dictatorship of painters...the dictatorship of a painter...to suppress all who have deceived us, to suppress the tricksters, to suppress the matter of deception, to suppress habits, to suppress charm, to suppress history, to suppress a lot of other things. But good sense will always carry the day. One ought above all to make a revolution against good sense! The true dictator will always be vanquished by the dictatorship of good sense...Perhaps not!

Translated by Brewster Ghiselin

From "Conversation avec Picasso," by Christian Zervos *in Cahiers d'Art,* 1935. By permission of the publishers of *Cahiers d'Art,* Paris.

EAST TO WEST

Yasuo Kuniyoshi

In 1925 and again in 1928 after my pictures had begun to sell we went abroad. There I admired and studied the old masters and traveled widely to see them. I was impressed by French contemporaries, especially for their keen understanding of their medium. I was excited about the things I saw, but in spite of persuasion on the part of Pascin and several other friends to stay longer in France, I was terribly glad to get back to New York. I found much to admire in French painters. There are so many little artists here, so few real painters. There they had so many fine painters.

The trip proved a great stimulus, enlarging my scope and vision. Almost everybody on the other side was painting directly from the object, something I hadn't done all these years. It was rather difficult to change my approach since up to then I had painted almost entirely from imagination and my memories of the past.

Throughout these many years of painting I have practiced starting my work from reality stating the facts before me. Then I paint without the object for a certain length of time, combining reality and imagination.

I have often obtained in painting directly from the object that which appears to be real results at the very first shot, but when that does happen, I purposely destroy what I have accomplished and re-do it over and over again. In other words that which comes easily I distrust. When I have condensed and simplified sufficiently I know then that I have something more than reality.

A word I often use is "felt," the meaning of which I try to get across in my painting. To me it means the realization of facts. For instance when painting a floor I want that floor to be a floor. Whatever object I am painting I try to realize its relation point by point.; the relation of myself to the object, and in the same way, point by point, the relation of the object to the background so as to make this object exist in space.

Comments upon the object or the fact of the object are not sufficient elements for a full expression. Each artist has to face the forces of nature and mould them together with his experience in order to create drama. Drama takes on different expressions according to the time and place.

I spend a long time drawing from the object although I never make a composition in smaller scale no matter how large a canvas I am working on. I start drawing right on the canvas, working very carefully at the beginning for the painting, and develop the drawing until it fully suggests the subject. This enables me to carry on with the painting without the object in front of me.

As time goes on colors take on a new significance. I don't use as many colors as I used to, but try more precisely to paint, in relation to color, so as to produce more color without using many colors. For luminosity I build a darker color on top of a lighter color. I believe in glazing to achieve depth and transparency of color.

I like to start as many canvases as I can during the summer. I carry them to a certain point so that when I start working on them again, usually back in New York in the winter, it means about six months have elapsed since I originally started the canvas. Therefore I sometimes have about a dozen canvases going at the same time. I never paint over, even a small area, if there are changes to be made. Instead I always scrape down to the canvas and rebuild again.

There are numerous problems that beset the artist in his work. Consciously or unconsciously each artist tries to solve them. Lately I have come to the stage where I actually take a problem and try to solve it. For instance I was interested in painting a dark object within the dark. In order to carry this out successfully it may take me several years. Once accomplished to my satisfaction, however, it becomes an integral part of me, enabling me to go on to another problem.

From "East to West," by Yasuo Kuniyoshi in the *Magazine of Art,* February, 1940. By permission of the author and the publishers of *Magazine of Art:* The American Federation of Arts, New York City.

BEFORE PARIS AND AFTER

Julian Levi

I find it rather difficult to write about my own painting. Briefly, I am seeking an integration between what I feel and what I have learned by objective criteria; an integration between the tired experienced eye and the childlike simple perception; but above all I hope to resolve the polarity which exists between an essentially emotional view of nature and a classical, austere sense of design. *"In truth, I have painted by opening my eyes day and night on the perceptible world, and also by closing them from time to time that I might better see the vision blossom and submit itself to orderly arrangement."* This quotation from an article by Georges Rouault, which appeared in Verve, is to me rich in meaning and summarizes, with Gallic brevity, precisely what I have been driving at.

It seems to me that almost every artist finds some subdivision of nature or experience more congenial to his temperament than any other. To me it has been the sea—or rather those regions adjacent to the sea—beaches, dunes, swampy coasts. I haven't the space to go into the roots of this particular nostalgia but it has been part of my life since early childhood.

As a secondary interest, I cherish the human physiognomy, the painting of people who, for diverse reasons, I find arresting. I seldom find my models among people of superlative beauty or symmetry. I am often fascinated by "brats" of eight or nine with stringy hair and querulous expressions...

In painting the sea coast I have tried to acquire as much objective knowledge of the subject as I possibly could. I know the people of those regions and I have become reasonably familiar with their activities. I have studied their fishing gear, their boats and assorted paraphernalia. I have learned how to sail (very badly, I regret to say) and the techniques of professional fishing. I don't lay great stress on the necessity of this kind of documentation but it does give me the feeling of being more closely related to what I have chosen to paint. There is another aspect of an artist's choice of his subject matter which I think could be profitably explored. It is that I believe he is affectively related to certain forms and designs. I believe his choice is channeled by the compulsion to find an objective vehicle for inward plastic images. I certainly do not know why, but I am stirred by certain geometrical relationships, certain rectangular forms and arabesques out of which grow particular harmonies and rhythms. In deciding what subject I shall paint I am irresistibly drawn to objects which contain the skeleton of this type of plastic structure. Whether I am spending the summer on Barnegat Bay or on Cape Cod or merely sketching along the Harlem River, I somehow contrive to find the exact set of lines and contours which this inner appetite demands.

I try to remember that painting at its best is a form of communication, that it is constantly reaching out to find response from an ideal and sympathetic audience. This I know is not accomplished by pictorial rhetoric nor by the manipulation of seductive paint surfaces. Nor is a good picture concocted out of theatrical props, beautiful subjects, or memories of other paintings. All these might astound but they will never communicate the emotional content or exaltation of life, which I believe an artist, by definition, has to accept as his task.

From "Before Paris and After," by Julian Levi in the *Magazine of Art,* December, 1940. By permission of the author and the publishers of *Magazine of Art:* The American Federation of Arts, New York City.

INSPIRATION TO ORDER

Max Ernst

It all started on August 10, 1925, by my recalling an incident of
my childhood when the sight of an imitation mahogany panel
opposite my bed had induced one of those dreams between sleeping
and waking. And happening to be at a seaside inn in wet weather
I was struck by the way the floor, its grain accentuated by many
scrubbings, obsessed my nervously excited gaze. So I decided to ex-
plore-the symbolism of the obsession, and to encourage my powers
of meditation and hallucination I took a series of drawings from the
floorboards by dropping pieces of paper on them at random and
then rubbing the paper with blacklead. As I looked carefully at the
drawings that I got in this way—some dark, others smudgily dim—I
was surprised by the sudden heightening of my visionary powers,
and by the dreamlike succession of contradictory images that came
one on top of another with the persistence and rapidity peculiar to
memories of love.

Now my curiosity was roused and excited, and I began an impar-
tial exploration, making use of every kind of material that happened
to come into my field of vision: leaves and their veins, frayed edges
of sacking, brushstrokes in a 'modern' painting, cotton unwound

from a cotton-reel, etc., etc. Then I saw human heads, many different beasts, a battle ending in a kiss *(the wind's sweetheart), rocks, sea and rain, earth-tremors, the sphinx in its stable, the small tables round about the earth, Caesar's shoulder-blade, false positions, a shawl covered with flowers of hoar frost, pampas.*

The *cuts of a whip, trickles of lava, fields of honour, inundations and seismic plants, scarecrows, the edge of the chestnut wood.*

> *Flashes of lightning before one's fourteenth year, vaccinated bread, conjugal diamonds, the cuckoo (origin of the pendulum), the meal of death, the wheel of light.*
> *A solar coinage system.*
> *The habits of leaves, the fascinating cyprus tree.*
> *Eve, the only one remaining to us.*

I put the first fruits of the *frottage* process together, from *sea and rain* to *Eve, the only one remaining to us,* and called it *Natural History.*

I stress the fact that, through a series of suggestions and transmutations arrived at spontaneously like hypnotic visions, drawings obtained in this way lose more and more of the character of the material being explored (wood, for instance). They begin to appear as the kind of unexpectedly clear images most likely to throw light on the first cause of the obsession, or at least to provide a substitute for it.

And so the *frottage* process simply depends on intensifying the mind's capacity for nervous excitement, using the appropriate technical means, excluding all conscious directing of the mind (towards reason, taste, or morals) and reducing to a minimum the part played by him formerly known as the 'author' of the work. The process, in consequence, shows up as a true equivalent of what we now call *automatic* writing. The author is present as a spectator, indifferent or impassioned, at the birth of his own work, and observes the phases of his own development. just as the poet's place, since the celebrated *Letter of a Clairvoyant,* consists in writing at the dictation of something that makes itself articulate within him, so the artist's role is to gather together and then give out that which makes itself *visible* within him. In devoting myself to this activity (or passivity)—later we called it *paranoic criticism*—and adapting *frottage,* which seemed at first only applicable to drawing, to the technical mediums of painting (for instance, scratching colours on a prepared coloured ground, over an uneven surface), and in trying all the time to reduce still more my own active participation in the making of a picture, so as to widen the active field of the mind's capacity for hallucination, I succeeded in being present as a spectator at the birth of all my works after August 10, 1925, the memorable day of the discovery of *frottage.* Being a man of 'ordinary constitution' (to use Rimbaud's terms) I have done my best to *make my soul monstrous.* A blind swimmer, I have made myself clairvoyant. I have seen. I have become the amazed lover of what I have seen, wanting to identify myself with it.

In 1930, when I had, with a passion that was yet systematic, composed my book, *The Hundred-headed Woman,* I had an almost daily visit from the *Head of the Birds,* called Loplop, a very special phantom of exceptional faithfulness, who is attached to my person. *He presented me with a heart in a cage, the sea in a cage, two petals, three leaves, a flower and a girl; and also the man with the black eggs, and the man with the red cloak.* One fine autumn afternoon he told me that one day a *Lacedaemonian had been asked to go and hear a man who could imitate the nightingale perfectly. The Lacedaemonian answered: I have often heard the nightingale itself.* One evening he told me some jokes that were not funny. Joke—it is better not to reward a fine action at all than to reward it badly. A soldier had both arms blown off in a battle. His colonel offered him half-a-crown. The soldier said to him: `I suppose, sir, you think I've only lost a pair of gloves.'

What is the mechanism of collage?

I think I would say that it amounts to *the exploitation of the chance meeting on a non-suitable plane of two mutually distant realities* (a paraphrase and generalization of the well-known quotation from Lautréamont *'Beautiful as the chance meeting upon a dissecting table of a sewing machine and an umbrella')* or, *more simply, the cultivation of systematic moving out of place on the lines of Andre Breton's theory: Super-reality must in any case be the function of our will to put everything completely out of place (naturally one could go so far as to put a hand out of place by isolating it from an arm, then the hand thereby gains, as a hand; and, what is more, when we speak of putting things out of place we are not thinking only of space.* (Warning to the reader in *The Hundred-headed Woman.)*

A complete, real thing, with a simple function apparently fixed once and for all (an umbrella), coming suddenly into the presence of another real thing, very different and no less incongruous (a sewing machine) in surroundings where both must feel out of place (on a dissecting table), escapes by this very fact from its simple function and its own identity; through a new relationship its false absolute will be transformed into a different absolute, at once true and poetic: the umbrella and the sewing machine will make love. The mechanism of the process seems to me to be laid bare by this very simple example. Complete transmutation followed by a pure act such as the act of love must necessarily occur every time the given facts make conditions favourable: *the pairing of two realities which apparently cannot be paired on a plane apparently not suited to them.* Speaking of the collage process in 1920 Breton wrote:

> It is the marvellous capacity to grasp two mutually distant realities without going beyond the field of our experience and to draw a spark from their juxtaposition; to bring with in reach of our senses abstract forms capable of the same intensity and enhancement as any others; and, depriving us of any system of reference, to set us at odds with our own memories. *(Preface to Max Ernst exhibition,* May, 1920.)

The two *processes,* frottage and *collage,* are so alike that without changing much I can use the same words to describe the discovery of the one that I used earlier for the other. One day, in 1919, being in wet weather at a seaside inn, I was struck by the way the pages of an illustrated catalogue obsessed my nervously excited gaze. It was a catalogue of objects for anthropological, microscopic, psychological, mineralogical and paleontological demonstration. I found here united elements such poles apart that the very incongruousness of the assembly started off a sudden intensification of my visionary faculties and a dreamlike succession of contradictory images—double, triple and multiple images coming one on top of the other with the persistence and rapidity peculiar to memories of love, and to the dreams that come between sleeping and waking. These images themselves suggested new ways for them to meet in a new unknown (the plane of unsuitability). All I had to do was to add, either by painting, or drawing, to the pages of the catalogue. And I had only to reproduce obediently what made itself visible within me, a colour, a scrawl, a landscape strange to the objects gathered in it, a desert, a sky, a geological event, a floor, a single line drawn straight to represent the horizon, to get a fixed and faithful image of my hallucination; to transform what had been commonplaces of advertising into dramas revealing my most secret desires.

I think I can say without over-statement that Surrealism has made it possible for painting to travel in seven league boots miles from

Renoir's three apples, Manet's four sticks of asparagus, Derain's little chocolate women, and the Cubist's tobacco packet. It has opened up a field of vision limited only by the mind's capacity for nervous excitement. It goes without saying that this has been a great blow to the critics, who are terrified to see the 'author's' importance being reduced to a minimum and the conception of talent abolished. Against them, however, we maintain that surrealist painting is within reach of all those who are attracted by true revelations and who are therefore prepared to help on inspiration and make it work to order.

We have no doubt that by yielding naturally to the business of subduing appearances and upsetting the relationships of 'realities' it is helping, with a smile on its lips, to hasten the general crisis of consciousness due in our time.

Translated by Myfanwy Evans

From "Inspiration to Order," by Max Ernst in *The Painter's Object,* by Myfanwy Evans. By permission of the publishers: John Lane the Bodley Head Limited, London.

MAKING PICTURES

D.H.Lawrence

One has to eat one's own words. I remember I used to assert, perhaps I even wrote it: Everything that can possibly be painted has been painted, every brush-stroke that can possibly be laid on canvas has been laid on. The visual arts are at a dead end. Then suddenly, at the age of forty, I begin painting myself and am fascinated.

Still, going through the Paris picture shops this year of grace, and seeing the Dufys and Chiricos, etc., and the Japanese Ito with his wish-wash nudes with pearl-button eyes, the same weariness comes over one. They are all so would-be, they make such efforts. They at least have nothing to paint. In the midst of them a graceful Friesz flower-piece, or a blotting-paper Laurencin, seems a masterpiece. At least here is a bit of *natural* expression in paint. Trivial enough, when compared to the big painters, but still, as far as they go, real.

What about myself, then! What am I doing, bursting into paint? I am a writer, I ought to stick to ink. I have found my medium of expression; why, at the age of forty, should I suddenly want to try another?

Things happen, and we have no choice. If Maria Huxley hadn't come rolling up to our house near Florence with four rather large canvases, one of which she had busted, and presented them to me because they had been abandoned in her house, I might never have started in on a real picture in my life. But those nice stretched canvases were too tempting. We had been painting doors and window-frames in the house, so there was a little stock of oil, turps and colour in powder, such as one buys from an Italian drogheria. There were several brushes for house-painting. There was a canvas on which the unknown owner had made a start-mud-grey, with the beginnings of a red-haired man. It was a grimy and ugly beginning, and the young man who had made it had wisely gone no further. He certainly had had no inner compulsion: nothing in him, as far as paint was concerned, or if there was anything in him, it had stayed in, and only a bit of the mud-grey "group" had come out.

So for the sheer fun of covering a surface and obliterating that mud-grey, I sat on the floor with the canvas propped against a chair—and with my house-paint brushes and colours in little casseroles. I disappeared into that canvas. It is to me the most exciting moment—when you have a blank canvas and a big brush full of wet colour, and you plunge. It is just like diving into a pond—then you start frantically to swim. So far as I am concerned, it is like swimming in a baffling current and being rather frightened and very thrilled, gasping and striking out for all you're worth. The knowing eye watches sharp as a needle; but the picture comes clean out of instinct, intuition and sheer physical action. Once the instinct and intuition gets into the brush-tip, the picture *happens,* if it is to be a picture at all.

At least, so my first picture happened—the one I have called "A Holy Family." In a couple of hours there it all was, man, woman, child, blue shirt, red shawl, pale room—all in the rough, but, as far as I am concerned, a picture. The struggling comes later. But the picture itself comes in the first rush, or not at all. It is only when the picture has come into being that one can struggle and make it grow to completion.

Ours is an excessively conscious age. We *know* so much, we feel so little. I have lived enough among painters and around studios to have had all the theories—and how contradictory they are—rammed down my throat. A man has to have a gizzard like an ostrich to digest all the brass-tacks and wire nails of modern art theories. Perhaps all the theories, the utterly indigestible theories, like nails in an ostrich's gizzard, do indeed help to grind small and make digestible all the emotional and aesthetic pabulum that lies in an artist's soul. But they can serve no other purpose. Not even corrective. The modern theories of art make real pictures impossible. You only get these ex-positions, critical ventures in paint, and fantastic negations. And the bit of fantasy that may lie in the negation—as in a Dufy or a Chirico is just the bit that has escaped theory and perhaps saves the picture. Theorise, theorise all you like—but when you start to paint, shut your theoretic eyes and go for it with instinct and intuition.

Myself, I have always loved pictures, the pictorial art. I never went to an art school, I have had only one real lesson in painting in all my life. But of course I was thoroughly drilled in "drawing," the solid-geometry sort, and the plaster-cast sort, and the pin-wire sort. I think the solid-geometry sort, with all the elementary laws of perspective, was valuable. But the pinwire sort and the plaster-cast light-and-shade sort was harmful. Plastercasts and pin-wire outlines were always so repulsive to me, I quite early decided I "couldn't draw." I couldn't draw, so I could never do anything on my own. When I did paint jugs of flowers or bread and potatoes, or cottages in a lane, copying from Nature, the result wasn't very thrilling. Nature was more or less of a plaster-cast to me-those plaster-cast heads of Minerva or figures of Dying Gladiators which so unnerved me as a youth. The "object," be it what it might, was always slightly repulsive to me once I sat down in front of it, to paint it. So, of course, I decided I couldn't really paint. Perhaps I can't. But I verily believe I can make pictures, which is to me all that matters in this respect. The art of painting consists in making pictures-and so many artists accomplish canvases without coming within miles of painting a picture.

I learnt to paint from copying other pictures—usually reproductions, sometimes even photographs. When I was a boy, how I concentrated over it! Copying some perfectly worthless scene reproduction in some magazine. I worked with almost dry water-colour, stroke by stroke, covering half a square-inch at a time, each square-inch perfect and completed, proceeding in a kind of mosaic advance, with no idea at all of laying on a broad wash. Hours and hours of intense concentration, inch by inch progress, in a method entirely wrong—and yet those copies of mine managed, when they were finished, to have a certain something that delighted me: a certain glow of life, which was beauty to me. A picture lives with the life you put into it. If you put no *life* into it—no thrill, no concentration of delight or exaltation of visual discovery—then the picture is dead, like so many canvases, no matter how much thorough and scientific work is put into it. Even if you only copy a purely banal reproduction of an old bridge, some sort of keen, delighted awareness of the old bridge or of its atmosphere, or the image it has kindled inside you, can go over on to the paper and give a certain touch of life to a banal conception.

It needs a certain purity of spirit to be an artist, of any sort. The motto which should be written over every School of Art is: "Blessed are the pure in spirit, for theirs is the kingdom of heaven." But by "pure in spirit" we mean pure in spirit. An artist may be a profligate and, from the social point of view, a scoundrel. But if he can paint a nude woman, or a couple of apples, so that they are a living image, then he was pure in spirit, and, for the time being, his was the kingdom of heaven. This is the beginning of all art, visual or literary or musical: be pure in spirit. It isn't the same as goodness. It is much more difficult and nearer the divine. The divine isn't only good, it is all things.

One may see the divine in natural objects; I saw it to-day, in the frail, lovely little camellia flowers on long stems, here on the bushy and splendid flower-stalls of the Ramblas in Barcelona. They were different from the usual fat camellias, more like gardenias, poised delicately, and I saw them like a vision. So now, I could paint them. But if I had bought a handful, and started in to paint them "from nature," then I should have lost them. By staring at them I should have lost them. I have learnt by experience. It is personal experience only. Some men can only get at a vision by staring themselves blind, as it were: like Cézanne; but staring kills my vision. That's why I could never "draw" at school. One was supposed to draw what one stared at.

The only thing one can look into, stare into, and see only vision, is the vision itself: the visionary image. That is why I am glad I never had any training but the self-imposed training of copying other men's pictures. As I grew more ambitious, I copied Leader's landscapes, and Frank Brangwyn's cartoon-like pictures, then Peter de Wint and Girtin watercolours. I can never be sufficiently grateful for the series of English watercolour painters, published by the *Studio* in eight parts, when I was a youth. I had only six of the eight parts, but they were invaluable to me. I copied them with the greatest joy, and found some of them extremely difficult. Surely I put as much labour into copying from those water-colour reproductions as most modern art students put into all their years of study. And I had enormous profit from it. I not only acquired a considerable technical skill in handling watercolour—let any man try copying the English water-colour artists, from Paul Sandby and Peter de Wint and Girtin, up to Frank Brangwyn and the impressionists like Brabazon, and he will see how much skill he requires—but also I developed my visionary awareness. And I believe one can only develop one's visionary awareness by close contact with the vision itself: that is, by knowing pictures, real vision pictures, and by dwelling on them, and really dwelling in them. It is a great delight, to dwell in a picture. But it needs a purity of spirit, a sloughing of vulgar sensation and vulgar interest, and above all, vulgar contact, that few people know how to perform. Oh, if art schools only taught that! If, instead of saying: This drawing is wrong, incorrect, badly drawn, etc., they would say: Isn't this in bad taste? isn't it insensitive? isn't that an insentient curve with none of the delicate awareness of life in it?—But art is treated all wrong. It is treated as if it were a science, which it is not. Art is a form of religion, minus the Ten Commandment business, which is sociological. Art is a form of supremely delicate awareness and atonement—meaning at-oneness, the state of being at one with the object. But is the great atonement in delight?—for I can never look on art save as a form of delight.

All my life I have from time to time gone back to paint, because it gave me a form of delight that words can never give. Perhaps the joy in words goes deeper and is for that reason more unconscious. The conscious delight is certainly stronger in paint. I have gone back to paint for real pleasure—and by paint I mean copying, copying either in oils or waters. I think the greatest pleasure I ever got came from copying Fra Angelico's "Flight into Egypt" and Lorenzetti's big picture of the Thebaid, in each case working from photographs and putting in my own colour; or perhaps even more a Carpaccio picture in Venice. Then I really learned what life, what powerful life has been put into every curve, every motion of a great picture. Purity of spirit, sensitive awareness, intense eagerness to portray an inward vision, how it all comes. The English water-colours are frail in comparison— and the French and the Flemings are shallow. The great Rembrandt I never tried to copy, though I loved him intensely, even more than I do now; and Rubens I never tried, though I always liked him so much, only he seemed so spread out. But I have copied Peter de Hooch, and Vandyck and others that I forget. Yet none of them gave me the deep thrill of the Italians, Carpaccio, or the lovely "Death of Procris" in the National Gallery, or that "Wedding" with the scarlet legs, in the Uffizi, or a Giotto from Padua. I must have made many copies in my day, and got endless joy out of them.

Then suddenly, by having a blank canvas, I discovered I could make a picture myself. That is the point, to make a picture on a blank canvas. And I was forty before I had the real courage to try. Then it became an orgy, making pictures.

I have learnt now not to work from objects, not to have models, not to have a technique. Sometimes, for a water-colour, I have worked direct from a model. But it always spoils the picture. I can only use a model when the picture is already made; then I can look at the model to get some detail which the vision failed me with, or to modify something which I feel is unsatisfactory and I don't know why. Then a model may give a suggestion. But at the beginning, a model only spoils the picture. The picture must all come out of the artist's inside, awareness of forms and figures. We can call it memory, but it is more than memory. It is the image as it lives in the consciousness, alive like a vision, but unknown. I believe many people have, in their consciousness, living images that would give them the greatest joy to bring out. But they don't know how to go about it. And teaching only hinders them.

To me, a picture has delight in it, or it isn't a picture. The saddest pictures of Piero della Francesca or Sodoma or Goya, have still that indescribable delight that goes with the real picture. Modern critics talk a lot about ugliness, but I never saw a real picture that seemed to me ugly. The theme may be ugly, there may be a terrifying, distressing, almost repulsive quality, as in El Greco. Yet it is all, in some strange way, swept up in the delight of a picture. No artist, even the gloomiest, ever painted a picture without the curious delight in image-making.

NOTES ON SCULPTURE
Henry Moore

I t is a mistake for a sculptor or a painter to speak or write very often about his job. It releases tension needed for his work. By trying to express his aims with rounded-off logical exactness, he can easily become a theorist whose actual work is only a caged-in exposition of conceptions evolved in terms of logic and words.

But though the nonlogical, instinctive, subconscious part of the mind must play its part in his work, he also has a conscious mind which is not inactive. The artist works with a concentration of his whole personality, and the conscious part of it resolves conflicts, organizes memories, and prevents him from trying to walk in two directions at the same time.

It is likely, then, that a sculptor can give, from his own conscious experience, clues which will help others in their approach to sculpture, and this article tries to do this, and no more. It is not a general survey of sculpture, or of my own development, but a few notes on some of the problems that have concerned me from time to time.

Three Dimensions

Appreciation of sculpture depends upon the ability to respond to form in three dimensions. That is, perhaps, why sculpture has been described as the most difficult of all arts; certainly it is more difficult than the arts which involve appreciation of flat forms, shape in only two dimensions. Many more people are 'form-blind' than colour-blind. The child learning to see first distinguishes only two-dimensional shape; it cannot judge distances, depths. Later, for its personal safety and practical needs, it has to develop (partly by means of touch) the ability to judge roughly three-dimensional distances. But having satisfied the requirements of practical necessity most people go no further. Though they may attain considerable accuracy in the perception of flat form, they do not make the further intellectual and emotional effort needed to comprehend form in its full spatial existence.

This is what the sculptor must do. He must strive continually to think of, and use form in its full spatial completeness. He gets the solid shape, as it were, inside his head—he thinks of it, whatever its size, as if he were holding it completely enclosed in the hollow of his hand. He mentally visualizes a complex form *from all round itself*: he knows while he looks at one side what the other side is like; he identifies himself with its centre of gravity, its mass, its weight; he realizes its volume, as the space that the shape displaces in the air.

And the sensitive observer of sculpture must also learn to feel shape simply as shape, not as description or reminiscence. He must, for example, perceive an egg as a simple single solid shape, quite apart from its significance as food, or from the literary idea that it will become a bird. And so with solids such as a shell, a nut, a plum, a pear, a tadpole, a mushroom, a mountain peak, a kidney, a carrot, a tree-trunk, a bird, a bud, a lark, a ladybird, a bullrush, a bone. From these he can go on to appreciate more complex forms or combinations of several forms.

Brancusi

Since Gothic, European sculpture had become overgrown with moss, weeds—all sorts of surface excrescences which completely concealed shape. It has been Brancusi's special mission to get rid of this overgrowth, and to make us once more shape-conscious. To do this he has had to concentrate on very simple direct shapes, to keep his sculpture, as it were, one-cylindered, to refine and polish a single shape to a degree almost too precious. Brancusi's work apart from its individual value has been of great historical importance in the development of contemporary sculpture. But it may now be no longer necessary to close down and restrict sculpture to the single (static) form unit. We can now begin to open out. To relate and combine together several forms of varied sizes, sections and direction, into one organic whole.

Shells and pebble—-being conditioned to respond to shapes

Although it is the human figure which interests me most deeply,

I have always paid great attention to natural forms, such as bones, shells, pebbles, etc. Sometimes, for several years running, I have been to the same part of the sea-shore—but each year a new shape of pebble has caught my eye, which the year before, though it was there in hundreds, I never saw. Out of the millions of pebbles passed in walking along the shore, I choose out to see with excitement only those which fit in with my existing form interest at the time. A different thing happens if I sit down and examine a handful one by one. I may then extend my form experience more by giving my mind time to become conditioned to a new shape.

There are universal shapes to which everybody is subconsciously conditioned and to which they can respond if their conscious control does not shut them off.

Holes in sculpture

Pebbles show Nature's way of working stone. Some of the pebbles I pick up have holes right through them.

When first working direct in a hard and brittle material like stone, the lack of experience and great respect for the material, the fear of ill-treating it, too often result in relief surface carving, with no sculptural power.

But with more experience the completed work in stone can be kept within the limitations of its material, that is, not be weakened beyond its natural constructive build, and yet be turned from an inert mass into a composition which has a full form existence, with masses of varied sizes and sections working together in spatial relationship.

A piece of stone can have a hole through it and not be weakened—if the hole is of a studied size, shape and direction. On the principle of the arch it can remain just as strong.

The first hole made through a piece of stone is a revelation.

The hole connects one side to the other, making it immediately more three-dimensional.

A hole can itself have as much shape-meaning as a solid mass. Sculpture in air is possible, where the stone contains only the hole, which is the intended and considered form.

The mystery of the hole—the mysterious fascination of caves in hillsides and cliffs.

Sizes and scale

There is a right physical size for every idea.

Pieces of good stone have stood about my studio for long periods, because, though I've had ideas which would fit their proportions and materials perfectly, their size was wrong.

There is a side to scale not to do with its actual physical size, its measurement in feet and inches—but connected with vision.

A carving might be several times over life size and yet be petty and small in feeling—and a small carving only a few inches in height can give the feeling of huge size and monumental grandeur, because the vision behind it is big. Example: Michael Angelo's drawings or a Masaccio Madonna—and the Albert Memorial.

Yet actual physical size has an emotional meaning. We relate everything to our own size, and our emotional response to size is controlled by the fact that men on the average are between five and six feet high.

An exact model to one-tenth scale of Stonehenge, where the stones would be less than us, would lose all its impressiveness.

Sculpture is more affected by actual size considerations than painting. A painting is isolated by a frame from its surroundings (unless it serves just a decorative purpose), and so retains more easily its own imaginary scale.

If practical considerations allowed me (cost of material, of transport, etc.) I should like to work on large carvings more often than I do. The average in-between size does not disconnect an idea enough from prosaic everyday life. The very small or the very large take on an added size emotion.

Recently I have been working in the country, where, carving in the open air, I find sculpture more natural than in a London studio, but it needs bigger dimensions. A large piece of stone or wood placed almost anywhere at random in a field, orchard or garden, immediately looks right and inspiring.

Drawing and Sculpture

My drawings are done mainly as a help towards making sculpture—as a means of generating ideas for sculpture, tapping oneself for the initial idea; and as a way of sorting out ideas and developing them.

Also, sculpture compared with drawing is a slow means of expression, and I find drawing a useful outlet for ideas which there is not time enough to realize as sculpture. And I use drawing as a method of study and observation of natural form (drawings from life, drawings of bones, shells, etc.).

And I sometimes draw just for its own enjoyment.

Experience, though, has taught me that the difference there is between drawing and sculpture should not be forgotten. A sculptural idea which may be satisfactory as a drawing always needs some alteration when translated into sculpture.

At one time whenever I made drawings for sculpture I tried to give them as much the illusion of real sculpture as I could—that is, I drew by the method of illusion, of light falling on a solid object. But now I find that carrying a drawing so far that it becomes a substitute for the sculpture either weakens the desire to do the sculpture, or is likely to make the sculpture only a dead realization of the drawing.

I now leave a wider latitude in the interpretation of the drawings I make for sculpture, and draw often in line and flat tones without the light and shade illusion of three dimensions; but this does not mean that the vision behind the drawing is only two-dimensional.

Abstraction and Surrealism

The violent quarrel between the abstractionists and the surrealists seems to me quite unnecessary. All good art has contained both abstract and surrealist elements, just as it has contained both classical and romantic elements—order and surprise, intellect and imagination, conscious and unconscious. Both sides of the artist's personality must play their part. And I think the first inception of a painting or a sculpture may begin from either end. As far as my own experience is concerned, I sometimes begin a drawing with no preconceived problem to solve, with only the desire to use pencil on paper, and make lines, tones and shapes with no conscious aim; but as my mind takes in what is so produced a point arrives where some idea becomes conscious and crystallizes, and then a control and ordering begins to take place.

Or sometimes I start with a set subject; or to solve, in a block of stone of known dimensions, a sculptural problem I've given myself, and then consciously attempt to build an ordered relationship of forms, which shall express my idea. But if the work is to be more than just a sculptural exercise, unexplainable jumps in the process of thought occur; and the imagination plays its part.

It might seem from what I have said of shape and form that I regard them as ends in themselves. Far from it. I am very much aware that associational, psychological factors play a large part in sculpture. The meaning and significance of form itself probably depends on the countless associations of man's history. For example, rounded forms convey an idea of fruitfulness, maturity, probably because the earth, women's breasts, and most fruits are rounded, and these shapes are important because they have this background in our habits of perception. I think the humanist organic element will always be for me of fundamental importance in sculpture, giving sculpture its vitality. Each particular carving I make takes on in my mind a human, or occasionally animal, character and personality, and this personality controls its design and formal qualities, and makes me satisfied or dissatisfied with the work as it develops.

My own aim and direction seems to be consistent with these beliefs, though it does not depend upon them. My sculpture is becoming less representational, less an outward visual copy, and so what some people would call more abstract; but only because I believe that in this way I can present the human psychological content of my work with the greatest directness and intensity.

From "Notes on Sculpture," by Henry Moore in *The Painter's Object,* by Myfanwy Evans. By permission of the publishers: John Lane the Bodley Head Limited, London.

COMPOSITION IN PURE MOVEMENT

Mary Wigman

Charged as I frequently am with "freeing" the dance from music, the question often arises, what can be the source and basic structure of my own dancing. I cannot define its principles more clearly than to say that the fundamental idea of any creation arises in me or, rather, out of me as a completely independent dance theme. This theme, however primitive or obscure at first, already contains its own development and alone dictates its singular and logical sequence. What I feel as the germinal source of any dance may be compared perhaps to the melodic or rhythmic "subject" as it is first conceived by a composer, or to the compelling image that haunts a poet. But beyond that I can draw no parallels. In working out a dance I do not follow the models of any other art, nor have I evolved a general routine for my own. Each dance is unique and free, a separate organism whose form is self-determined.

Neither is my dancing abstract, in intention at any rate, for its origin is not in the mind. If there is an abstract effect it is incidental. On the other hand my purpose is not to "interpret" the emotions. Grief, joy, fear, are terms too fixed and static to describe the sources of my work. My dances flow rather from certain states of being, different stages of vitality which release in me a varying play of the emotions, and in themselves dictate the distinguishing atmospheres of the dances.

I can at this moment clearly recall the origin of my *Festlicher Rhythmus*. Coming back from the holidays, rested, restored by sun and fresh air, I was eager to begin dancing again. When I stepped into the studio and saw my co-workers there waiting for me, I beat my hands together and out of this spontaneous expression of happiness, of joy, the dance developed.

My first tentative attempts to compose were made when I was studying the Dalcroze system. Though I have always had a strong feeling for music it seemed from the very start most natural for me to express my own nature by means of pure movement. Perhaps it was just because there was so much musical work to be done at that time, that all these little dances and dance studies took form without music. A German painter observing my modest experiments advised me to go to Munich and work with Von Laban who was also interested in such dancing. On Laban's system of gymnastics I founded my body technic; and during this period of apprenticeship I continued the gradual evolution of my own work.

After years of trial I have come to realize in a very final way, that for me the creation of a dance to music already written cannot be complete and satisfactory. I have danced with several of the great European orchestras, and to music (always generically dance music) old and new. I have even attempted to work out Hindemith's *Daemon,* and some compositions of Bartok, Kodaly, and other contemporaries. But while music easily evokes in me a dance reaction, it is in the development of the dance that a great divergence so often occurs. For usually a dance idea, a "theme," however inspired, by a state of feeling, or indirectly by music, sets up independent reactions. The theme calls for its own development. It is in working this out that I find my dance parting company with the music. The parallel development of the dance with the already completely worked out musical idea is what I find in most instances to be functionally wrong. Each dance demands organic autonomy.

So I have come gradually to feel my way toward a new re-integration of music with the dance. I do not create a dance and then order music written for it. As soon as I conceive a theme, and before it is completely defined, I call in my musical assistants. Catching my idea, and observing me for atmosphere, they begin to improvise with me. Every step of the development is built up co-operatively. Experiments are made with various instruments, accents, climaxes, until we feel the work has indissoluble unity.

My *Pastorale* was developed in the following way: I came into my studio one day and sank down with a feeling of complete relaxation. Out of a sense of deepest peace and quietude I began slowly to move my arms and body. Calling to my assistants I said, "I do not know if anything will come of this feeling, but I should like a reed instrument that would play over and over again a simple little tune, not at all important, always the same one." Then with the monotonous sound of the little tune, with its gentle lyric suggestion, the whole dance took form. Afterwards we found that it was built on six-eighths time, neither myself nor the musician being conscious of the rhythm until we came to the end.

The monumental *Totenmal* which we presented in Munich last year was accompanied by a whole orchestra of percussion instruments. During the period of preparation these instruments were handled by dancers. The improvisation of dancing and music was so dovetailed that in the long hours of practice the girls dancing constantly changed places with those making the music. The final result was one of the greatest possible harmony. In group creations, as in my individual work, movement and sound are always evolved together.

Working with a group my effort is to seek out a common feeling. I present the main idea, each one improvises. No matter how wide the range of individuality, I must find some common denominator from these different emanations of personality. Thus, on the rock of basic feeling, I slowly build each structure.

Of course all that I have said here should be accepted as a very personal credo. I do not propose to erect a general system for I am a firm believer in individual freedom. Creative work will always assume new and varying forms. Any profound expression of self for which its creator assumes responsibility in the most complete sense must give authentic impetus to a new or an old idea in art.

From "Composition in Pure Movement," by Mary Wigman in *Modern Music,* January-February, 1946. By permission of the author and the publishers of *Modern Music:* The League of Composers, New York City.

DEDICATION OF THE RIVAL LADIES

John Dryden

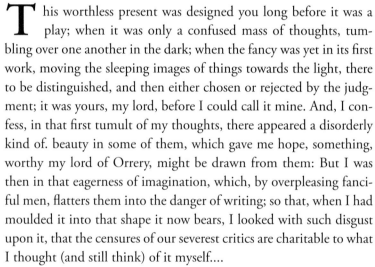

This worthless present was designed you long before it was a play; when it was only a confused mass of thoughts, tumbling over one another in the dark; when the fancy was yet in its first work, moving the sleeping images of things towards the light, there to be distinguished, and then either chosen or rejected by the judgment; it was yours, my lord, before I could call it mine. And, I confess, in that first tumult of my thoughts, there appeared a disorderly kind of. beauty in some of them, which gave me hope, something, worthy my lord of Orrery, might be drawn from them: But I was then in that eagerness of imagination, which, by overpleasing fanciful men, flatters them into the danger of writing; so that, when I had moulded it into that shape it now bears, I looked with such disgust upon it, that the censures of our severest critics are charitable to what I thought (and still think) of it myself....

The advantages which rhyme has over blank verse are so many, that it were lost time to name them....But that benefit which I consider most in it, because I have not seldom found it, is, that it bounds and circumscribes the fancy. For imagination in a poet is a faculty so wild and lawless, that, like an high-ranging spaniel, it must have clogs tied to it, lest it outrun the judgment. The great easiness of blank verse renders the poet too luxuriant; he is tempted to say many things, which might better be omitted, or at least shut up in fewer words; but when the difficulty of artful rhyming is interposed, where the poet commonly confines his sense to his couplet, and must contrive that sense into such words, that the rhyme shall naturally follow them, not they the rhyme; the fancy then gives leisure to the judgment to come in, which, seeing so heavy a tax imposed, is ready to cut off all unnecessary expenses. This last consideration has already answered an objection which some have made, that rhyme is only an embroidery of sense, to make that, which is ordinary in itself, pass for excellent with less examination. But certainly, that, which most regulates the fancy, and gives the judgment its busiest employment, is like to bring forth the richest and clearest thoughts.

From "To the Right Honourable Roger, Earl of Orrery," dedicatory letter to "The Rival-Ladies," by John Dryden in *The Works of John Dryden,* revised and corrected by George Saintsbury. Croscup & Sterling Company, New York City.

THE PROCESS OF INSPIRATION

Jean Cocteau

O ften the public forms an idea of inspiration that is quite false, almost a religious notion. Alas! I do not believe that inspiration falls from heaven. I think it rather the result of a profound indolence and of our incapacity to put to work certain forces in ourselves. These unknown forces work deep within us, with the aid of the elements of daily life, its scenes and passions, and, when they burden us and oblige us to conquer the kind of somnolence in which we indulge ourselves like invalids who try to prolong dream and dread resuming contact with reality, in short when the work that makes itself in us and in spite of us demands to be born, we can believe that this work comes to us from beyond and is offered us by the gods. The artist is more slumberous in order that he shall not work. By a thousand ruses, he prevents his nocturnal work from coming to the light of day.

For it is at this moment that consciousness must take precedence over the unconscious and that it becomes necessary to find the means which permit the unformed work to take form, to render it visible to all. To write, to conquer ink and paper, accumulate letters and paragraphs, divide them with periods and commas, is a different matter from carrying around the dream of a play or of a book.

"More light" was the last phrase of Goethe. This phrase assumes meaning when one considers the struggle of Goethe against the shadow and that existence which he consecrated to clarifying the least recesses of his being and to repulsing the charm of the dog and the wolf. I bow before certain scenes of Faust, Part II, that of the fall of Euphorion, for example, in which Goethe reaches the state of grace, in full possession of himself. It would be inexact to accuse an artist of pride when he declares that his work requires somnambulism. The poet is at the disposal of his night. His role is humble, he must clean house and await its due visitation.

The play that I am producing at the Theatre de l'OEuvre, *The Knights o f the Round Table,* is a visitation of this sort. I was sick and tired of writing, when one morning, after having slept poorly, I woke with a start and witnessed, as from a seat in a theater, three acts which brought to life an epoch and characters about which I had no documentary information and which I regarded moreover as forbidding.

Long afterward, I succeeded in writing the play and I divined the circumstances that must have served to incite me.

Translated by Brewster Ghiselin

From "Procès de l'Inspiration," in *Le Foyer des Artistes,* by Jean Cocteau. By permission of the publishers: Librairie Plon, Les Petits-Fils de Plon et Nourrit, Paris.

PREFACE TO SECOND
EDITION OF LYRICAL BALLADS
William Wordsworth

What is a Poet? To whom does he address himself? And what
language is to be expected from him? He is a man speaking
to men: a man, it is true, endowed with more lively sensibility, more
enthusiasm and tenderness, who has a greater knowledge of human
nature, and a more comprehensive soul, than are supposed to be
common among mankind; a man pleased with his own passions and
volitions, and who rejoices more than other men in the spirit of life
that is in him; delighting to contemplate similar volitions and passions as manifested in the goings-on of the Universe, and habitually
impelled to create them where he does not find them. To these qualities he has added a disposition to be affected more than other men
by absent things as if they were present; an ability of conjuring up in
himself passions, which are indeed far from being the same as those
produced by real events, yet (especially in those parts of the general
sympathy which are pleasing and delightful) do more nearly resemble the passions produced by real events, than anything which, from
the motions of their own minds merely, other men are accustomed
to feel in themselves: whence, and from practice, he has acquired a
greater readiness and power in expressing what he thinks and feels,

and especially those thoughts and feelings which, by his own choice, or from the structure of his own mind, arise in him without immediate external excitement...

Not that I always began to write with a distinct purpose formally conceived; but habits of meditation have, I trust, so prompted and regulated my feelings, that my descriptions of such objects as strongly excite those feelings, will be found to carry along with them a *purpose.* If this opinion be erroneous, I can have little right to the name of a Poet. For all good poetry is the spontaneous overflow of powerful feelings: and though this be true, Poems to which any value can be attached were never produced on any variety of subjects but by a man who, being possessed of more than usual organic sensibility, had also thought long and deeply. For our continued influxes of feeling are modified and directed by our thoughts, which are indeed the representatives of all our past feelings; and as, by contemplating the relation of these general representatives to each other, we discover what is really important to men, so, by the repetition and continuance of this act, our feelings will be connected with important subjects, till at length, if we be originally possessed of much sensibility, such habits of mind will be produced, that, by obeying blindly and mechanically the impulses of those habits, we shall describe objects, and utter sentiments, of such a nature, and in such connection with each other, that the understanding of the reader must necessarily be in some degree enlightened, and his affections strengthened and purified...

I have said that poetry is the spontaneous overflow of powerful feelings: it takes its origin from emotion recollected in tranquillity: the emotion is contemplated till, by a species of reaction, the tranquility gradually disappears, and an emotion, kindred to that which was before the subject of contemplation, is gradually produced, and does itself actually exist in the mind. In this mood successful composition generally begins, and in a mood similar to this it is carried on...

From "Preface to the Second Edition of Several of the Foregoing Poems, Published, with an Additional Volume, under the Title of 'Lyrical Ballads,'" by William Wordsworth in *The Complete Poetical Works of William Wordsworth,* with an introduction by John Morley. Macmillan and Company, 1895, London and New York City.

PREFATORY NOTE TO *KUBLA KAHN*

Samuel Taylor Coleridge

The following fragment is here published at the request of a poet of great and deserved celebrity, and, as far as the Author's own opinions are concerned, rather as a psychological curiosity, than on the ground of any supposed *poetic* merits.

In the summer of the year 1797, the Author, then in ill health, had retired to a lonely farm-house between Porlock and Linton, on the Exmoor confines of Somerset and Devonshire. In consequence of a slight indisposition, an anodyne had been prescribed, from the effects of which he fell asleep in his chair at the moment that he was reading the following sentence, or words of the same substance, in "Purchas's Pilgrimage:" "Here the Khan Kubla commanded a palace to be built, and a stately garden thereunto. And thus ten miles of fertile ground were inclosed with a wall." The Author continued for about three hours in a profound sleep, at least of the external senses, during which time he has the most vivid confidence, that he could not have composed less than from two to three hundred lines; if that indeed can be called composition in which all the images rose up before him as things, with a parallel production of the correspondent expressions, without any sensation or consciousness of effort.

On awaking he appeared to himself to have a distinct recollection of the whole, and taking his pen, ink, and paper, instantly and eagerly wrote down the lines that are here preserved. At this moment he was unfortunately called out by a person on business from Porlock, and detained by him above an hour, and on his return to his room, found, to his no small surprise and mortification, that though he still retained some vague and dim recollection of the general purport of the vision, yet, with the exception of some eight or ten scattered lines and images, all the rest had passed away like the images on the surface of a stream into which a stone has been cast, but alas! without the after restoration of the latter!

> *Then all the charm*
> *Is broken—all that phantom-world so fair*
> *Vanishes, and a thousand circlets spread,*
> *And each mis-shape the other. Stay awhile,*
> *Poor youth! who scarcely dar'st lift up thine eyes—*
> *The stream will soon renew its smoothness, soon*
> *The visions will return! And lo, he stays,*
> *And soon the fragments dim of lovely forms*
> *Come trembling back, unite, and now once more*
> *The pool becomes a mirror.*

Yet from the still surviving recollections in his mind, the Author has frequently purposed to finish for himself what had been originally, as it were, given to him. But the tomorrow is yet to come.

From the prefatory note to "Kubla Khan" by Samuel Taylor Coleridge in *The Poetical Works of Samuel Taylor Coleridge,* edited by James Dykes Campbell. Macmillan and Company, 1895, London and New York City

THE NAME AND NATURE OF POETRY

A. E. Housman

Meaning is of the intellect, poetry is not. If it were, the eighteenth century would have been able to write it better. As matters actually stand, who are the English poets of that age in whom pre-eminently one can hear and recognise the true poetic accent emerging clearly from the contemporary dialect? These four: Collins, Christopher Smart, Cowper, and Blake. And what other characteristic had these four in common? They were mad. Remember Plato: 'He who without the Muses' madness in his soul comes knocking at the door of poesy and thinks that art will make him anything fit to be called a poet, finds that the poetry which he indites in his sober senses is beaten hollow by the poetry of madmen.'

That the intellect is not the fount of poetry, that it may actually hinder its production, and that it cannot even be trusted to recognise poetry when produced, is best seen in the case of Smart. Neither the prize founded in this University by the Rev. Thomas Seaton nor the successive contemplation of five several attributes of the Supreme Being could incite him to good poetry while he was sane. The only poem by which he is remembered, a poem which came to its own in the kinder climate of the nineteenth century and has inspired one of the best poems of the twentieth, was written, if not, as tradition says, in actual confinement, at any rate very soon after release; and when the eighteenth century, the age of sanity and intelligence, collected his poetical works, it excluded this piece as 'bearing melancholy proofs of the recent estrangement of his mind.'

Collins and Cowper, though they saw the inside of madhouses, are not supposed to have written any of their poetry there; and Blake was never mad enough to be locked up. But elements of their nature were more or less insurgent against the centralised tyranny of the intellect, and their brains were not thrones on which the great usurper could sit secure. And so it strangely came to pass that in the eighteenth century, the age of prose and of unsound or unsatisfying poetry, there sprang up one well of the purest inspiration. For me, the most poetical of all poets is Blake. I find his lyrical note as beautiful as Shakespeare's and more beautiful than anyone else's; and I call him more poetical than Shakespeare, even though Shakespeare has so much more poetry, because poetry in him preponderates more than in Shakespeare over everything else, and instead of being confounded in a great river can be drunk pure from a slender channel of its own. Shakespeare is rich in thought, and his meaning has power of itself to move us, even if the poetry were not there: Blake's meaning is often unimportant or virtually non-existent, so that we can listen with all our hearing to his celestial tune.

Even Shakespeare, who had so much to say, would sometimes pour out his loveliest poetry in saying nothing.

> *Take O take those lips away*
> *That so sweetly were forsworn,*
> *And those eyes, the break of day,*
> *Lights that do mislead the morn;*
> *But my kisses bring again,*
> *bring again,*
> *Seals of love, but seal'd in vain,*
> *seal'd in vain.*

That is nonsense; but it is ravishing poetry. When Shakespeare fills such poetry with thought, and thought which is worthy of it, as in *Fear no more the heat o' the sun* or *O mistress mine, where art thou roaming?* Those songs, the very summits of lyrical achievement, are indeed greater and more moving poems, but I hardly know how to call them more poetical.

Now Blake again and again, as Shakespeare now and then, gives us poetry neat, or adulterated with so little meaning that nothing except poetic emotion is perceived and matters.

> *Hear the voice of the Bard,*
> *Who present, past, and future sees;*

Whose ears have heard The Holy Word
  That walk'd among the ancient trees,

Calling the lapsèd soul
  And weeping in the evening dew;
That might control The starry pole,
  And fallen, fallen light renew.

O Earth, O Earth, return!
  Arise from out the dewy grass;
Night is worn,
And the morn
  Rises from the slumberous mass.

Turn away no more;
  Why wilt thou turn away?
The starry floor,
The watery shore
  Is giv'n thee till the break of day.'

That mysterious grandeur would be less grand if it were less mysterious; if the embryo ideas which are all that it contains should endue form and outline, and suggestion condense itself into thought.

> Memory, hither come
>> And tune your merry notes;
> And while upon the wind
>> Your music floats
>
> I'll pore upon the stream
> Where sighing lovers dream,
> And fish for fancies as they pass
> Within the watery glass.

That answers to nothing real; memory's merry notes and the rest are empty phrases, not things to be imagined; the stanza does but entangle the reader in a net of thoughtless delight. The verses which I am now going to read probably possessed for Blake a meaning, and his students think that they have found it; but the meaning is a poor foolish disappointing thing in comparison with the verses themselves.

> My Spectre around me night and day
> Like a wild beast guards my way;
> My Emanation far within
> Weeps incessantly for my sin.

A fathomless and boundless deep,
There we wander, there we weep;
On the hungry craving wind
My Spectre follows thee behind.

He scents thy footsteps in the snow
Wheresoever thou dost go:
Through the wintry hail and rain
When wilt thou return again?

Dost thou not in pride and scorn
Fill with tempests all my morn,
And with jealousies and fears
Fill my pleasant nights with tears?

Seven of my sweet loves thy knife
Has bereaved of their life.
Their marble tombs I built with tears
And with cold and shuddering fears.

Seven more loves weep night and day
Round the tombs where my loves lay,
And seven more loves attend each night
Around my couch with torches bright.

And seven more loves in my bed
Crown with wine my mournful head,
Pitying and forgiving all
Thy transgressions great and small.

When wilt thou return and view
My loves, and them to life renew?
When wilt thou return and live?
When wilt thou pity as I forgive?

I am not equal to framing definite ideas which would match that magnificent versification and correspond to the strong tremor of unreasonable excitement which those words set up in some region deeper than the mind. Lastly take this stanza, addressed 'to the Accuser who is the God of this World.'

Tho' thou art worship'd by the names divine
    Of Jesus and Jehovah, thou art still.
The Son of Morn in weary Night's decline,
    The lost traveller's dream under the hill.

It purports to be theology: what theological sense, if any, it may have, I cannot imagine and feel no wish to learn: it is pure and self-existent poetry, which leaves no room in me for anything besides.

In most poets, as I said, poetry is less often found thus disengaged from its usual concomitants, from certain things with which it naturally unites itself and seems to blend indistinguishably. For instance:

> *Sorrow, that is not sorrow, but delight;*
> *And miserable love, that is not pain*
> *To hear of, for the glory that redounds*
> *Therefrom to human kind, and what we are.*

The feeling with which those lines are read is composite, for one constituent is supplied by the depth and penetrating truth of the thought. Again:

> *Though love repine and reason chafe,*
> * There came a voice without reply,--*
> *'Tis man's perdition to be safe,*
> * When for the truth he ought to die.'*

Much of the emotion kindled by that verse can be referred to the nobility of the sentiment. But in these six simple words of Milton—

Nymphs and shepherds, dance no more—

What is it that can draw tears, as I know it can, to the eyes of more readers than one? What in the world is there to cry about? Why have the mere words the physical effect of pathos when the sense of the passage is blithe and gay? I can only say, because they are poetry, and find their way to something in man which is obscure and latent, something older than the present organisation of his nature, like the patches of fen which still linger here and there in the drained lands of Cambridgeshire.

Poetry indeed seems to me more physical than intellectual. A year or two ago, in common with others, I received from America a request that I would define poetry. I replied that I could no more define poetry than a terrier can define a rat, but that I thought we both recognised the object by the symptoms which it provokes in us. One of these symptoms was described in connexion with another object by Eliphaz the Temanite: 'A spirit passed before my face: the hair of my flesh stood up.' Experience has taught me, when I am shaving of a morning, to keep watch over my thoughts, because, if a line of poetry strays into my memory, my skin bristles so that the razor ceases to act. This particular symptom is accompanied by a shiver down the spine; there is another which consists in a constriction of the throat and a precipitation of water to the eyes; and there is a third which I can only describe by borrowing a phrase from one of Keats's last letters, where he says, speaking of Fanny Brawne, 'everything that reminds me of her goes through me like a spear.' The seat of this sensation is the pit of the stomach.

My opinions on poetry are necessarily tinged, perhaps I should say tainted, by the circumstance that I have come into contact with it on two sides. We were saying a while ago that poetry is a very wide term, and inconveniently comprehensive: so comprehensive is it that it embraces two books, fortunately not large ones, of my own. I know how this stuff came into existence; and though I have no right to assume that any other poetry came into existence in the same way, yet I find reason to believe that some poetry, and quite good poetry, did. Wordsworth for instance says that poetry is the spontaneous overflow of powerful feelings, and Burns has left us this confession, 'I have two or three times in my life composed from the wish rather than the impulse, but I "never succeeded to any purpose:' In short I think that the production of poetry, in its first stage, is less an active than a passive and involuntary process; and if I were obliged, not to define poetry, but to name the class of things to which it belongs, I should call it a secretion; whether a natural secretion, like turpentine in the fir, or a morbid secretion, like the pearl in the oyster. I think that my own case, though I may not deal with the material so cleverly as the oyster does, is the latter; because I have seldom written poetry unless I was rather out of health, and the experience, though pleasurable, was generally agitating and exhausting. If only that you may know what to avoid, I will give some account of the process.

Having drunk a pint of beer at luncheon—beer is a sedative to the brain, and my afternoons are the least intellectual portion of my life—I would go out for a walk of two or three hours. As I went along, thinking of nothing in particular, only looking at things around me and following the progress of the seasons, there would flow into my mind, with sudden and unaccountable emotion, sometimes a line or two of verse, sometimes a whole stanza at once, accompanied, not preceded, by a vague notion of the poem which they were destined to form part of. Then there would usually be a lull of an hour or so, then perhaps the spring would bubble up again. I say bubble up, because, so far as I could make out, the source of the suggestions thus proffered to the brain was an abyss which I have already had occasion to mention, the pit of the stomach. When I got home I wrote them down, leaving gaps, and hoping that further inspiration might be forthcoming another day. Sometimes it was, if I took my walks in a receptive and expectant frame of mind; but sometimes the poem had to be taken in hand and completed by the brain, which was apt to be a matter of trouble and anxiety, involving trial and disappointment, and sometimes ending in failure. I happen to remember distinctly the genesis of the piece which stands last in my first volume. Two of the stanzas, I do not say which, came into my head, just as they are printed, while I was crossing the corner of Hampstead Heath between the Spaniard's Inn and the footpath to Temple Fortune. A third stanza came with a little coaxing after tea. One more was needed, but it did not come: I had to turn to and compose it myself, and that was a laborious business. I wrote it thirteen times, and it was more than a twelvemonth before I got it right.

From *The Name and Nature of Poetry*, by A. E. Housman. By permission of the publishers: Cambridge University Press, American Branch, New York City.

THE COURSE IN
POETICS: FIRST LESSON

Paul Valéry

My first concern must be to explain the word "Poetics" which I have restored to its quite primitive sense, not that now in use. It came to mind and seemed to me the only proper one to designate the kind of study I propose to carry on in this Course.

This term is ordinarily taken to mean any account or collection of rules, conventions, or precepts dealing with the composition of lyric or dramatic poems, or even the making of verse. But we may find that the word has grown far enough out of use in this sense, along with the thing it names, to be given another.

Not very long ago, all the arts were subject, each according to its nature, to certain obligatory forms or modes imposed on all works of the same genre; these could be and had to be learned, as we do the syntax of a language. It was not thought that the effect a work might produce, however powerful or happy, was enough to justify the work and assure it a universal value. The fact did not carry with it the right. It had been recognized very early that there were, in each of the arts, practices to be recommended, observances and restrictions which best favor the success of an artist's purpose, and which it was to his own interest to know and respect.

But gradually, and on the authority of very great men, the idea of a sort of legality crept in and took the place of what had been, at first, recommendations of empirical origin. Reason put rigor into the rules. They were expressed in precise formulas; the critic armed himself with them; and this paradoxical result followed, that an artistic discipline which set up reasoned difficulties in the way of the artist's impulses came into great and lasting favor because of the extreme facility it offered in judging and classifying works, by simple reference to a code or well defined canon.

These formal rules offered a further facility to those who wished to produce works. Very strict and even very severe conditions relieve the artist of a number of the most delicate decisions and of many responsibilities in the matter of form, while they sometimes excite him to discoveries to which complete freedom could never have led him.

But whether we deplore or rejoice at the fact, the era of authority in the arts is rather long since past, and the word "Poetics" now arouses in us scarcely more than the notion of troublesome and old-fashioned rules. For that reason I have thought it possible to recover the word in a sense derived from its etymology, although I have not dared to pronounce it *Poietics,* as the physiologists do when they speak of hematopoietic or galactopoietic functions. Rather it is in short the quite simple notion of *making* that I wish to express. The making, the *poiein,* that I wish to consider is the kind that results in some finished work; I shall shortly limit it to the kind of works we have agreed to call *works of the mind.* I mean those which the mind likes to make for its own use, employing to that end any physical means that can serve.

Like the simple act of which I have just spoken, any work may or may not lead us to meditate on the process of its creation, may or may not give rise to a more or less pronounced, more or less exacting attitude of inquiry, which makes of creation itself a problem.

Such a study does not force itself upon us. We may think it is vain, and we may even consider my claim fanciful. Furthermore: certain minds will find it not only vain but harmful; and they may even owe it to themselves to find it so. One can imagine for example that a poet may legitimately fear that he might undermine his original powers, or his immediate productivity, by making an analysis of them. He instinctively refuses to plumb their depths otherwise than through the exercise of his art; he refuses to master them by demonstrative reason. It is credible that our simplest act, our most familiar gesture could not be performed, that the least of our powers might become an obstacle to us if we had to bring it before the mind and know it thoroughly in order to exercise it.

Achilles cannot win over the tortoise if he meditates on space and time.

On the contrary, however, it may happen that we take such keen interest in this inquiry and that we attach such high importance to its pursuit, that we may be brought to consider with more satisfaction, and even with more passion, *the act of making than the thing made.*

It is on this point, Gentlemen, that my undertaking must necessarily be distinguished from that carried on by Literary History on the one hand, and on the other by textual and literary Criticism.

Literary History looks for the outwardly verified circumstances in which works were composed, appeared, and produced their effects. It informs us about authors, about the vicissitudes of their life and their work, in so far as these are visible things which have left traces that may be discovered, coordinated, and interpreted. It collects traditions and documents.

I do not need to remind you with what erudition and originality of views such a course was professed from this very chair by your eminent colleague M. Abel Lefranc. But a knowledge of authors and their times, a study of the succession of literary phenomena can only excite us to conjecture what may have happened in the minds of those who have done what was necessary to get themselves inscribed in the annals of the History of Letters. If they succeeded in doing so, it was through the concurrence of two conditions which may always be considered as independent: one is necessarily the production of the work itself, the other is the production of a certain value in the work by those who have known and liked it once it is produced, those who have enforced its reputation and assured its transmission, its conservation, its ulterior life.

I have just pronounced the words "value" and "production." I shall dwell on them for a moment.

If we would undertake to explore the domain of the creative mind, we must not be afraid to stand, at first, on the most general considerations, since they are the ones that will allow us to advance without having to retrace our steps too often, and will offer us the greatest number of analogies, that is the greatest number of approximate expressions for the description of facts and ideas which most often, by their very nature, escape any attempt at direct definition. That is why I call attention to borrowing a few words from Economics: I shall perhaps find it convenient to assemble under the single terms *production* and *producer* the various activities and persons that will occupy us, if we wish to treat what they have in common without distinguishing between their different kinds. It will be no less convenient, without specifying whether we are speaking of reader or hearer or spectator, to combine all these participants in works of all kinds under the economic term *consumer.*

As for the notion of value, we are well aware that in the world of the mind it plays a role of the first order, comparable to the one it plays in the economic world, although spiritual value is much more subtle than economic since it is bound up with needs infinitely more varied, and not measurable as the needs of our physiological life are. *The Iliad* is still known, and gold has remained for so many centuries a more or less simple but rather remarkable and generally venerated substance, for the reason that rarity, inimitability, and a few other properties distinguish gold and *The Iliad,* making of them privileged objects, standards of *value.*

Without insisting on my economic comparison, it is clear that the idea of work, and such ideas as the creation and accumulation of wealth, or supply and demand, occur quite naturally in the domain that concerns us.

As much by their similarity as by their different uses, these notions under the same names remind us that in two orders of facts which seem very distinct from one another, problems of the relation of persons to their social milieu arise. Besides, just as there is an economic analogy, and for the same reason, there is also a political analogy between the phenomena of organized intellectual life and those of public life. There is a whole policy of intellectual power, an internal policy (quite internal, of course), and an external policy, the latter falling within the province of Literary History, of which it should form one of the principal objects.

Politics and economics thus generalized are notions that, from the first moment we look at the world of the mind, when we still might expect to consider it a system perfectly isolable during the phase of creating its works, are necessary notions, and seem profoundly present in most of the mind's creations, and always hovering in the vicinity of its acts.

At the very heart of the scholar's or artist's thought, even the one most absorbed in his search, who seems most confined to his own

153

sphere and face to face with what is most self and most impersonal, there is present some strange anticipation of the external reactions to be provoked by the work now in the making: it is difficult for a man to be alone.

The effect of this presence can always be assumed, without fear of error; but it may be combined so subtly with other factors of the work, sometimes so well disguised, that it is almost impossible to isolate it.

Nevertheless, we know that the real meaning of a certain choice or a certain effort on the part of a creator often lies outside the work itself, and is the result of amore or less conscious concern with the effect to be produced and with its consequences for the producer. Thus, while it is at work, the mind is constantly going and coming from Self to Other; what its innermost being produces is modified by a peculiar awareness of the judgment of others. Therefore, in our reflection on a work, we may take one or the other of these two mutually exclusive attitudes. If we mean to proceed with as much rigor as such a subject allows, we must require ourselves to distinguish very carefully between investigation into the creation of a work and study of the production of its value, that is the effects it may produce here or there, in such and such a head, at such and such a time. To demonstrate this point, it is sufficient to remark that what we can really know or think we know, in any domain, is nothing else than what we can either *observe* or *do*, ourselves, and that it is impossible to bring together in one and the same condition, and in one and the same attention, the observation of the mind that produces the work and the observation of the mind that produces a certain value in the work. No eye is capable of observing both these functions at once; producer and consumer are two essentially separate systems. The work is for one the *terminus,* for the other the *origin* of developments which may be as foreign as you please to one another.

We must conclude that any judgment that announces a relation in three terms between the producer, the work and the consumer—and judgments of this kind are not rare in criticism—is an illusory judgment which can have no meaning and which is immediately destroyed by the slightest reflection. We can only consider the work's relation to its producer, or on the other hand its relation to the one whom it affects once it is made. The action of the first and the reaction of the second can never meet. The idea each has of the work is incompatible with the other's.

Hence arise very frequent surprises, a few of which are advantageous. There are mistakes that are creative. There are many effects-and among them the most powerful-which require the absence of any direct correspondence between the two activities concerned. A certain work, for example, is the fruit of long labor; it combines a large number of trials, repetitions, rejections, and choices. It has taken months, even years of reflection, and it may also presuppose the experience and attainments of a whole lifetime. Now, the effect of this work may take no more than a few moments to declare itself. A glance will suffice to appreciate a considerable monument, to feel its shock. In two hours all the calculations of the tragic poet, all the labor he has spent in ordering the effects of his play, shaping every line of it one by one; or again, all the harmonic and orchestral combinations contrived by the composer; or all the meditations of the philosopher, the long years he has put into curbing, controlling, withholding his thought until he could perceive and accept its definitive order, all these acts of faith, all these acts of choice, all these mental transactions finally reach the stage of the finished work, to strike, astonish, dazzle or disconcert the mind of the *Other,* who is suddenly subjected to the excitement of this enormous charge of intellectual labor. All this makes a *disproportionate act.*

One may (very roughly, of course) compare this effect to the fall, in a few seconds, of a mass which had been carried up, piece by piece, to the top of a tower without regard to the time or the number of trips.

It is in this way that we get the impression of superhuman power. But as you know, the effect does not always come off; it sometimes happens, in intellectual mechanics, that the tower is too high, or the mass too great, and we get a negative result, or none at all.

Let us suppose, however, that the big effect comes off. Those persons who have felt it, those who have been, if you will, overwhelmed by its power and perfections, by the large number of lucky strokes, the piling up of happy surprises, cannot, and in fact must not imagine all the internal labor, the possibilities discarded, the long process of picking out suitable components, the delicate reasoning whose conclusions appear to be reached by magic, in a word, the amount of inner life treated by the chemist of the creative mind, or sorted out of mental chaos by some Maxwellian demon; and so those same persons are led to imagine a being of great powers, capable of working all these wonders with no more effort than it takes to do anything at all.

What the work produces in us, then, is incommensurable with our own powers of immediate production. Besides, certain elements of the work which have come to the author by some happy chance may be attributed to a singular virtue of his mind. In this way the consumer becomes a producer in his turn: at first, a producer of the value of the work; and next, because he immediately applies the principal of causality (which at bottom is only a naive expression of one of the mind's modes of production), he becomes a producer of the value of the imaginary being who made the thing he admires.

Perhaps if great men were as conscious as they are great there would be no great men in their own eyes.

Thus, and this is what I have been coming to, this example, although very special, shows us that for works to have their effects, the producer and the consumer must each be independent or ignorant of the other's thoughts and conditions. The secrecy and surprise which tacticians often recommend in their writings are here naturally assured.

To sum up, when we speak of works of the mind, we mean either the terminus of a certain activity or the origin of a certain other activity, and that makes two orders of incommunicable effects, each of which requires of us a special adaptation incompatible with the other.

What remains is the work itself, as a tangible thing. This is a third consideration, quite different from the other two.

We shall now regard a work as an object, as pure *object,* that is to say without putting into it any more of ourselves than may apply indifferently to all objects: an attitude clearly marked by the absence of any production of value.

What can we do to this object which, this time, can do nothing to us? But we can do something to it. We can measure it according to its spacial or temporal nature; we can count the words in a text or the syllables in a line; we can confirm that a certain book appeared at a certain date; that a certain picture is a copy of a certain other; that there is a half line of Lamartine to be found in Thomas, or that a certain page of Victor Hugo has, ever since 1645, belonged to an obscure Father Francis. We may note that a certain piece of reasoning is a fallacy, that this sonnet is incorrect; that the drawing of that arm is in defiance of anatomy, and that a certain use of words is strange. All this is the result of operations that may be classed as purely material operations since they amount to ways of superimposing the work, or fragments of the work, upon some model.

This treatment of works of the mind does not distinguish them from all other possible works. It places them and keeps them in the order of things, and imposes upon them a defined existence. That is the point to remember:

All that we can define is at once set off from the producing mind in opposition to it. The mind turns whatever it defines into matter it can work on, or a tool it can work with.

Whatever it has clearly defined, the mind places out of its own reach, and in so doing, shows that it knows itself and that it trusts only what is not itself.

These distinctions in the notion of a work which I have just proposed to you, and which divide it, not in any search for subtlety but by the easiest sort of reference to immediate observation, aim to bring out the idea which is now going to serve to introduce my analysis of the production of works of the mind.

All that I have said so far may be condensed into these few words: *works of the mind exist only in action.* Beyond this action, what remains is only an object that has no particular relation to the mind. Transport the statue you admire among a people sufficiently different from your own, and -it becomes an insignificant stone. The Parthenon is only a small quarry of marble. And when the text of a poet is used as a collection of grammatical difficulties, or examples, it ceases at once to be a work of the mind, since the use to which it is put is entirely foreign to the conditions of its creation, and since in addition it is denied the consumer value that gives meaning to such a work.

A poem on paper is nothing more than a piece of writing that may be used for anything that can be done with a piece of writing. But among all its possibilities there is one, and only one, which can finally put this text under conditions that will give it the force and form of action. A poem is a discourse that requires and sustains continuous connection between the *voice* that is and the *voice that is coming and must come*. And this voice must be such that it seems prescribed and excites the affective state of which the text itself is the unique verbal expression. Take away the voice and the voice required, and everything becomes arbitrary. The poem is changed into a sequence of signs held together only by the fact that they have been traced on paper one after another.

For these reasons I shall not cease to condemn the detestable practice of misusing those works best fitted to create and develop a feeling for poetry among young people, the practice of treating poems as things, of chopping them up as if their composition were nothing, of allowing if not requiring them to be recited in the way you have all heard, to be used as memory or spelling tests; in a word, of abstracting the essence of these works, that which makes them what they are and not something else, that which gives them their own quality and necessity.

It is the performance of the poem which is the poem. Without this, these rows of curiously assembled words are but inexplicable fabrications.

Works of the mind, poems or other, can be related only to *that which gives birth to that which gave them birth themselves,* and to absolutely nothing else. No doubt, divergencies may arise among the poetic interpretations of a poem, among the impressions and meanings, or rather among the resonances provoked in one or another reader by the action of the work. But now this banal remark, upon reflection, must take on an importance of the first order: the possible diversity of legitimate effects of a work is the very mark of the mind. It corresponds, moreover, to the plurality of ways that occurred to the author during his labor of production. The fact is that every act of the mind itself is always somehow accompanied by a certain more or less perceptible atmosphere of indetermination.

I must beg you to excuse this expression. I do not find a better.

Let us imagine ourselves in a state of transport from a work of art, one of those works which compel us to desire them all the more, the more we possess them, or the more they possess us. We now find ourselves divided between feelings arising in remarkable alternation and contrast. We feel on the one hand that the work acting upon us suits us so well that we cannot imagine it as different. In certain cases of supreme satisfaction, we even feel that we are being transformed in some profound way, becoming someone whose sensibility is capable of such fullness of delight and immediate comprehension. But we feel no less strongly, and as it were through some quite other sense, that the phenomenon which causes and develops this state in us, inflicts its power upon us, might not have been, and even ought not to have been, and is in fact improbable.

All the while that our enjoyment or our joy is real, real as a fact, the existence and formation of the means (that is, the work which generates our sensation) seem to us accidental. Its existence appears to be the result of some extraordinary chance, or some sumptuous gift of fortune, and it is in this (let us not forget to remark) that a particular analogy may be found between the effect of a work of art and that of certain aspects of nature: some geological feature, or a fleeting combination of light and vapor in the evening sky.

At times we are unable to imagine that a certain man, like one of us, could be the author of so extraordinary a blessing, and the glory we give him is the expression of our inability.

But whatever details may go into those games or dramas played in the mind of the producer, all must be brought to completion in the visible work and find in this very fact a final and absolute determination. This end is the outcome of a succession of inner changes which are as disordered as you please but which must necessarily be reconciled at the moment when the hand moves to write, under one unique command, whether happy or not. Now this hand, this external act, necessarily resolves for better or worse that state of indetermination of which I spoke. The producing mind seems to be elsewhere, seeking to impress upon its work a character quite different from its own. In a finished work, it hopes to escape the instability, the incoherence, the inconsequence which it recognizes in itself and which constitute its most frequent condition. To that end, it counters interruptions from every direction and of every kind which it must undergo at every moment. It absorbs an infinite variety of incidents; it rejects any substitutions of image, sensation, impulse, and idea that cut across other ideas. It struggles against what it is obliged to accept, produce, or express; in short, against its own nature and its accidental and instantaneous activity.

During its meditation it hums around its own center. The least thing is enough to divert it. St. Bernard observes: *Odoratus impedit cogitationem.* Even in the best head, contradiction is the rule, correct sequence is the exception. And this very correctness is a logician's artifice, an artifice which, like all others which the mind contrives against itself, consists in giving material shape to the elements of thought, which it calls "concepts," turning them into circles and domains, thus conferring upon these intellectual objects a duration independent of the vicissitudes of the mind; for logic after all is only a speculation on the permanence of notations.

But here is a very astonishing situation: the dispersion always threatening the mind contributes almost as importantly to the production of the work as concentration itself. The mind at work, struggling against its own mobility, against its own constitutional restlessness and diversity, against the dissipation or natural decay of any specialized attitude, on the other hand finds incomparable resources in this very condition itself. The instability, incoherence, inconsequence of which I spoke, which trouble and limit the mind in any sustained effort of construction or composition, are just as surely also treasures of possibility, whose riches it senses in its vicinity at the very moment when it is consulting itself. These are the mind's reserves, from which anything may come, its reasons for hoping that the solution, the signal, the image, or the missing word may be nearer at hand than it seems. The mind can always feel in the darkness around it the truth or the decision it is looking for, which it knows to be at the mercy of the slightest thing, of that very meaningless disorder which seemed to divert it and banish it indefinitely.

Sometimes what we wish to see appear to our minds (even a simple memory) is like some precious object we might hold and feel of through a wrapping of cloth that hides it from our eyes. It is and is not ours, and the least incident may reveal it. Sometimes we invoke what ought to exist, having defined it by its conditions. We demand it, being faced with some peculiar combination of elements all equally imminent to the mind and yet no one of which will stand out and satisfy our need. We beg of our minds some show of inequality. We hold up our desire before the mind as one places a magnet over a composite mixture of dust from which a particle of iron will suddenly jump out. In the order of mental things, there seem to be certain very mysterious relations between *the desire and the event. I do* not wish to say that the mind's desire creates a sort of field, much more complex than a magnetic field, which might have the power to call up what suits us. This image is only one way of expressing a fact of observation to which I shall return later. But however clear, evident, forceful, or beautiful the spiritual event may be which terminates our expectation, completes our thought, or removes our doubt, still nothing is irrevocable. Here, the moment to come has absolute power over what the preceding moment produces. That is because the mind when reduced to its own sole substance does not have the power to *finish,* and absolutely cannot bind itself by itself.

When we say that our opinion on a certain point is definitive, we say this in order to make it so: we have recourse to others. The sound of our voice is much more assuring to us than the firm inner remark which our voice pretends, aloud, that we have formed. When we think we have completed a certain thought, we never feel sure that we could come back to it without either improving or spoiling what we had finished. It is in this that the life of the mind is divided against itself as soon as it sets to work. Every work requires acts of will (although it always includes a number of components in which what we call the *will* has no part). But when our will, our expressed power, tries to turn upon the mind itself and make it obey, the result is always a simple arrest, the maintenance or perhaps the renewal of certain conditions.

In fact, we can act directly only upon the freedom of the mind's processes. We can lessen the degree of that freedom, but as for the rest, I mean as for the changes and substitutions still possible under our constraint, we must simply wait until what we desire appears, because that is all we can do. *We have no means of getting exactly what we wish from ourselves.*

For that exactness, or desired result, is of the same mental substance as our desire, and it may be they interfere with each other in acting simultaneously. We know that it happens fairly often that some desired solution comes to us after an interval of relaxed interest in the problem, as it were a reward for the freedom given to the mind.

What I have just said, although it applies more especially to the producer, may also be observed in the consumer of the work. In the latter the production of value, for example the comprehension, the interest aroused, the effort he may expend to possess the work more completely, would give rise to similar observations.

Whether I fasten on the page I must write or the one I wish to understand, in both cases I enter upon a phase of diminished freedom. But in both cases the restriction of my freedom may give rise to two quite opposite results. Sometimes my task itself excites me to pursue it; far from resenting it as a difficulty or a departure from the most natural course of my mind, I give myself to it and advance in such lively fashion along the path of my purpose that the sensation of fatigue is diminished, up to the moment when suddenly it actually beclouds my thought, shuffles the deck of ideas to set up again the normal disorder of short-term exchanges, the state of dispersive and restful indifference.

At other times, however, constraint is uppermost; the maintenance of direction is more and more difficult, the labor involved becomes more perceptible than its result, the means are opposed to the end, and the tension of the mind must be fed from resources more and more precarious and more and more unlike the ideal object whose power and action they must maintain, at the expense of fatigue rapidly becoming unbearable. That is the great contrast between two uses of the mind. It will serve to show you that the care I have taken to specify that works must be considered only as acts of production or consumption, was entirely consistent with what may be observed; while, on the other hand, it furnishes us the means of making a very important distinction between works of the mind.

Among these works, usage has created a category called works of art. It is not very easy to define this term, if indeed we need to define it. In the first place, I see nothing in the *production* of works which clearly forces me to create a category for the work of art. I find everywhere, in our minds, attention, tentative efforts, unexpected clarity and dark passages, improvisations and trials, or very hurried repetitions. On every hearth of the mind there are both fire and ashes; prudence and imprudence, method and its opposite; chance in a thousand forms. Artists, scholars, all are alike in the details of the strange life of thought. It may be said that at any particular moment the functional difference between minds at work is imperceptible. But if we turn our attention to the effects of works already finished, we discover in certain ones a particularity that groups them, differentiates them from all others. A certain work taken by itself may be divided into parts that are wholes, each able to create a desire and satisfy it. The work offers us in each of its parts, *food and appetite* at once. It continually awakens in us both thirst and a fountain. In return for the freedom we give up, it rewards us by making us love the captivity it imposes upon us and by giving us the feeling of a delightful kind of immediate knowledge; all the while, expending *to our great satisfaction* our own energy, which it evokes in a way so compatible with the highest performance of our organic resources that the sensation of effort itself becomes intoxicating and we feel ourselves possessors in being magnificently possessed.

So the more we give, the more we wish to give, all the while thinking we are receiving. The illusion of acting, expressing, discovering, understanding, solving, mastering, animates us.

All these effects, which are sometimes prodigious, are quite instantaneous, like everything that plays upon our sensibility; they attack directly the strategic points commanding our affective life, and through it make us intellectually available; they accelerate, retard, or even regularize our various functions whose accord or discord gives us in the end all the possible modulations on the sensation of living, from flat calm up to tempest.

The very tone of the 'cello, with many people, exercises real visceral persuasion. There are words whose frequency in an author's work reveals to us that for him they are endowed with far more resonance, and thus with positively creative power, than they are in general. This is one of those personal valuations, *those great values for one alone,* which certainly play a very handsome role in those productions of the mind in which singularity is an element of the first importance. These considerations will serve to clarify somewhat the constitution of poetry, which is rather mysterious. It is strange that one should exert himself to formulate a discourse which must simultaneously obey perfectly incongruous conditions: musical, rational, significant, and suggestive; conditions which require a continuous and repeated connection between rhythm and syntax, between *sound* and *sense.*

These parts are without any conceivable relation to one another. Yet we must give the illusion of their profound intimacy. What good is all this? The observance of rhythms, rimes, and verbal melody hampers the direct movement of my thought, and in fact keeps me from saying what I wish....*But what do I wish to say?* That is the question.

The answer is that in this case we have to wish what we must wish in order that thought, language and its conventions, on the one hand, all borrowed from the life around us, and on the other, the rhythm and accents of the voice, which are directly personal things, may be brought into accord; and this accord requires mutual sacrifices, the most remarkable of which is the one that must be voluntarily made by thought.

Some day I shall explain how this change shows in the language of poets, and how there is a poetic language in which words are no longer the words of free practical usage. They are no longer held together by the same attractions; they are charged with two different values operating simultaneously and of equivalent importance: their sound and their instantaneous psychic effect. They remind us then of those complex numbers in geometry; the coupling of the *phonetic variable* with the *semantic variable* creates problems of extension and convergence which poets solve blindfold—but they solve them (and that is the essential thing), from time to time... *From Time to Time,* that is the point! There lies the uncertainty, there lies the disparity between persons and times. That is our capital fact. I shall have to return to it at length; for all art, whether poetic or not, consists in defending oneself against the disparity of the moment.

All I have just outlined in this summary examination of the general notion of a work must lead me at last to indicate the point of view I have chosen, from which to explore this immense domain, the making of works of the mind. We have tried, in a few moments, to give you an idea of the complexity of these questions, where it may be said that everything happens at once, where what is deepest in man is combined with a number of external factors.

All may be summed up in this formula: that in the making of a work, an act comes in contact with the indefinable.

A voluntary act, which in every one of the arts is very complex, often requiring long labor, the most absorbed attention, and very precise knowledge, must adapt itself, in the making of art, to a state of being in itself quite irreducible, to a kind of definite expression, which does not refer to any localizable object, but which may itself be determined, and achieved by a system of uniformly determined acts; all this resulting in a work whose effect must be to set up an analogous state of being in someone else—I do not say a similar state, since we shall never know about that, but one analogous to the initial state of the producer.

Thus, on the one hand the *indefinable,* on the other hand a necessarily finite *act;* on the one hand *a state,* sometimes a single sensation producing value and impulse, a state whose sole character is to correspond to no finite term of our experience; on the other hand an *act,* that is to say the essence of determination, since an act is a miraculous escape from the closed world of the possible into the universe of fact; and this act is frequently produced despite the mind with all its precise knowledge—arising from the chaotic as Minerva arose fully armed from the mind of Jupiter, an old image still full of meaning! With the artist, it happens in fact—when the circumstances are favorable—that the inner impulse to production gives him, at once and inseparably, the motive, the immediate external aim, and the means and technical requirements for the act. In general a creative situation is set up in which there is a more or less lively exchange between requirements, knowledge, intentions, means, all mental and instrumental things, all the elements of action, in one act whose stimulus is not situated in the world where the aims of ordinary action are found, and consequently can furnish us with no foresight that may determine the formula of acts to be accomplished in order to locate it with certainty.

And it was when I finally came to conceive this quite remarkable fact (though seldom remarked, it seems) I mean the performance of an act, as the outcome, the issue, the final determination of a state which is inexpressible in finite terms (that is to say which exactly cancels its causal sensation), that I resolved to adopt as the general form of this Course the most general possible type of human action. I thought it best at all costs to set a simple line, a sort of geodetic path through the observations and ideas that surround this innumerable subject, knowing that in a study which has not before, to my knowledge, been taken up in its entirety, it is illusory to seek any intrinsic order, any line of development involving no repetition which would permit us to list problems according to the progression of some variable, for such a variable does not exist.

When the mind is in question, everything is in question; all is disorder, and every reaction against that disorder is of the same kind as itself. For the fact is that disorder is the condition of the mind's fertility: it contains the mind's promise, since its fertility depends on the unexpected rather than the expected, depends rather on what we do not know, and because we do not know it, than what we know. How could it be otherwise? The domain I am trying to survey is limitless, but the whole is reduced to human proportions at once if we take care to stick to our own experience, to the observations we have ourselves made, to the means we have tested. I try never to forget that every man is the measure of things.

Translated by Jackson Mathews

From "The Course in Poetics: First Lesson," by Paul Valéry, translated by Jackson Mathews, in the Southern Review, Winter, 1940, volume 5, no. 3. By permission of the translator, who has kindly revised his translation for this publication, and the publishers of the *Southern Review:* Louisiana State University Press, Baton Rouge, Louisiana.

THREE PIECES ON THE CREATIVE PROCESS
William Butler Yeats

The Thinking of the Body

Those learned men who are a terror to children and an igno-
minious sight in lovers' eyes, all those butts of a traditional hu-
mour where there is something of the wisdom of peasants, are mathematicians, theologians, lawyers, men of science of various kinds.
They have followed some abstract reverie, which stirs the brain only
and needs that only, and have therefore stood before the looking-
glass without pleasure and never known those thoughts that shape
the lines of the body for beauty or animation, and wake a desire for
praise or for display.

There are two pictures of Venice side by side in the house where
I am writing this, a Canaletto that has little but careful drawing,
and a not very emotional pleasure in clean bright air, and a Franz
Francken, where the blue water, that in the other stirs one so little,
can make one long to plunge into the green depth where a cloud
shadow falls. Neither painting could move us at all, if our thought
did not rush out to the edges of our flesh, and it is so with all good
art, whether the Victory of Samothrace which reminds the soles of
our feet of swiftness, or the Odyssey that would send us out under

174

the salt wind, or the young horsemen on the Parthenon, that seem happier than our boyhood ever was, and in our boyhood's way. Art bids us touch and taste and hear and see the world, and shrinks from what Blake calls mathematic form, from every abstract thing, from all that is of the brain only, from all that is not a fountain jetting from the entire hopes, memories, and sensations of the body. Its morality is personal, knows little of any general law, has no blame for Little Musgrave, no care for Lord Barnard's house, seems lighter than a breath and yet is hard and heavy, for if a man is not ready to face toil and risk, and in all gaiety of heart, his body will grow unshapely and his heart lack the wild will that stirs desire. It approved before all men those that talked or wrestled or tilted under the walls of Urbino, or sat in the wide window-seats discussing all things, with love ever in their thought, when the wise Duchess ordered all, and the Lady Emilia gave the theme.

Preface to *The King of the Great Clock Tower*

A year ago I found that I had written no verse for two years; I had never been so long barren; I had nothing in my head, and there used to be more than I could write. Perhaps Coole Park where I had escaped from politics, from all that Dublin talked of, when it was shut, shut me out from my theme; or did the subconscious drama that was my imaginative life end with its owner? but it was more likely that I had grown too old for poetry. I decided to force myself to write, then take advice. In 'At Parnell's Funeral' I rhymed passages from a lecture I had given in America; a poem upon mount Meru came spontaneously, but philosophy is a dangerous theme; then I was barren again. I wrote the prose dialogue of *The King of The Great Clock Tower* that I might be forced to make lyrics for its imaginary people. When I had written all but the last lyric I went a considerable journey partly to get the advice of a poet not of my school who would, as he did some years ago, say what he thought. I asked him to dine, tried to get his attention. 'I am in my sixty-ninth year' I said, 'probably I should stop writing verse, I want your opinion upon some verse I have written lately.' I had hoped he would ask me to read it but he would not speak of art, or of literature, or of anything related to them. I had however been talking to his latest disciple and knew that his opinions had not changed: Phidias had corrupted sculpture, we had nothing of true Greece but certain Nike dug up out of the foundations of the Parthenon, and that corruption ran through all our art; Shakespeare and Dante had corrupted literature, Shakespeare by his too abounding sentiment, Dante by his compromise with the Church.

He said apropos of nothing "Arthur Balfour was a scoundrel," and from that on would talk of nothing but politics. All the other modern statesmen were more or less scoundrels except `Mussolini and that hysterical imitator of his, Hitler.' When I objected to his violence he declared that Dante considered all sins intellectual, even sins of the flesh, he himself refused to make the modern distinction between error and sin. He urged me to read the works of Captain Douglas who alone knew what caused our suffering. He took my manuscript and went away denouncing Dublin as 'a reactionary hole' because I had said that I was re-reading Shakespeare, would go on to Chaucer, and found all that I wanted of modern life in 'detection and the wild west.' Next day his judgement came and that in a single word 'Putrid.'

Then I took my verses to a friend of my own school, and this friend said "go on just like that. Plays like *The Great Clock Tower* always seem unfinished but that is no matter. Begin plays without knowing how to end them for the sake of the lyrics. I once wrote a play and after I had filled it with lyrics abolished the play." Then I brought my work to two painters and a poet until I was like Panurge consulting oracles as to whether he should get married and rejecting all that did not confirm his own desire.

> *God guard me from those thoughts men think*
> *In the mind alone,*
> *He that sings a lasting song*
> *Thinks in a marrow bone;*
>
> *From all that makes a wise old man*
> *That can be praised of all;*

O what am I that I should not seem
For the song's sake a fool.

I pray—for fashion's word is out
And prayer comes round again—
That I may seem though I die old
A foolish, passionate man.

Long-Legged Fly

That civilisation may not sink,
Its great battle lost,
Quiet the dog, tether the pony
To a distant post;
Our master Caesar is in the tent
Where the maps are spread,
His eyes fixed upon nothing,
A hand under his head.
Like a long-legged fly upon the stream
His mind moves upon silence.

That the topless towers be burnt
And men recall that face,

Move most gently if move you must
In this lonely place.
She thinks, part woman, three parts a child,
That nobody looks; her feet
Practise a tinker shuffle
Picked up on a street.
Like a long-legged fly upon the stream
Her mind moves upon silence.

That girls at puberty may find
The first Adam in their thought,
Shut the door of the Pope's chapel,
Keep those children out.
There on that scaffolding reclines
Michael Angelo.
With no more sound than the mice make
His hand moves to and fro.
Like a long-legged fly upon the stream
His mind moves upon silence.

THE PROCESS OF MAKING POETRY

AmyLowell

In answering the question, How are poems made? my instinctive answer is a flat 'I don't know.' It makes not the slightest difference that the question as asked me refers solely to my own poems, for I know as little of how they are made as I do of any one else's. What I do know about them is only a millionth part of what there must be to know. I meet them where they touch consciousness, and that is already a considerable distance along the road of evolution.

Whether poetry is the fusion of contradictory ideas, as Mr. Graves believes, or the result and relief of emotional irritation and tension, as Sara Teasdale puts it, or the yielding to a psychical state verging on day-dream, as Professor Prescott has written a whole book to prove, it is impossible for any one to state definitely. All I can confidently assert from my own experience is that it is not day-dream, but an entirely different psychic state and one peculiar to itself.

The truth is that there is a little mystery here, and no one is more conscious of it than the poet himself. Let us admit at once that a poet is something like a radio aerial—he is capable of receiving messages on waves of some sort; but he is more than an aerial, for he possesses the capacity of transmuting these messages into those patterns of words we call poems.

It would seem that a scientific definition of a poet might put it something like this: a man of an extraordinarily sensitive and active subconscious personality, fed by, and feeding, a non-resistant consciousness. A common phrase among poets is, 'It came to me.' So hackneyed has this become that one learns to suppress the expression with care, but really it is the best description I know of the conscious arrival of a poem.

Sometimes the external stimulus which has produced a poem is known or can be traced. It may be a sight, a sound, a thought, or an emotion. Sometimes the consciousness has no record of the initial impulse, which has either been forgotten or springs from a deep, unrealized memory. But whatever it is, emotion, apprehended or hidden, is a part of it, for only emotion can rouse the subconscious into action. How carefully and precisely the subconscious mind functions, I have often been a witness to in my own work. An idea will come into my head for no apparent reason; 'The Bronze Horses,' for instance. I registered the horses as a good subject for a poem; and, having so registered them, I consciously thought no more about the matter. But what I had really done was to drop my subject into the subconscious, much as one drops a letter into the mail-box. Six months later, the words of the poem began to come into my head, the poem-to use my private vocabulary—was 'there.'

Some poets speak of hearing a voice speaking to them, and say that they write almost to dictation. I do not know whether my early scientific training is responsible for my using a less picturesque vocabulary, or whether their process really differs from mine. I do not hear a voice, but I do hear words pronounced, only the pronouncing is toneless. The words seem to be pronounced in my head, but with nobody speaking them. This is an effect with which I am familiar, for I always *hear* words even when I am reading to myself, and still more when I am writing. In writing, I frequently stop to read aloud what I have written, although this is really hardly necessary, so clearly do the words sound in my head.

The subconscious is, however, a most temperamental ally. Often he will strike work at some critical point and not another word is to be got out of him. Here is where the conscious training of the poet comes in, for he must fill in what the subconscious has left, and fill it in as much in the key of the rest as possible. Every long poem is sprinkled with these *lacunae;* hence the innumerable rewritings which most poems undergo. Sometimes the sly subconscious partner will take pity on the struggling poet and return to his assistance; sometimes he will have nothing to do with that particular passage again. This is the reason that a poet must be both born and made. He must be born with a subconscious factory always working for him or he never can be a poet at all, and he must have knowledge and talent enough to 'putty' up his holes—to use Mr. Graves's expression. Let no one undervalue this process of puttying; it is a condition of good poetry. Of the many first manuscript drafts of great poets that have passed through my hands in the last twenty-five years, I have seen none without its share of putty, and the one of all most worked over is Keats's 'The Eve of St. Agnes:

Long poems are apt to take months preparing in the subconscious mind; in the case of short poems, the period of subconscious gestation may be a day or an instant, or any time between. Suddenly words are there, and there with an imperious insistence which brooks no delay. They must be written down immediately or an acute suffering comes on, a distress almost physical, which is not relieved until the poem is given right of way. I never deny poems when they come; whatever I am doing, whatever I am writing, I lay it aside and attend to the arriving poem. I am so constituted that poems seldom come when I am out of doors, or actively engaged in company. But when I am alone, an idea contingent upon something I have seen or done when I am out will announce itself, quite as though it had been biding its time until it had me quiescent and receptive.

I seldom compose in my head. The first thing I do when I am conscious of the coming of a poem is to seek paper and pencil. It seems as though the simple gazing at a piece of blank paper hypnotized me into an awareness of the subconscious. For the same reason, I seldom correct poems while walking or driving; I find that the concentration needed for this is in the nature of trance (although that is too exaggerated a word for it), and must not be broken into by considerations of where I am going or what station I am to get out at.

This state of semi-trance is not surprising when we think of short poems; what is curious is that the trancelike state can hold over interruptions in the case of long poems. When a poem is so long that days or weeks are needed to write it, the mere sitting down to continue it produces the requisite frame of mind, which holds (except for the *lacunae* I have spoken of) throughout its correction. On the other hand, no power will induce it if the subconscious is not ready; hence the sterile periods known to all poets.

I do believe that a poet should know all he can. No subject is alien to him, and the profounder his knowledge in any direction, the more depth will there be to his poetry. I believe he should be thoroughly grounded in both the old and the new poetic forms, but I am firmly convinced that he must never respect tradition above his intuitive self. Let him be sure of his own sincerity above all, let him bow to no public acclaim, however alluring, and then let him write with all courage what his subconscious mind suggests to him.

From "The Process of Making Poetry," in *Poetry and Poets,* by Amy Lowell. By permission of the publishers: Houghton Mifflin Company, Boston.

THE MAKING
OF A POEM

Stephen Spender

Apology

I t would be inexcusable to discuss my own way of writing poetry unless I were able to relate this to a wider view of the problems which poets attempt to solve when they sit down at a desk or table to write, or walk around composing their poems in their heads. There is a danger of my appearing to put across my own experiences as the general rule, when every poet's way of going about his work and his experience of being a poet are different, and when my own poetry may not be good enough to lend my example any authority.

Yet the writing of poetry is an activity which makes certain demands of attention on the poet and which requires that he should have certain qualifications of ear, vision, imagination, memory and so on. He should be able to think in images; he should have as great a mastery of language as a painter has over his palate, even if the range of his language be very limited. All this means that, in ordinary society, a poet has to adapt himself, more or less consciously, to the demands of his vocation, and hence the peculiarities of poets and the condition of inspiration which many people have said is near to madness. One poet's example is only his adaptation of his personality to the demands of poetry, but if it is clearly stated it may help us to understand other poets, and even something of poetry.

Today we lack very much a whole view of poetry, and have instead many one-sided views of certain aspects of poetry which have been advertised as the only aims which poets should attempt. Movements such as free verse, imagism, surrealism, expressionism, personalism and so on, tend to make people think that poetry is simply a matter of not writing in metre of rhyme, or of free association, or of thinking in images, or of a kind of drawing room madness (surrealism) which corresponds to drawing room communism. Here is a string of ideas: Night, dark, stars, immensity, blue, voluptuous, clinging, columns, clouds, moon, sickle, harvest, vast camp fire, hell. Is this poetry? A lot of strings of words almost as simple as this are set down on the backs of envelopes and posted off to editors or to poets by the vast army of amateurs who think that to be illogical is to be poetic, with that fond question. Thus I hope that this discussion of how poets work will imply a wider and completer view of poets.

Concentration

The problem of creative writing is essentially one of concentration, and the supposed eccentricities of poets are usually due to mechanical habits or rituals developed in order to concentrate. Concentration, of course, for the purpose of writing poetry, is different from the kind of concentration required for working out a sum. It is a focussing of the attention in a special way, so that the poet is aware of all the implications and possible developments of his idea, just as one might say that a plant was not concentrating on developing mechanically in one direction, but in many directions, towards the warmth and light with its leaves, and towards the water with its roots, all at the same time.

Schiller liked to have a smell of rotten apples, concealed beneath the lid of his desk, under his nose when he was composing poetry. Walter de la Mare has told me that he must smoke when writing. Auden drinks endless cups of tea. Coffee is my own addiction, besides smoking a great deal, which I hardly ever do except when I am writing. I notice also that as I attain a greater concentration, this tends to make me forget the taste of the cigarette in my mouth, and then I have a desire to smoke two or even three cigarettes at a time, in order that the sensation from the outside may penetrate through the wall of concentration which I have built round myself.

For goodness sake, though, do not think that rotten apples or cigarettes or tea have anything to do with the quality of the work of a Schiller, a de la Mare, or an Auden. They are a part of a concentration which has already been attained rather than the causes of concentration. De la Mare once said to me that he thought the desire to smoke when writing poetry arose from a need, not of a stimulus, but to canalize a distracting leak of his attention away from his writing towards the distraction which is always present in one's environment. Concentration may be disturbed by someone whistling in the street or the ticking of a clock. There is always a slight tendency of the body to sabotage the attention of the mind by providing some distraction. If this need for distraction can be directed into one channel—such as the odor of rotten apples or the taste of tobacco or tea—then other distractions outside oneself are put out of competition.

Another possible explanation is that the concentrated effort of writing poetry is a spiritual activity which makes one completely forget, for the time being, that one has a body. It is a disturbance of the balance of body and mind and for this reason one needs a kind of anchor of sensation with the physical world. Hence the craving for a scent or taste or even, sometimes, for sexual activity. Poets speak of the necessity of writing poetry rather than of a liking for doing it. It is spiritual compulsion, a straining of the mind to attain heights surrounded by abysses and it cannot be entirely happy, for in the most important sense, the only reward worth having is absolutely denied: for, however confident a poet may be, he is never quite sure that all his energy is not misdirected nor that what he is writing is great poetry. At the moment when art attains its highest attainment it reaches beyond its medium of words or paints or music, and the artist finds himself realizing that these instruments are inadequate to the spirit of what he is trying to say.

Different poets concentrate in different ways. In my own mind I make a sharp distinction between two types of concentration: one is immediate and complete, the other is plodding and only completed by stages. Some poets write immediately works which, when they are written, scarcely need revision. Others write their poems by stages, feeling their way from rough draft to rough draft, until finally, after many revisions, they have produced a result which may seem to have very little connection with their early sketches.

These two opposite processes are vividly illustrated in two examples drawn from music: Mozart and Beethoven. Mozart thought out symphonies, quartets, even scenes from operas, entirely in his head—often on a journey or perhaps while dealing with pressing problems—and then he transcribed them, in their completeness, onto paper. Beethoven wrote fragments of themes in note books which he kept beside him, working on and developing them over years. Often his first ideas were of a clumsiness which makes scholars marvel how he could, at the end, have developed from them such miraculous results.

Thus genius works in different ways to achieve its ends. But although the Mozartian type of genius is the more brilliant and dazzling, genius, unlike virtuosity, is judged by greatness of results, not by brilliance of performance. The result must be the fullest development in a created aesthetic form of an original moment of insight, and it does not matter whether genius devotes a lifetime to producing a small result if that result be immortal. The difference between two types of genius is that one type (the Mozartian) is able to plunge the greatest depths of his own experience by the tremendous effort of a moment, the other (the Beethovenian) must dig deeper and deeper into his consciousness, layer by layer. What counts in either case is the vision which sees and pursues and attains the end; the logic of the artistic purpose.

A poet may be divinely gifted with a lucid and intense and purposive intellect; he may be clumsy and slow; that does not matter, what matters is integrity of purpose and the ability to maintain the purpose without losing oneself. Myself, I am scarcely capable of immediate concentration in poetry. My mind is not clear, my will is weak, I suffer from an excess of ideas and a weak sense of form. For every poem that I begin to write, I think of at least ten which I do not write down at all. For every poem which I do write down, there are seven or eight which I never complete.

The method which I adopt therefore is to write down as many ideas as possible, in however rough a form, in note books. (I have at least twenty of these, on a shelf beside my desk, going back over fifteen years.) I then make use of some of the sketches and discard others.

The best way of explaining how I develop the rough ideas which I use, is to take an example. Here is a Notebook begun in 1944. About a hundred pages of it are covered with writing, and from this have emerged about six poems. Each idea, when it first occurs is given a number. Sometimes the ideas do not get beyond one line. For example No. 3 (never developed), is the one line:

A language of flesh and roses.

I shall return to this line in a few pages, when I speak of inspiration. For the moment, I turn to No. 13, because here is an idea which has been developed to its conclusion. The first sketch begins thus:

a) There are some days when the sea lies like a harp
Stretched flat beneath the cliffs. The waves
Like wires burn with the sun's copper glow
[all the murmuring blue every silent]
Between whose spaces every image
Of sky [field and] hedge and field and boat
Dwells like the huge face of the afternoon.
[Lies]
When the heat grows tired, the afternoon
Out of the land may breathe a sigh
[Across these wires like a hand. They vibrate
With]
Which moves across those wires like a soft hand
[Then the vibration]
Between whose spaces the vibration holds
Every bird-cry, dog's bark, man-shout
And creak of rollock from the land and sky
With all the music of the afternoon.

192

Obviously these lines are attempts to sketch out an idea which exists clearly enough on some level of the mind where it yet eludes the attempt to state it. At this stage, a poem is like a face which one seems to be able to visualize clearly in the eye of memory, but when one examines it mentally or tries to think it out, feature by feature, it seems to fade.

The idea of this poem is a vision of the sea. The faith of the poet is that if this vision is clearly stated it will be significant. The vision is of the sea stretched under a cliff. On top of the cliff there are fields, hedges, houses. Horses draw carts along lanes, dogs bark far inland, bells ring in the distance. The shore seems laden with hedges, roses, horses and men, all high above the sea, on a very fine summer day when the ocean seems to reflect and absorb the shore. Then the small strung-out glittering waves of the sea lying under the shore are like the strings of a harp which catch the sunlight. Between these strings lies the reflection of the shore. Butterflies are wafted out over the waves, which they mistake for the fields of the chalky landscape, searching them for flowers. On a day such as this, the land, reflected in the sea, appears to enter into the sea, as though it lies under it, like Atlantis. The wires of the harp are like a seen music fusing seascape and landscape.

Looking at this vision in another way, it obviously has symbolic value. The sea represents death and eternity, the land represents the brief life of the summer and of one human generation which passes into the sea of eternity. But let me here say at once that although the poet may be conscious of this aspect of his vision, it is exactly what he wants to avoid stating, or even being too concerned with. His job is to recreate his vision, and let it speak its moral for itself. The poet must distinguish clearly in his own mind between that which most definitely must be said and that which must not be said. The unsaid inner meaning is revealed in the music and the tonality of the poem, and the poet is conscious of it in his knowledge that a certain tone of voice, a certain rhythm, are necessary.

In the next twenty versions of the poem I felt my way towards the clarification of the seen picture, the music and the inner feeling. In the first version quoted above, there is the phrase in the second and third lines:

> *The waves*
> *Like wires burn with the sun's copper glow.*

This phrase fuses the image of the sea with the idea of music, and it is therefore a key-phrase, because the theme of the poem is the fusion of the land with the sea. Here, then are several versions of these one and a quarter lines, in the order in which they were written:

> *b) The waves are wires*
> *Burning as with the secret song of fires*

c) The day burns in the trembling wires
   With a vast music golden in the eyes

d) The day glows on its trembling wires
   Singing a golden music in the eyes

e) The day glows on its burning wires
   Like waves o f music golden to the eyes.

f) Afternoon burns upon its wires
   Lines of music dazzling the eyes

g) Afternoon gilds its tingling wires
   To a visual silent music of the eyes

In the final version, these two lines appear as in the following stanza:

h) There are some days the happy ocean lies
   Like an unfingered harp, below the land.

Afternoon gilds all the silent wires
Into a burning music of the eyes.

On mirroring paths between those fine-strung fires

The shore, laden with roses, horses, spires,
Wanders in water, imaged above ribbed sand.

Inspiration

The hard work evinced in these examples, which are only a fraction of the work put into the whole poem, may cause the reader to wonder whether there is no such thing as inspiration, or whether it is merely Stephen Spender who is uninspired. The answer is that everything in poetry is work except inspiration, whether this work is achieved at one swift stroke, as Mozart wrote his music, or whether it is a slow process of evolution from stage to stage. Here again, I have to qualify the word 'work,' as I qualified the word 'concentration': the work on a line of poetry may take the form of putting a version aside for a few days, weeks or years, and then taking it up again, when it may be found that the line has, in the interval of time, almost rewritten itself.

Inspiration is the beginning of a poem and it is also its final goal. It is the first idea which drops into the poet's mind and it is the final idea which he at last achieves in words. In between this start and this winning post there is the hard race, the sweat and toil.

Paul Valéry speaks of the *'une ligne donnée'* of a poem. One line is given to the poet by God or by nature, the rest he has to discover for himself.

My own experience of inspiration is certainly that of a line or a phrase or a word or sometimes something still vague, a dim cloud of an idea which I feel must be condensed into a shower of words. The peculiarity of the key word or line is that it does not merely attract, as, say, the word 'braggadocio' attracts. It occurs in what seems to be an active, male, germinal form as though it were the centre of a statement requiring a beginning and an end, and as though it had an impulse in a certain direction. Here are examples:

A language of flesh and roses.

This phrase (not very satisfactory in itself) brings to my mind a whole series of experiences and the idea of a poem which I shall perhaps write some years hence. I was standing in the corridor of a train passing through the Black Country. I saw a landscape of pits and pitheads, artificial mountains, jagged yellow wounds in the earth; everything transformed as though by the toil of an enormous animal or giant tearing up the earth in search of prey or treasure. Oddly enough, a stranger next to me in the corridor echoed my inmost thought. He said: "Everything there is man-made." At this moment the line flashed into my head:

A language of flesh and roses.

The sequence of my thought was as follows: the industrial land-scape which seems by now a routine and act of God which enslaves both employers and workers who serve and profit by it, is actually the expression of man's will. Men willed it to be so, and the pitheads, slag-heaps and the ghastly disregard of anything but the pursuit of wealth, are a symbol of modern man's mind. In other words, the world which we create—the world of slums and telegrams and newspapers—is a kind of language of our inner wishes and thoughts. Although this is so, it is obviously a language which has got outside our control. It is a confused language, an irresponsible senile gibberish. This thought greatly distressed me, and I started thinking that if the phenomena created by humanity are really like words in a language, what kind of language do we really aspire to? All this sequence of thought flashed into my mind with the answer which came before the question: *A language of flesh and roses.*

I hope this example will give the reader some idea of what I mean by inspiration. Now the line, which I shall not repeat again, is a way of thinking imaginatively. If the line embodies some of the ideas which I have related above, these ideas must be further made clear in other lines. That is the terrifying challenge of poetry. Can I think out the logic of images? How easy it is to explain here the poem that I would have liked to write! How difficult it would be to write it. For writing it would imply living my way through the imaged experience of all these ideas, which here are mere abstractions, and such an effort of imaginative experience requires a lifetime of patience and watching.

Here is an example of a cloudy form of thought germinated by

the word *cross,* which is the key word of the poem which exists formlessly in my mind. Recently my wife had a son. On the first day that
I visited her after the boy's birth, I went by bus to the hospital. Passing through the streets on the top of the bus, they all seemed very
clean, and the thought occurred to me that everything was prepared
for our child. Past generations have toiled so that any child born
today inherits, with his generation, cities, streets, organization, the
most elaborate machinery for living. Everything has been provided
for him by people dead long before he was born. Then, naturally
enough, sadder thoughts colored this picture for me, and I reflected how he also inherited vast maladjustments, vast human wrongs.
Then I thought of the child as like a pin-point of present existence,
the moment incarnate, in whom the whole of the past, and all possible futures cross. This word cross somehow suggested the whole
situation to me of a child born into the world and also of the form
of a poem about his situation. When the word *cross* appeared in the
poem, the idea of the past should give place to the idea of the future
and it should be apparent that the *cross* in which present and future
meet is the secret of an individual human existence. And here again,
the unspoken secret which lies beyond the poem, the moral significance of other meanings of the word `cross' begins to glow with its
virtue that should never be said and yet should shine through every
image in the poem.

This account of inspiration is probably weak beside the accounts that other poets might give. I am writing of my own experience, and my own inspiration seems to me like the faintest flash of insight into the nature of reality beside that of other poets whom I can think of. However, it is possible that I describe here a kind of experience which, however slight it may be, is far truer to the real poetic experience than Aldous Huxley's account of how a young poet writes poetry in his novel *Time Must Have a Stop*. It is hard to imagine anything more self-conscious and unpoetic than Mr. Huxley's account.

Memory

If the art of concentrating in a particular way is the discipline necessary for poetry to reveal itself, memory exercised in a particular way is the natural gift of poetic genius. The poet, above all else, is a person who never forgets certain sense-impressions which he has experienced and which he can re-live again and again as though with all their original freshness.

All poets have this highly developed sensitive apparatus of memory, and they are usually aware of experiences which happened to them at the earliest age and which retain their pristine significance throughout life. The meeting of Dante and Beatrice when the poet was only nine years of age is the experience which became a symbol in Dante's mind around which the *Divine Comedy* crystallized. The experience of nature which forms the subject of Wordsworth's poetry was an extension of a childhood vision of `natural presences' which surrounded the boy Wordsworth. And his decision in later life to live in the Lake District was a decision to return to the scene of these childhood memories which were the most important experiences in his poetry. There is evidence for the importance of this kind of memory in all the creative arts, and the argument certainly applies to prose which is creative. Sir Osbert Sitwell has told me that his book *Before the Bombardment,* which contains an extremely civilized and satiric account of the social life of Scarborough before and during the last war, was based on his observations of life in that resort before he had reached the age of twelve.

It therefore is not surprising that although I have no memory for telephone numbers, addresses, faces and where I have put this morning's correspondence, I have a perfect memory for the sensation of certain experiences which are crystallized for me around certain associations. I could demonstrate this from my own life by the overwhelming nature of associations which, suddenly aroused, have carried me back so completely into the past, particularly into my childhood, that I have lost all sense of the present time and place. But the best proofs of this power of memory are found in the odd lines of poems written in note books fifteen years ago. A few fragments of unfinished poems enable me to enter immediately into the experiences from which they were derived, the circumstances in which they were written, and unwritten feelings in the poem that were projected but never put into words.

...Knowledge of a full sun
That runs up his big sky, above
The hill, then in those trees and throws
His smiling on the turf.

That is an incomplete idea of fifteen years ago, and I remember exactly a balcony of a house facing a road, and, on the other side of the road, pine trees, beyond which lay the sea. Every morning the sun sprang up, first of all above the horizon of the sea, then it climbed to the tops of the trees and shone on my window. And this memory connects with the sun that shines through my window in London now in spring and early summer. So that the memory is not exactly a memory. It is more like one prong upon which a whole calendar of similar experiences happening throughout years, collect. A memory once clearly stated ceases to be a memory, it becomes perpetually present, because every time we experience something which recalls it, the clear and lucid original experience imposes its formal beauty on the new experiences. It is thus no longer a memory but an experience lived through again and again.

Turning over these old note books my eye catches some lines, in a projected long poem, which immediately re-shape themselves into the following short portrait of a woman's face:

Her eyes are gleaming fish
Caught in her nervous face, as if in a net.
Her hair is wild and fair, haloing her cheeks
Like a fantastic flare of Southern sun.
There is madness in her cherishing her children.
Sometimes, perhaps a single time in years,
Her wandering fingers stoop to arrange some flowers
Then in her hands her whole life stops and weeps.

It is perhaps true to say that memory is the faculty of poetry, because the imagination itself is an exercise of memory. There is nothing we imagine which we do not already know. And our ability to imagine is our ability to remember what we have already once experienced and to apply it to some different situation. Thus the greatest poets are those with memories so great that they extend beyond their strongest experiences to their minutest observations of people and things far outside their own self-centredness (the weakness of memory is its self-centredness: hence the narcissistic nature of most poetry).

Here I can detect my own greatest weakness. My memory is defective and self-centred. I lack the confidence in using it to create situations outside myself, although I believe that, in theory, there are very few situations in life which a poet should not be able to imagine, because it is a fact that most poets have experienced almost every situation in life. I do not mean by this that a poet who writes about a Polar Expedition has actually been to the North Pole. I mean, though, that he has been cold, hungry, etc., so that it is possible for him by remembering imaginatively his own felt experiences to know what it is like to explore the North Pole. That is where I fail. I cannot write about going to the North Pole.

Faith

It is evident that a faith in their vocation, mystical in intensity, sustains poets. There are many illustrations from the lives of poets to show this, and Shakespeare's sonnets are full of expressions of his faith in the immortality of his lines.

>From my experience I can clarify the nature of this faith. When I was nine, we went to the Lake District, and there my parents read me some of the poems of Wordsworth. My sense of the sacredness of the task of poetry began then, and I have always felt that a poet's was a sacred vocation, like a saint's. Since I was nine, I have wanted to be various things, for example, Prime Minister (when I was twelve). Like some other poets I am attracted by the life of power and the life of action, but I am still more repelled by them. Power involves forcing oneself upon the attention of historians by doing things and occupying offices which are, in themselves, important, so that what is truly powerful is not the soul of a so-called powerful and prominent man but the position which he fills and the things which he does.

Similarly, the life of `action' which seems so very positive is, in fact, a selective, even a negative kind of life. A man of action does one thing or several things because he does not do something else. Usually men who do very spectacular things fail completely to do the ordinary things which fill the lives of most normal people, and which would be far more heroic and spectacular perhaps, if they did not happen to be done by many people. Thus in practice the life of action has always seemed to me an act of cutting oneself off from life.

Although it is true that poets are vain and ambitious, their vanity and ambition is of the purest kind attainable in this world, for the saint renounces ambition. They are ambitious to be accepted for what they ultimately are as revealed by their inmost experiences, their finest perceptions, their deepest feelings, their uttermost sense of truth, in their poetry. They cannot cheat about these things, because the quality of their own being is revealed not in the noble sentiments which their poetry expresses, but in sensibility, control of language, rhythm and music, things which cannot be attained by a vote of confidence from an electorate, or by the office of Poet Laureate. Of course, work is tremendously important, but, in poetry, even the greatest labor can only serve to reveal the intrinsic qualities of soul of the poet as he really is.

Since there can be no cheating, the poet, like the saint, stands in all his works before the bar of a perpetual day of judgment. His vanity of course is pleased by success, though even success may contribute to his understanding that popularity does not confer on him the favorable judgment of all the ages which he seeks. For what does it mean to be praised by one's own age, which is soaked in crimes and stupidity, except perhaps that future ages, wise where we are foolish, will see him as a typical expression of this age's crimes and stupidity? Nor is lack of success a guarantee of great poetry, though there are some who pretend that it is. Nor can the critics, at any rate beyond a certain limited point of technical judgment, be trusted.

The poet's faith is therefore, firstly, a mystique of vocation, secondly, a faith in his own truth, combined with his own devotion to a task. There can really be no greater faith than the confidence that one is doing one's utmost to fulfill one's high vocation, and it is this that has inspired all the greatest poets. At the same time this faith is coupled with a deep humility because one knows that, ultimately, judgment does not rest with oneself. All one can do is to achieve nakedness, to be what one is with all one's faculties and perceptions, strengthened by all the skill which one can acquire, and then to stand before the judgment of time.

In my Notebooks, I find the following Prose Poem, which expresses these thoughts:

Bring me peace bring me power bring me assurance. Let me reach the bright day, the high chair, the plain desk, where my hand at last controls the words, where anxiety no longer undermines me. If I don't reach these I'm thrown to the wolves, I'm a restless animal wandering from place to place, from experience to experience.

Give me the humility and the judgment to live alone with the deep and rich satisfaction of my own creating: not to be thrown into doubt by a word of spite or disapproval.

In the last analysis don't mind whether your work is good or bad so long as it has the completeness, the enormity of the whole world which you love.

Song

Inspiration and song are the irreducible final qualities of a poet which make his vocation different from all others. Inspiration is an experience in which a line or an idea is given to one, and perhaps also a state of mind in which one writes one's best poetry. Song is far more difficult to define.

It is the music which a poem as yet unthought of will assume, the empty womb of poetry for ever in the poet's consciousness, waiting for the fertilizing seed.

Sometimes, when I lie in a state of half-waking half-sleeping, I am conscious of a stream of words which seem to pass through my mind, without their having a meaning, but they have a sound, a sound of passion, or a sound recalling poetry that I know. Again sometimes when I am writing, the music of the words I am trying to shape takes me far beyond the words, I am aware of a rhythm, a dance, a fury, which is as yet empty of words.

In these observations, I have said little about headaches, midnight oil, pints of beer or of claret, love affairs, and so on, which are supposed to be stations on the journeys of poets through life. There is no doubt that writing poetry, when a poem appears to succeed, results in an intense physical excitement, a sense of release and ecstasy. On the other hand, I dread writing poetry, for, I suppose, the following reasons: a poem is a terrible journey, a painful effort of concentrating the imagination; words are an extremely difficult medium to use, and sometimes when one has spent days trying to say a thing clearly one finds that one has only said it dully; above all, the writing of a poem brings one face to face with one's own personality with all its familiar and clumsy limitations. In every other phase of existence, one can exercise the orthodoxy of a conventional routine: one can be polite to one's friends, one can get through the day at the office, one can pose, one can draw attention to one's position in society, one is—in a word—dealing with men. In poetry, one is wrestling with a god.

Usually, when I have completed a poem, I think 'this is my best poem,' and I wish to publish it at once. This is partly because I only write when I have something new to say, which seems more worth while than what I have said before, partly because optimism about my present and future makes me despise my past. A few days after I have finished a poem, I relegate it to the past of all my other wasted efforts, all the books I do not wish to open.

Perhaps the greatest pleasure I have got from poems that I have written is when I have heard some lines quoted which I have not at once recognized. And I have thought 'how good and how interesting,' before I have realized that they are my own.

In common with other creative writers I pretend that I am not, and I am, exceedingly affected by unsympathetic criticism, whilst praise usually makes me suspect that the reviewer does not know what he is talking about. Why are writers so sensitive to criticism? Partly, because it is their business to be sensitive, and they are sensitive about this as about other things. Partly, because every serious creative writer is really in his heart concerned with reputation and not with success (the most successful writer I have known, Sir Hugh Walpole, was far and away the most unhappy about his reputation, because the 'highbrows' did not like him). Again, I suspect that every writer is secretly writing for *someone,* probably for a parent or teacher who did not believe in him in childhood. The critic who refuses to 'understand' immediately becomes identified with this person, and the understanding of many admirers only adds to the writer's secret bitterness if this one refusal persists.

Gradually one realizes that there is always this someone who will not like one's work. Then, perhaps, literature becomes a humble exercise of faith in being all that one can be in one's art, of being more than oneself, expecting little, but with a faith in the mystery of poetry which gradually expands into a faith in the mysterious service of truth.

Yet what failures there are! And how much mud sticks to one; mud not thrown by other people but acquired in the course of earning one's living, answering or not answering the letters which one receives, supporting or not supporting public causes. All one can hope is that this mud is composed of little grains of sand which will produce pearls.

From "The Making of a Poem," by Stephen Spender in *Partisan Review,* Summer, 1946. By permission of Mr. Spender's agents: Harold Matson, New York City, and A. D. Peters, London; and the publishers of *Partisan Review,* New York City.

THE BIRTH OF A POEM

Brewster Ghiselin

No doubt poems may be written in different ways; and one of these precludes much examination, since the poem seems to issue from the dark of the mind without much awareness of how it comes. As John Peale Bishop has observed, all writing is to some degree automatic. But there is sometimes a very full consciousness of the process, or of such of its aspects as are open to introspection.

Many artists and thinkers have written about the creative process as they have observed it in themselves. Yet there are not many very full accounts of the production of specific works. Perhaps the most nearly complete is contained in Henri Poincaré's essay "Mathematical Creation." And probably the best known is Poe's account of the writing of "The Raven," which is possibly insincere. Even if the honesty of the reporter is unquestioned, his method, of recollection and introspection, is hazardous. Yet it seems to be the only approach that reveals the creative activities in any illuminating relation to the complex of meanings, the work of art or other invention, that is developed amid them.

Once the work is begun, a poem may be completed in a few minutes—or it may take years. "Bath of Aphrodite" was produced in four writings: two pieces of verse, one of prose, and the final composition of thirty-three lines of verse, in which were included some of the meaning and substance of the earlier efforts, augmented and re-formed.

The first fragment, "Anadyomene," was set down with only a few changes in September, 1938:

> In the autumn of this glass-sharp sea
> Her thighs curved like the Venus's-shell
> Wade and submerge, shine
> Wavering in trapped light;
> She returns to her own mystery,
> The sea from which she arose.

What I was trying to say was, I suppose, what I finally managed to say in the ultimate poem—or something like it. Unfortunately I could not know this. I could only note the discontent, frustration, and disappointment mingled with the excitement of realization that the lines gave me.

For they did realize something. In some measure, they satisfied a need I had felt again and again, often associated with images of swimmers or waders in the ocean. It was as if the human beings in the dark water surfaced with light were words of strangely moving sound suggesting a marvelous import, which despite every effort I could not understand.

But now I began to understand, mainly through grasping the intellectual form of the poem: an idea of the return of Aphrodite, or Venus, the foam-born, into the sea. Hence the title "Anadyomene," the one who rises from the sea, an epithet of Aphrodite by which her origin is remembered.

The image is of Venus; perhaps like the Botticellian figure standing on the shoreward shell, which can never cease to affect our sensibility. But now she is seen advancing into the waves. Behind her is the land, where she has sojourned and become human. Now she rides no magical shell blown by rose-scattering winds. She is only a woman wading into the ocean on an autumn morning.

Yet in that image of a woman are qualities which the divine Aphrodite was created to embody. Her thighs are curved like the Venus's-shell, the antique cowry, whose wave-shedding forms suggest the collaborations of life and the sea and whose wheat-grain shape is the natural symbol of fecundity and of love. Entering the water, she is returning to something obscured or lost while she was on the land: her own mystery, her proper self. In a return to her Anadyomenean nature, without ceasing to be a woman in the real and present world, she is made whole again.

The form, therefore, is a comment on our knowledge and on the abstractions by which we live. It is a way of saying that a woman may be something more than our current definitions comprehend.

But in this first fragment these matters are imperfectly conveyed. All beginning and end, the poem is scarcely ample enough to engage the mind. And the auditory form is weak: it fails to establish firmly and fully moods and images and the relations between them. The structure does not realize very much.

Besides, there is something of primary importance in the poem which is not at all clear: the meaning of the sea in relation to that image of a woman in the fullness of her being. For the sea is not simply a means, picturesque but arbitrary, of relating the woman to the goddess. The sea is some sort of creative mystery relative to the woman and goddess alike, and of large significance. The obscurity of this meaning was for me the central failure of the fragmentary poem.

The writing, however, was finished, at least for the time being. In that first form it was no more than an intimation, like an embryonic heartbeat. The poem was as yet unborn.

II

One morning weeks later, some words came to my mind and I wrote them down, three lines mainly about transient shore birds such as are seen along the California coast in late summer and early autumn. I had had that coast much in mind, an exciting and satisfying image. It was natural that I should write about it. The lines flew into my mind as casually and effortlessly as the shore birds of the coast fly across one's vision out of the light and foam mist. I saw an image of the wader, and birds flashing past her in the lighted morning, and in the same instant I had the lines:

> And what are these...visitors that pass her?
> Shore birds with wings like thin
> Fins against the morning.

Having written that, I saw through those wings the light of the whole coast.

Often a poem is written with the eye-intent upon an object that isn't there, before it. Such an object must be excitingly significant, capable of making the mind glow about it. Half the trick then lies in keeping the object spotted in the central furnacelight of the aroused excitement while the construction of the poem goes on in relative shadow, as if it were a thing of slight importance. For under these circumstances the structure may be played with freely and irreverently. Because the structure then never becomes an absolute, all the freedom of the mind's action is preserved to the last moment of the creative labor. To intensely imagine the wader in the sun and sealight of the coast was therefore an important part of the process of bringing forth the poem.

But I wrote no more that day—I forget why; perhaps I was on the way to teach a class. I watched those birds go down the shore and saw the red and yellow cliffs of Torrey Pines rise in the light behind them. The imagined scene was taking shape in the only way that can succeed: according to promptings that are secret because they are of the mind's wholeness. The whole activity of the mind always transcends the specific activity that forms the pattern of any moment of consciousness. The mind, moreover, belongs to time—at least when it is sane. The maintenance of its sanity requires its orderly implication in the processes of the world. And therefore it must give itself to change. The order inherited from any preceding moment often will not perfectly adjust it to the realities of the present moment, the pressures of the instant. Then, to make possible a new adjustment, the closed system of the inherited order—the accepted pattern of consciousness—must be broken. Of itself it will not alter, it must be penetrated from without. It must be washed over, flooded, drowned, and perhaps dissolved, in the greater activity of the whole mind. This is the disordering that makes order possible, out of which all living order comes.

Because the creation of a poem involves a reordering of consciousness, its development cannot be forced and regulated wholly by an effort of conscious authority. Often one must wait for the development. As Paul Valéry has pointed out, one must allow the mind the liberty of its own process. That is perhaps what Keats had in mind when he said poetry should come "as naturally as the leaves to a tree, [or] it had better not come at all." We may not suppose that he meant that poetry should be written without effort or with little. For we know from his manuscripts that he labored to make his poems complete and right. He reworked whole passages, tried variant readings, struck out a word to put another in its place-and sometimes struck out that and wrote in the first again. As every poet does.

I waited a long time for my two fragments to come to something. Sometimes I repeated the three lines, and less often the earlier ones, partly in expectation of revising them, but mostly in order to rouse the images that made me feel my life. One day I noticed that I was saying instead of "visitors" "visitants." I was not quite sure of the new word, but it seemed right. Doubtless I had known the meaning once, for the dictionary reassured me: it meant a visitor, and more specifically a migratory bird.

III

In a way, those fragments of verse were preparation for certain passages in a story I began to write that winter: "Death of the Past," published the following year in *Story* magazine. In the story, a character remembers a woman wading into the ocean:
"... now he remembered her bathing under the red cliffs of Torrey Pines,where the cry of the surf on the flat sand is one unceasing call as in a shell. Mist rises from the many breakers falling or pushing their foam before them, and in the lighted mist Ann wades ankle-deep the slow shoreward wash the dark sand shows through; she wades the first ribbed pools deepening to her knees, leaping up her thighs; she leans against a wave, wades deeper, lies forward into the

next bank of foam.

"He had often watched her thus entering the water. She had revealed by her act and form unphrasable relations of man to woman and woman to the sea."

The description does not exist for itself, of course. It is intended to define and make more concrete the relation between the two characters; to prepare for the development of a similar relation between one of those characters and a third; and to suggest a feeling of some profound acceptance.

The passage required a small amount of revision before I got it right. I remember being pleased because it embodied more accurately and fully what I had been trying to bring to life in the fragmentary poems. For its purpose in the story it seemed right. But the meaning of the sea in relation to the woman, and, as I now saw, to human beings generally, remained almost as obscure as ever.

IV

"Death of the Past" is the prose twin of the poem—perhaps the Siamese twin, since they are joined by the ligature of a phrase. Both were finished in the summer of 1939. One Saturday morning in the midst of a too busy summer session, I was impelled to work on the poem. I remember mostly the inconvenience: if I suppressed the impulse it might not come again. I laid other work aside and by Sunday evening I had got the poem into what proved to be its final form:

Bath of Aphrodite
She rises among boulders. Naked, alone,
In freshets of the seacliff wind she stands;
She comes rose-golden over the color of stones,
Down to the wide plane of the seaward sand.

And what are these ... visitants that pass her?
Shorebirds with wings like thin
Fins against the morning.

She wades in shallows warmer than the air
And sees the long push of the promised foam,
She feels the chill that draws her breath like fear,
And wading slowly feels for the deeper cold....

What voices twitter and fade along that shore?
The godwit and the killdeer and the curlew,
The turnstone and the willet.

And now the water is silvering to her knees.
Over the sunmarks flurried about her feet
She sees a hundred harmless fishes flit
In the autumn of the glass-sharp morning sea.

What birds are those that ride the rising seas?
Slow shorelong pelicans
Fanned by the shoreward green.

Her thighs curved like the Venus's-shell submerge,
She wades into deep waves, her body drowns
Up to the lifted breasts and lifting arms;
Foam floats the tendrils of her tightening curls.

What birds are these that fall with never a swerve?
Far waves where morning burns,
Terns shatter into glass.

Now the rich moment, as she leans and swims
Folded into a hissing slope of foam:
The sea receives the shape that once it gave:
Her gold and roses to its dazzle of waves,
The shadow of all her secrets to its shade.

It may seem strange that so short a poem should take so much time to write. The condition of the crowded two pages of the penciled manuscript explains why: it is blurred with repeated erasures, strawed with deletions, spattered with glosses and variants. It appears almost as full of doubt as of decision.

And the lines are in disorder. Near the top of the first page are the three lines about the shore birds. That was the nucleus of the poem, the first finished element of its structure and a clue to the mood. Six lines are scrawled in above it. One has been mauled, wrecked, and crossed out. Its condition is significant, for it contains the traces of a formative meditation, one of those difficult, time-consuming researches into the relation between the depths of the excited mind and the possibilities of the medium, whereby the worker little by little shapes his structure and clarifies his creative intention. For that intention is not ever quite clear in the beginning; it only becomes so upon the completion of the poem. The poem is its only exact and explicit definition.

The line in question is not quite legible in every part and in all its variant forms. But it is clearly the prototype of the second line of the completed poem. The earliest legible reading was:

Lapped in the struggles of the silken wind.

In writing the prose passage of the story, I had intended to suggest, as I have said, a certain feeling of acceptance. In this line I tried to suggest that feeling by giving a sense of the touch and pressure upon the flesh of the enclosing and dynamic air. The word "struggles" gave the willful violence of the wind, "silken" smoothed the touch to sensuousness, "lapped" made the touch everywhere complete, so that the relation was nowhere denied. But the line was nevertheless not quite satisfying. I tried another form:

Lapped in the silken struggles of the air.

This opened the line out at the end: the long vowel of "air" trailed off in the soft continuant of the "r." And this gave a sense of the open extent of the atmosphere: space widened and I could feel the sky. But "silken struggles" seemed oversensuous. This was not what I wanted and I restored the earlier version:

Lapped in the struggles of the silken wind.

What was wrong with it? Perhaps "silken" was wrong even in this less emphatic position. It has precious and indoor connotations. Whereas I was trying to create a sense of fresh and casual contact with the natural world.

I knew, moreover, that I was going to build my poem to give expression to that sense of coming into touch with the natural world, most finally and fully through the symbolic immersion of my swimmer in the sea. There was plenty of time to create the desired impression. And I saw now that there was something wrong in trying to create it fully in the early part of the poem. For it was a part of the climactic development of the vision. Enough, if I could anticipate the water in the handling of the image of the wind. Instead of the wide air, I put the wind-rebuffing cliffs behind the woman, the hard and fixed forms of the land which she is about to turn away from to the flow of wind and water:

In freshets of the seacliff wind she stands.

Now I began to see more clearly and fully what I was trying to say: that she belonged both to the land and to the water, to the fixed and the flowing. I saw her colored with the earth colors of rose and gold, walking over the color of the earth:

She comes rose-golden over the color of stones,
Down to the wide plane of the seaward sand.

Perhaps because she has lived too much in consciousness of the land, the world of finished and separate forms, she turns in need of balance to the enfolding flow of the water. I saw too why the season must be autumn, the season of dissolving forms. The very birds are those of autumn and of the margin between the two worlds of land and sea. But as she wades deeper the voices of the shore birds dwindle to faint twitters and are gone. She moves a little fearful into the unknown unchartable water, sees the birds of the lifted surf, the pelicans, and those that feed beyond it, the terns. The sea receives her wholly, body and psyche, to itself:

> *Her gold and roses to its dazzle of waves,*
> *The shadow of all her secrets to its shade.*

As earlier she was seen to have qualities of the land, earth colors and fixed form, so she is seen now to have predominantly the qualities of the water, its movement of lighted surfaces over secret depths.

Thus the immersion symbolizes also the woman's acceptance of her full nature, of the reality of her inner life as well as of the outer world. But in her body and consciousness the elements are unified in a particular life. Whereas the salt indeterminate ocean flood is the universal reservoir of elements, the image of death—but also of all new possibility, and hence of the life fountain itself. As Aphrodite, she is conceived as having risen out of the ocean, her flesh and spirit having formed out of its clear flow. So in her turning seaward she is remembering the mystery of birth and creation, and reestablishing in their relation of dependence upon the formative source the things that have been formed. And therefore her wading into the sea is an indication of her readiness for self-transcendence; it is an act of submission to life, including what is unknown and uncontrollable in life, and a recognition that her being is grounded in something larger and richer than the personal body and ego.

224

I did not understand all these things and grasp their significance before I wrote the final lines. The writing was an aspect of the act of understanding. And of course I do not insist that all these meanings will appear more or less fully to the readers of the poem, though I should like to think that they will.

V

The poem did not compose itself as directly and easily as this summary suggests. There were formal problems requiring continual manipulation of the materials, at the same time offering difficulties and providing a challenge and stimulant. The poem was moving from the first toward an embodiment of an idea and impression of that integral unity of man with the restless universe and in all the elements of his own changeful being which is fullness of life. The formal intention, sensed more than thought, must therefore be to create through the process which constitutes the structure of the poem an impression of richness and variety and change in combination with a high degree of integration.

To this end, the patterns of rime are made in different ways: by using various sorts of echoes besides ordinary rime and by placing them at the beginning or center of some lines as well as at the end, by varying the rime schemes, and by superimposing on one scheme a suggestion of one or more others, as in the first quatrain. The primary stanzas, those defined for the eye as well as the ear, are linked into a continuous chain by rime or rime substitutes and are further contradicted or countered by means of stanzas defined by rime patterns that overlap the printed divisions in various ways. Thus every quatrain is extended by the line following, which belongs to the group by reason of length as well as rime, and the succeeding three-foot lines are extended by means of a rime on the third stress of the following pentameter.

These and most other structures were created with forethought and worked out in full consciousness. Some, such as the pattern made by the initial rimes, *fins, turn, fanned, terns,* I did not see until the poem was finished, but I hesitate to call them accidental. Some appeared without conscious intention and were then elaborated, or justified and allowed to stand. When first set down, the line:

The godwit and the killdeer and the curlew

looked like a pentameter. But when I tried to shorten the line to the required trimeter, I was dissatisfied. Though perhaps the reasoning by which I persuaded myself that the line was right as it stood is rationalization, it seemed that it read equally well as a trimeter, the second and third foot being paeons, or as a pentameter. It occurred to me besides that the structure reinforced the impression I had been working for, not only in adding another to the sort of feet used and in forming a union of the longer line with the shorter, but in suggesting two other systems of prosody, the dipodic and accentual. For the line reminds the ear of their typical music, and it may easily be scanned, and read, according to either: the dipodic or the accentual. I will say nothing about the effect of all this on the next line.

Though it is not always by calculation, it seems nevertheless by the strictest intent that the form is what it is. As in the human body, the parts tend to merge into one another without absolute demarcation, often have multiple functions, are at the same time one thing and another thing, escaping the outlines of any one pattern applied in abstract analysis. Thus they may suggest also the nature of the spiritual, the wholeness and the fullness of complete experience.

VI

In the poem the meanings made explicit in my analysis subsist in the form of impressions not primarily intellectual, yet with intellectual implications. Certainly any adequate poetic statement must have directly or indirectly its weight of meaning for the intellect. Yet it is the intellectual meaning which chiefly comes clear in an expository account such as this one. Beside the actual poem even the most exhaustive description should be seen to be a relatively barren abstraction.

From "The Birth of a Poem," by Brewster Ghiselin in Poetry: A Magazine of Verse, October, 1946. By permission of the publishers of Poetry, Chicago.

NARCISSUS
AS NARCISSUS

Allen Tate

On this first occasion, which will probably be the last, of my writing about my own verse, I could plead in excuse the example of Edgar Allan Poe, who wrote about himself in an essay called "The Philosophy of Composition." But in our age the appeal to authority is weak, and I am of my age. What I happen to know about the poem that I shall discuss is limited. I remember merely my intention in writing it; I do not know whether the poem is good; and I do not know its obscure origins.

How does one happen to write a poem: where does it come from? That is the question asked by the psychologists or the geneticists of poetry. Of late I have not read any of the genetic theories very attentively: years ago I read one by Mr. Conrad Aiken; another, I think, by Mr. Robert Graves; but I have forgotten them. I am not ridiculing verbal mechanisms, dreams, or repressions as origins of poetry; all three of them and more besides may have a great deal to do with it. Nor should I ignore Mr. I. A. Richards, whose theories I have read a great deal: to him a poem seems to induce a kind of ideal harmony out of the greatest number of our appetites, which ordinarily jangle, and the reader gets the same harmony or "ordering of the mind" second-hand—only it is really as good as first-hand since the poet differs from the mere reader by the fine hair of his talent for constructing appetitive harmonies in words. While this theory may be false, I can only say that, given a few premises which I shall not discuss, it is logical : I do not care whether it is false or true. Other psychological theories say a good deal about compensation. A poem is an indirect effort of a shaky man to justify himself to happier men, or to present a superior account of his relation to a world that allows him but little certainty, and would allow equally little to the happier men if they did not wear blinders—according to the poet. For example, a poet might be a man who could not get enough self-justification out of being an automobile salesman (whose certainty is a fixed quota of cars every month) to rest comfortably upon it. So the poet, who wants to be something that he cannot be, and is a failure in plain life, makes up fictitious versions of his predicament that are interesting even to other persons because nobody is a perfect automobile salesman. Everybody, alas, suffers a little...I constantly read this kind of criticism of my own verse. According to its doctors, my one intransigent desire is to have been a Confederate general, and because I could not or would not become anything else, I set up for poet and began to invent fictions about the personal ambitions that my society has no use for.

Although a theory may not be "true," it may make certain insights available for a while; and I have deemed it proper to notice theories of the genetic variety because a poet talking about himself is often expected, as the best authority, to explain the origins of his poems. But persons interested in origins are seldom quick to use them. Poets, in their way, are practical men; they are interested in results. What is the poem, after it is written? That is the question. Not where it came from, or why. The Why and Where can never get beyond the guessing stage because, in the language of those who think it can, poetry cannot be brought to "laboratory conditions." The only real evidence that any critic may bring before his gaze is the finished poem. For some reason most critics have a hard time fixing their minds directly under their noses, and before they see the object that is there they use a telescope upon the horizon-to see where it came from. They are woodcutters who do their job by finding out where the ore came from in the iron of the steel of the blade of the axe that Jack built. I do not say that this procedure is without its own contributory insights; but the insights are merely contributory and should not replace the poem, which is the object upon which they must be focused. A poem may be an instance of morality, of social conditions, of psychological history; it may instance all its qualities, but never one of them alone, nor any two or three; nor ever less than all.

Genetic theories, I gather, have been cherished academically with detachment. Among "critics" they have been useless and not quite disinterested: I have myself found them applicable to the work of poets whom I do not like. That is the easiest way.

I say all this because it seems to me that my verse or anybody else's is merely a way of knowing something: if the poem *is* a real creation, it is a kind of knowledge that we did not possess before. It is not knowledge "about" something else; the poem is the fullness of that knowledge. We know the particular poem, not what it says that we can restate. In a manner of speaking, the poem is its own knower, neither poet nor reader knowing anything that the poem says apart from the words of the poem. I have expressed this view elsewhere in other terms, and it has been accused of aestheticism or art for art's sake. But let the reader recall the historic position of Catholicism: *nulla salus extra ecclesiam.* That must be religion*ism.* There is probably nothing wrong with art for art's sake if we take the phrase seriously, and not take it to mean the kind of poetry written in England forty years ago. Religion always ought to transcend any of its particular uses; and likewise the true art for art's sake view can be held only by persons who are always looking for things that they can respect apart from use (though they may be useful), like poems, fly-rods, and formal gardens...These are negative postulates, and I am going to illustrate them with some commentary on a poem called "Ode to the Confederate Dead."

II

That poem is "about" solipsism, a philosophical doctrine which says that we create the world in the act of perceiving it; or about

Narcissism, or any other *ism* that denotes the failure of the human personality to function objectively in nature and society. Society (and "nature" as modern society constructs it) appears to offer limited fields for the exercise of the whole man, who wastes his energy piecemeal over separate functions that ought to come under a unity of being. (Until the last generation, only certain women were whores, having been set aside as special instances of sex amid a social scheme that held the general belief that sex must be part of a whole; now the general belief is that sex must be special.) Without unity we get the remarkable self-consciousness of our age. Everybody is talking about this evil, and a great many persons know what ought to be done to correct it. As a citizen I have my own prescription, but as a poet I am concerned with the experience of "solipsism." And an experience *of* it is not quite the same thing as a philosophical statement *about* it.

I should have trouble connecting solipsism and the Confederate dead in a rational thesis; I should make a fool of myself in the discussion, because I know no more of the Confederate dead or of solipsism than hundreds of other people. (Possibly less: the dead Confederates may be presumed to have a certain privacy; and as for solipsism, I blush in the presence of philosophers, who know all about Bishop Berkeley; I use the term here in its strict etymology.) And if I call this interest in one's ego Narcissism, I make myself a logical ignoramus, and I take liberties with mythology. I use Narcissism to mean only preoccupation with self; it may be love or hate. But a good psychiatrist knows that it means self-love only, and otherwise he can talk about it more coherently, knows more about it than I shall ever hope or desire to know. He would look at me professionally if I uttered the remark that the modern squirrel cage of our sensibility, the extreme introspection of our time, has anything whatever to do with the Confederate dead.

But when the doctor looks at literature it is a question whether he sees it: the sea boils and pigs have wings because in poetry all things are possible—if you are man enough. They are possible because in poetry the disparate elements are not combined in logic, which can join things only under certain categories and under the law of contradiction; they are combined in poetry rather as experience, and experience has decided to ignore logic, except perhaps as another field of experience. Experience means conflict, our natures being what they are, and conflict means drama. Dramatic experience is not logical; it may be subdued to the kind of coherence that we indicate when we speak, in criticism, of form. Indeed, as experience, this conflict is always a logical contradiction, or philosophically an antinomy. Serious poetry deals with the fundamental conflicts that cannot be logically resolved: we can state the conflicts rationally, but reason does not relieve us of them. Their only final coherence is the formal re-creation of art, which "freezes" the experience as permanently as a logical formula, but without, like the formula, leaving all but the logic out.

Narcissism and the Confederate dead cannot be connected logically, or even historically; even were the connection an historical fact, they would not stand connected as art, for no one experiences raw history. The proof of the connection must lie, if anywhere, in the experienced conflict which is the poem itself. Since one set of references for the conflict is the historic Confederates, the poem, if it is successful, is a certain section of history made into experience, but only on this occasion, and on these terms: even the author of the poem has no experience of its history apart from the occasion and the terms.

It will be understood that I do not claim even a partial success in the junction of the two "ideas" in the poem that I am about to discuss. I am describing an intention, and the labor of revising the poem-a labor spread over ten years-fairly exposes the lack of confidence that I have felt and still feel in it. All the tests of its success in style and versification would come in the end to a single test, and answer, yes or no, to the question: Assuming that the Confederates and Narcissus are not yoked together by mere violence, has the poet convinced the reader that, on the specific occasion of this poem, there is a necessary yet hitherto undetected relation between them? By necessary I mean dramatically relevant, a relation "discovered" in terms of the particular occasion, not historically argued or philosophically deduced. Should the question that I have just asked be answered yes, then this poem or any other with its specific problem could be said to have form: what was previously a merely felt quality of life has been raised to the level of experience—it has become specific, local, dramatic, "formal"—that is to say, *in*-formed.

III

The structure of the Ode is simple. Figure to yourself a man stopping at the gate of a Confederate graveyard on a late autumn afternoon. The leaves are falling; his first impressions bring him the "rumor of mortality"; and the desolation barely allows him, at the beginning of the second stanza, the conventionally heroic surmise that the dead will enrich the earth, "where these memories grow." From those quoted words to the end of that passage he pauses for a baroque meditation on the ravages of time, concluding with the figure of the "blind crab." This creature has mobility but no direction, energy but no purposeful world to use it in: in the entire poem there are only two explicit symbols for the looked-in ego; the crab is the first and less explicit symbol, a mere hint, a planting of the idea that will become overt in its second instance—the jaguar towards the end. The crab is the first intimation of the nature of the moral conflict upon which the drama of the poem develops: the cut-off-ness of the modern "intellectual man" from the world.

The next long passage or "strophe," beginning "You know who have waited by the wall," states the other term of the conflict. It is the theme of heroism, not merely moral heroism, but heroism in

235

the grand style, elevating even death from mere physical dissolution into a formal ritual: this heroism is a formal ebullience of the human spirit in an entire society, not private, romantic illusion—something better than moral heroism, great as that may be, for moral heroism, being personal and individual, may be achieved by certain men in all ages, even ages of decadence. But the late Hart Crane's commentary, in a letter, is better than any I can make; he described the theme as the "theme of chivalry, a tradition of excess (not literally excess, rather active faith) which cannot be perpetuated in the fragmentary cosmos of today—'those desires which should be yours tomorrow,' but which, you know, will not persist nor find any way into action."

The structure then is the objective frame for the tension between the two themes, "active faith" which has decayed, and the "fragmentary cosmos" which surrounds us. (I must repeat here that this is not a philosophical thesis; it is an analytical statement of a conflict that is concrete within the poem.) In contemplating the heroic theme the man at the gate never quite commits himself to the illusion of its availability to him. The most that he can allow himself is the fancy that the blowing leaves are charging soldiers, but he rigorously returns to the refrain: "Only the wind"—or the "leaves flying." I suppose it is a commentary on our age that the man at the gate never quite achieves the illusion that the leaves are heroic men, so that he may identify himself with them, as Keats and Shelley too easily and too beautifully did with nightingales and west winds. More than this, he cautions himself, reminds himself repeatedly of his subjective prison, his solipsism, by breaking off the half-illusion and coming back to the refrain of wind and leaves—a refrain that, as Hart Crane said, is necessary to the "subjective continuity."

These two themes struggle for mastery up to the passage:

> *We shall say only the leaves whispering*
> *In the improbable mist of nightfall—*
> *which is near the end.*

It will be observed that the passage begins with a phrase taken from the wind-leaves refrain—the signal that it has won. The refrain has been fused with the main stream of the man's reflections, dominating them; and he cannot return even to an ironic vision of the heroes. There is nothing but death, the mere naturalism of death at that—spiritual extinction in the decay of the body. Autumn and the leaves are death; the men who exemplified in a grand style an "active faith" are dead; there are only the leaves.

> *Shall we then worship death...*
> *... set up the grave*
> *In the house? The ravenous grave...*
> *that will take us before our time?*

The question is not answered, although as a kind of morbid romanticism it might, if answered affirmatively, provide the man with an illusory escape from his solipsism; but he cannot accept it. Nor has he been able to live in his immediate world, the fragmentary cosmos. There is no practical solution, no solution offered for the edification of moralists. (To those who may identify the man at the gate with the author of the poem I would say: He differs from the author in not accepting a "practical solution," for the author's dilemma is perhaps not quite so exclusive as that of the meditating man.) The main intention of the poem has been to make dramatically visible the conflict, to concentrate it, to present it, in Mr. R. P. Blackmur's phrase, as "experienced form"—not as a logical dilemma.

The closing image, that of the serpent, is the ancient symbol of time, and I tried to give it the credibility of the commonplace by placing it in a mulberry bush-with the faint hope that the silkworm would somehow be implicit. But time is also death. If that is so, then space, or the Becoming, is life; and I believe there is not a single spatial symbol in the poem. "Seaspace" is allowed the "blind crab"; but the sea, as appears plainly in the passage beginning, "Now that the salt of their blood..." is life only in so far as it is the source of the lowest forms of life, the source perhaps of all life, but life undifferentiated, halfway between life and death. This passage is a contrasting inversion of the conventional

> *... inexhaustible bodies that are not*
> *Dead, but feed the grass...*

the reduction of the earlier, literary conceit to a more naturalistic figure derived from modern biological speculation. These "buried Caesars" will not bloom in the hyacinth but will only make saltier the sea.

The wind-leaves refrain was added to the poem in 1930, nearly five years after the first draft was written. I felt that the danger of adding it was small because, implicit in the long strophes of meditation, the ironic commentary on the vanished heroes was already there, giving the poem such dramatic tension as it had in the earlier version. The refrain makes the commentary more explicit, more visibly dramatic, and renders quite plain, as Hart Crane intimated, the subjective character of the imagery throughout. But there was another reason for it, besides the increased visualization that it imparts to the dramatic conflict. It "times" the poem better, offers the reader frequent pauses in the development of the two themes, allows him occasions of assimilation; and on the whole—this was my hope and intention—the refrain makes the poem seem longer than it is and thus eases the concentration of imagery—without, I hope, sacrificing a possible effect of concentration.

IV

I have been asked why I called the poem an ode. I first called it an elegy. It is an ode only in the sense in which Cowley in the seventeenth century misunderstood the real structure of the Pindaric ode. Not only are the meter and rhyme without fixed pattern, but in another feature the poem is even further removed from Pindar than Abraham Cowley was: a purely subjective meditation would not even in Cowley's age have been called an ode. I suppose in so calling it I intended an irony: the scene of the poem is not a public celebration, it is a lone man by a gate.

The dominant rhythm is "mounting," the dominant meter iambic pentameter varied with six-, four-, and three-stressed lines; but this was not planned in advance for variety. I adapted the meter to the effect desired at the moment. The model for the irregular rhyming was "Lycidas," but other models could have served. The rhymes in a given strophe I tried to adjust to the rhythm and the texture of feeling and image. For example, take this passage in the second strophe:

> *Autumn is desolation in the plot*
> *Of a thousand acres where these memories grow*
> *>From the inexhaustible bodies that are not*
> *Dead, but feed the grass row after rich row.*
> *Think of the autumns that have come and gone!—*
> *Ambitious November with the humors of the year,*
> *With a particular zeal for every slab,*
> *Staining the uncomfortable angels that rot*

On the slabs, a wing chipped here, an arm there:
The brute curiosity o f an angel's stare
Turns you, like them, to stone,
Transforms the heaving air
Till plunged to a heavier world below
You shift your sea-space blindly
Heaving, turning like the blind crab.

There is rhymed with *year* (to many persons, perhaps, only a half-rhyme), and I hoped the reader would unconsciously assume that he need not expect further use of that sound for some time. So when the line, "The brute curiosity of an angel's stare," comes a moment later, rhyming with *year-there,* I hoped that the violence of image would be further reinforced by the repetition of a sound that was no longer expected. I wanted the shock to be heavy; so I felt that I could not afford to hurry the reader away from it until he had received it in full. The next two lines carry on the image at a lower intensity: the rhyme, "Transforms the heaving *air,*" prolongs the moment of attention upon that passage, while at the same time it ought to begin dissipating the shock, both by the introduction of a new image and by reduction of the "meaning" to a pattern of sound, the ere-rhymes. I calculated that the third use of that sound (stare) would be a surprise, the fourth (air) a monotony. I purposely made the end words of the third from last and last lines—below and crab—delayed rhymes for row and slab, the last being an internal and half-dissonant rhyme for the sake of bewilderment and incompleteness, qualities by which the man at the gate is at the moment possessed.

This is elementary but I cannot vouch for its success. As the dramatic situation of the poem is the tension that I have already described, so the rhythm is an attempt at a series of "modulations" back and forth between a formal regularity, for the heroic emotion, and a broken rhythm, with scattering imagery, for the failure of that emotion. This is "imitative form," which Yvor Winters deems a vice worth castigation. I have pointed out that the passage, "You know who have waited by the wall," presents the heroic theme of "active faith"; it will be observed that the rhythm, increasingly after "You who have waited for the angry resolution," is almost perfectly regular iambic, with only a few initial inversions and weak endings. The passage is meant to convey a plenary vision, the actual presence, of the exemplars of active faith: the man at the gate at that moment is nearer to realizing them than at any other in the poem; hence the formal rhythm. But the vision breaks down; the wind-leaves refrain supervenes; and the next passage, "Turn your eyes to the immoderate past," is the irony of the preceding realization. With the self-conscious historical sense he turns his eyes into the past. The next passage after this, beginning, "You hear the shout..." is the failure of the vision in both phases, the pure realization and the merely historical. He cannot "see" the heroic virtues; there is wind, rain, leaves. But there is sound; for a moment he deceives himself with it. It is the noise of the battles that he has evoked. Then comes the figure of the rising sun of those battles; he is "lost in that orient of the thick and fast," and he curses his own moment, "the setting sun." The "setting sun" I tried to use as a triple image, for the decline of the heroic age and for the actual scene of late afternoon, the latter being. not only natural desolation but spiritual desolation as well. Again for a moment he thinks he hears the battle shout, but only for a moment; then the silence reaches him.

Corresponding to the disintegration of the vision just described, there has been a breaking down of the formal rhythm. The complete breakdown comes with the images of the "mummy" and the "hound bitch." (Hound bitch because the hound is a hunter, participant of a formal ritual.) The failure of the vision throws the man back upon himself, but upon himself he cannot bring to bear the force of sustained imagination. He sees himself in random images (random to him, deliberate with the author) of something lower than he ought to be: the human image is only that of preserved death; but if he is alive he is an old hunter, dying. The passages about the mummy and the bitch are deliberately brief—slight rhythmic stretches. (These are the only verses I have written for which I thought of the movement first, then cast about for the symbols.)

I believe the term modulation denotes in music the uninterrupted shift from one key to another: I do not know the term for change of rhythm without change of measure. I wish to describe a similar change in verse rhythm; it may be convenient to think of it as modulation of a certain kind. At the end of the passage that I have been discussing the final words are "Hears the wind only." The phrase closes the first main division of the poem. I have loosely called the longer passages strophes, and if I were hardy enough to impose the classical organization of the lyric ode upon a baroque poem, I should say that these words bring to an end the Strophe, after which must come the next main division, or Antistrophe, which was often employed to answer the matter set forth in the Strophe or to present it from another point of view. And that is precisely the significance of the next main division, beginning: "Now that the salt of their blood..." But I wanted this second division of the poem to arise out of the collapse of the first. It is plain that it would not have suited my purpose to round off the first section with some sort of formal rhythm; so I ended it with an unfinished line. The next division must therefore begin by finishing that line, not merely in meter but with an integral rhythm. I will quote the passage:

> *The hound bitch*
> *Toothless and dying, in a musty cellar*
> Hears the wind only.

> *Now that the salt of their blood*

> *Stiffens the saltier oblivion of the sea,*
> *Seals the malignant purity of the flood....*

The caesura, after *only*, is thus at the middle of the third foot. (I do not give a full stress to *wind*, but attribute a "hovering stress" to wind and the first syllable of *only*.) The reader expects the foot to be completed by the stress on the next word, Now, as in a sense it is; but the phrase, "Now that the salt of their blood," is also the beginning of a new movement; it is two "dactyls" continuing more broadly the falling rhythm that has prevailed. But with the finishing off of the line with *blood*, the mounting rhythm is restored; the whole line from *Hears* to *blood* is actually an iambic pentameter with liberal inversions and substitutions that were expected to create a counter-rhythm within the line. From the caesura on, the rhythm is new; but it has—or was expected to have—an organic relation to the preceding rhythm; and it signals the rise of a new statement of the theme. I have gone into this passage in detail—I might have chosen another—not because I think it is successful, but because I labored with it; if it is a failure, or even an uninteresting success, it ought to offer as much technical instruction to other persons as it would were it both successful and interesting. But a word more: the broader movement introduced by the new rhythm was meant to correspond, as a sort of Antistrophe, to the earlier formal movement beginning, "You know who have waited by the wall." It is a new formal movement with new feeling and new imagery. The heroic but precarious illusion of the earlier movement has broken down into the personal symbols of the mummy and the hound; the pathetic fallacy of the leaves as charging soldiers and the conventional "buried Caesar" theme have become rotten leaves and dead bodies wasting in the earth, to return after long erosion to the sea. In the midst of this naturalism, what shall the man say? What shall all humanity say in the presence of decay? The two themes, then, have been struggling for mastery; the structure of the poem thus exhibits the development of two formal passages that contrast the two themes. The two formal passages break down, the first shading into the second ("Now that the salt of their blood..."), the second one concluding with the figure of the jaguar, which is presented in a distracted rhythm left suspended at the end from a weak ending-the word *victim*. This figure of the jaguar is the only explicit rendering of the Narcissus motif in the poem, but instead of a youth gazing into a pool, a predatory beast stares at a jungle stream, and leaps to devour himself.

The next passage begins:

> *What shall we say who have knowledge*
> *Carried to the heart?*

This is Pascal's war between heart and head, between *finesse and géométrie*. Should the reader care to think of these lines as the gathering up of the two themes, now fused, into a final statement, I should see no objection to calling it the Epode. But upon the meaning of the lines from here to the end there is no need for further commentary. I have talked about the structure of the poem, not its quality. One can no more find the quality of one's own verse than one can find its value, and to try to find either is like looking into a glass for the effect that one's face has upon other persons.

If anybody ever wished to know anything about this poem that he could not interpret for himself, I suspect that he is still in the dark. I cannot believe that I have illuminated the difficulties that some readers have found in the style. But then I cannot, have never been able to, see any difficulties of that order. The poem has been much revised. I still think there is much to be said for the original *barter* instead of *yield* in the second line, and for *Novembers* instead of *November* in line fifteen. The revisions were not undertaken for the convenience of the reader but for the poem's own clarity, so that, word, phrase, line, passage, the poem might at worst come near its best expression.

From "Narcissus as Narcissus," in *Reason in Madness,* by Allen Tate. Copyright 1935, 1936, 1937, 1938, 1940, 1941 by the author. By permission of the publishers: G. P. Putnam's Sons, New York.

REMEMBERING
HART CRANE

Malcolm Cowley

S ome years ago in the *New Republic,* I told how Hart Crane used
to write his poems. But since the poems are still being read,
nine years after his suicide, in April, 1932, and since the meaning
of his life is still being argued about, the story is worth repeating in
more detail.

There would be a Sunday afternoon party on Tory Hill, near
Patterson, New York, in Slater Brown's unpainted and unremodeled
farmhouse. I can't remember any of the jokes that were made, or why
we laughed at them so hard; I can remember only the general atmosphere of youth and poverty and high spirits. Hart would be laughing twice as hard as the rest of us in the big, low-ceilinged kitchen;
he would be drinking twice as much hard cider and contributing
more than his share of the crazy metaphors and overblown epithets.
Gradually he would fall silent and a little later we would find that
he had disappeared. In lulls that began to interrupt the laughter,
now Hart was gone, we would hear a new hubbub through the walls
of the next room—the phonograph playing a Cuban rumba, the
typewriter clacking simultaneously; then the phonograph would

run down and the typewriter stop while Hart changed the record, perhaps to a torch song, perhaps to Ravel's "Bolero." Sometimes he stamped across the room, declaiming to the four walls and the slow spring rain.

An hour later, after the rain had stopped, he would appear in the kitchen or on the croquet court, his face brick-red, his eyes burning, his already iron-gray hair bristling straight up from his skull. He would be chewing a five-cent cigar which he had forgotten to light. In his hands would be two or three sheets of typewritten manuscript, with words crossed out and new lines scrawled in. "Read that," he would say. "Isn't that the *grrrea*test poem ever written!"

We would read it obediently, Allen Tate perhaps making a profound comment. The rest of us would get practically nothing out of it except the rhythm like that of a tom-tom and a few startling images. But we would all agree that it was absolutely superb. In Hart's state of exaltation there was nothing else we could say without driving him to rage or tears.

But this story, which I have told before, contains neither the real beginning nor the real end. I later discovered that Hart would have been meditating over that particular poem for months or even years, scribbling verses on pieces of paper that he carried in his pockets and meanwhile waiting for the moment of pure inspiration when he could put them all together. In his patience he reminded me of another friend, a famous killer of woodchucks, who instead of shooting at them from a distance with a high-powered rifle, and probably missing them, used to frighten them into their holes and wait till they came out again. Sometimes when they were slow about it, he said that he used to charm them out by playing his mouth-organ. In the same fashion, Hart tried to charm his inspiration out of its hiding place by drinking and laughing and playing the phonograph.

As for the end of the story, it might be delayed for several weeks. Painfully, perseveringly—and dead sober—Hart would revise his new poem, clarifying its images, correcting its meter and searching through dictionaries and thesauruses for exactly the right word. "The seal's wide spindrift gaze toward paradise," in the second of his "Voyages," was the result of a search that lasted for several days; I was then working in the same office and can remember his roar of jubilation when he found the word "spindrift" in *Webster's Unabridged.* Even after the poem had been completed, the manuscript mailed to *Poetry* or the *Dial* and perhaps accepted, he would still have changes to make. In the formal sense, he was badly educated, having left high school before he was graduated and having filled his head since then with an assortment of sometimes profound but uncoordinated knowledge. He was not even very intelligent, in the conventional sense of the word; as a problem-solving animal he was less than competent. But nobody I knew, and very few people in the history of literature, were willing to spend so much time in perfecting a single poem to the moment of what seemed to be absolute rightness.

PREFACE TO THE SPOILS OF POYNTON

Henry James

I t was years ago, I remember, one Christmas Eve when I was dining with friends: a lady beside me made in the course of talk one of those allusions that I have always found myself recognising on the spot as "germs." The germ, wherever gathered, has ever been for me the germ of a "story," and most of the stories straining to shape under my hand have sprung from a single small seed, a seed as minute and wind-blown as that casual hint for "The Spoils of Poynton" dropped unwitting by my neighbour, a mere floating particle in the stream of talk. What above all comes back to me with this reminiscence is the sense of the inveterate minuteness, on such happy occasions, of the precious particle—reduced, that is, to its mere fruitful essence. Such is the interesting truth about the stray suggestion, the wandering word, the vague echo, at touch of which the novelist's imagination winces as at the prick of some sharp point: its virtue is all in its needle-like quality, the power to penetrate as finely as possible. This fineness it is that communicates the virus of suggestion, anything more than the minimum of which spoils the operation. If one is given a hint at all designedly one is sure to be given too much; one's subject is in the merest grain, the speck of truth, of beauty, of reality, scarce visible to the common eye—since, I firmly hold, a good eye for a subject is anything but usual. Strange and attaching, certainly, the consistency with which the first thing to be done for the communicated and seized idea is to reduce almost to nought the form, the air as of a mere disjoined and lacerated lump of life, in which we may have happened to meet it. Life being all inclusion and confusion, and art being all discrimination and selection, the latter, in search of the hard latent *value* with which alone it is concerned, sniffs round the mass as instinctively and unerringly as a dog suspicious of some buried bone. The difference here, however, is that, while the dog desires his bone but to destroy it, the artist finds in *his* tiny nugget, washed free of awkward accretions and hammered into a sacred hardness, the very stuff for a clear affirmation, the happiest chance for the indestructible. It at the same time amuses him again and again to note how, beyond the first step of the actual case, the case that constitutes for him his germ, his vital particle, his grain of gold, life persistently blunders and deviates, loses herself in the sand. The reason is of course that life has no direct sense whatever for the subject and is capable, luckily for us, of nothing but splendid waste. Hence the opportunity for the sublime economy of art, which rescues, which saves, and hoards and "banks," investing and reinvesting these fruits of toil in wondrous useful "works" and thus making up for us, desperate spendthrifts that we all naturally are, the most princely of incomes. It is the subtle secrets of that system, however, that are meanwhile the charming study, with an endless attraction, above all in the question—endlessly baffling indeed—of the method at the heart of the madness; the madness, I mean, of a zeal, among the reflective sort, so disinterested. If life, presenting us the germ, and left merely to herself in such a business, gives the case away, almost always, before we can stop her, what are the signs for our guidance, what the primary laws for a saving selection, how do we know when and where to intervene, where do we place the beginnings of the wrong or the right deviation? Such would be the elements of an enquiry upon which, I hasten to say, it is quite forbidden me here to embark: I but glance at them in evidence of the rich pasture that at every turn surrounds the ruminant critic. The answer may be after all that mysteries here elude us, that general considerations fail or mislead, and that even the fondest of artists need ask no wider range than the logic of the particular case. The particular case, or in other words his relation to a given subject, once the relation is established, forms in itself a little world of exercise and agitation. Let him hold himself perhaps supremely fortunate if he can meet half the questions with which that air alone may swarm.

So it was, at any rate, that when my amiable friend, on the Christmas Eve, before the table that glowed safe and fair through the brown London night, spoke of such an odd matter as that a good lady in the north, always well looked on, was at daggers drawn with her only son, ever hitherto exemplary, over the ownership of the

valuable furniture of a fine old house just accruing to the young man
by his father's death, I instantly became aware, with my "sense for the
subject," of the prick of inoculation; the *whole* of the virus, as I have
called it, being infused by that single touch. There had been but ten
words, yet I had recognised in them, as in a flash, all the possibilities
of the little drama of my "spoils," which glimmered then and there
into life; so that when in the next breath I began to hear of action
taken, on the beautiful ground, by our engaged adversaries, tipped
each, from that instant, with the light of the highest distinction, I
saw clumsy Life again at her stupid work. For the action taken, and
on which my friend, as I knew she would, had already begun all
complacently and benightedly further to report, I had absolutely,
and could have, no scrap of use; one had been so perfectly qualified
to say in advance: "It's the perfect little workable thing, but she'll
strangle it in the cradle, even while she pretends, all so cheeringly, to
rock it; wherefore I'll stay her hand while yet there's time." I didn't,
of course, stay her hand—there never is in such cases "time"; and I
had once more the full demonstration of the fatal futility of Fact. The
turn taken by the excellent situation—excellent, for development, if
arrested in the right place, that is in the germ—had the full measure
of the classic ineptitude; to which with the full measure of the artistic
irony one could once more, and for the thousandth time, but take
off one's hat. It was not, however, that this in the least mattered,
once the seed had been transplanted to richer soil; and I dwell on

that almost inveterate redundancy of the wrong, as opposed to the ideal right, in any free flowering of the actual, by reason only of its approach to calculable regularity.

If there was nothing regular meanwhile, nothing more so than the habit of vigilance, in my quickly feeling where interest would really lie, so I could none the less acknowledge afresh that these small private cheers of recognition made the spirit easy and the temper bland for the confused whole. I "took" in fine, on the spot, to the rich bare little fact of the two related figures, embroiled perhaps all so sordidly; and for reasons of which I could most probably have given at the moment no decent account. Had I been asked why they were, in that stark nudity, to say nothing of that ugliness of attitude, "interesting," I fear I could have said nothing more to the point, even to my own questioning spirit, than "Well, you'll see!" By which of course I should have meant "Well, *I* shall see"—confident meanwhile (as against the appearance or the imputation of poor taste) that interest would spring as soon as one should begin really to see *anything*. That points, I think, to a large part of the very source of interest for the artist: it resides in the strong consciousness of his seeing all for himself. He has to borrow his motive, which is certainly half the battle; and this motive is his ground, his site and his foundation. But after that he only lends and gives, only builds and piles high, lays together the blocks quarried in the deeps of his imagination and on his personal premises. He thus remains all the while in intimate commerce

with his motive, and can say to himself—what really more than anything else inflames and sustains him—that he alone has the secret of
the particular case, he alone can measure the truth of the direction
to be taken by his developed data. There can be for him, evidently,
only one logic for these things; there can be for him only one truth
and one direction—the quarter in which his subject most completely
expresses itself. The careful ascertainment of how it shall do so, and
the art of guiding it with consequent authority—since this sense of
"authority" is for the master-builder the treasure of treasures, or at
least the joy of joys—renews in the modern alchemist something like
the old dream of the secret of life.

Extravagant as the mere statement sounds, one seemed accordingly
to handle the secret of life in drawing the positive right truth out of
the so easy muddle of wrong truths in which the interesting possibilities of that "row," so to call it, between mother and son over their
household gods might have been stifled. I find it odd to consider, as
I thus revert, that I could have had none but the most general war-
rant for "seeing anything in it," as the phrase would have been; that
I couldn't in the least, on the spot, as I have already hinted, have
justified my faith. One thing was "in it," in the sordid situation, on
the first blush, and one thing only—though this, in its limited way,
no doubt, a curious enough value: the sharp light it might project on
that most modern of our current passions, the fierce appetite for the
upholsterer's and joiner's and brazier's work, the chairs and tables,

the cabinets and presses, the material odds and ends, of the more labouring ages. A lively mark of our manners indeed the diffusion of this curiosity and this avidity, and full of suggestion, clearly, as to their possible influence on other passions and other relations. On the face of it the "things" themselves would form the very centre of such a crisis; these grouped objects, all conscious of their eminence and their price, would enjoy, in any picture of a conflict, the heroic importance. They would have to be presented, they would have to be painted—arduous and desperate thought; something would have to be done for them not too ignobly unlike the great array in which Balzac, say, would have marshalled them: *that* amount of workable interest at least would evidently be "in it."

It would be wrapped in the silver tissue of some such conviction, at any rate, that I must have laid away my prime impression for a rest not disturbed till long afterwards, till the year 1896, I make out, when there arose a question of my contributing three "short stories" to *The Atlantic Monthly;* or supplying rather perhaps a third to complete a trio two memhers of which had appeared. The echo of the situation mentioned to me at our Christmas Eve dinner awoke again, I recall, at that touch—I recall, no doubt, with true humility, in view of my renewed mismeasurement of my charge. Painfully associated for me had "The Spoils of Poynton" remained, until recent re-perusal, with the awkward consequence of that fond error. The subject had emerged from cool reclusion all suffused with a flush of meaning; thanks to which irresistible air, as I could but plead in the event, I found myself—as against a mere commercial austerity—beguiled and led on. The thing had "come," the flower of conception had bloomed—all in the happy dusk of indifference and neglect; yet, strongly and frankly as it might now appeal, my idea wouldn't surely overstrain a *natural* brevity. A story that couldn't possibly be long would have inevitably to be "short," and out of the depths of that delusion it accordingly began to struggle. To my own view, after the "first number," this composition (which in the magazine bore another title) conformed but to its nature, which was not to transcend a modest amplitude; but, dispatched in installments, it felt itself eyed, from month to month, I seem to remember, with an editorial ruefulness excellently well founded—from the moment such differences of sense could exist, that is, as to the short and the long. The sole impression it made, I woefully gathered, was that of length, and it has till lately, as I say, been present to me but as the poor little "long" thing.

It began to appear in April, 1896, and, as is apt blessedly to occur for me throughout this process of revision, the old, the shrunken concomitants muster again as I turn the pages. They lurk between the lines; these serve for them as the barred seraglio-windows behind which, to the outsider in the glare of the Eastern street, forms indistinguishable seem to move and peer; "association" in fine bears upon them with its infinite magic. Peering through the lattice from without inward I recapture a cottage on a cliffside, to which, at the earliest approach of the summer-time, redoubtable in London through the luxuriance of still other than "natural" forces, I had betaken myself to finish a book in quiet and to begin another in fear. The cottage was, in its kind, perfection; mainly by reason of a small paved terrace which, curving forward from the cliff-edge like the prow of a ship, overhung a view as level, as purple, as full of rich change, as the expanse of the sea. The horizon was in fact a band of sea; a small red-roofed town, of great antiquity, perched on its sea-rock, clustered within the picture off to the right; while above one's head rustled a dense summer shade, that of a trained and arching ash, rising from the middle of the terrace, brushing the parapet with a heavy fringe and covering the place like a vast umbrella. Beneath this umbrella and really under exquisite protection "The Spoils of Poynton" managed more or less symmetrically to grow.

I recall that I was committed to begin, the day I finished it, short of dire penalties, "The Other House"; with which work, however, of whatever high profit the considerations springing from it might be too, we have nothing to do here—and to the felt jealousy of which, as that of a grudging neighbour, I allude only for sweet recovery of the fact, mainly interesting to myself I admit, that the rhythm of the earlier book shows no flurry of hand. I "liked" it—the earlier book: I venture now, after years, to welcome the sense of that amenity as well; so immensely refreshing is it to be moved, in any case, toward these retrospective simplicities. Painters and writers, I gather, are, when easily accessible to such appeals, frequently questioned as to those of their productions they may most have delighted in; but the profession of delight has always struck me as the last to consort, for the artist, with any candid account of his troubled effort—ever the sum, for the most part, of so many lapses and compromises, simplifications and surrenders. Which is the work in which he hasn't surrendered, under dire difficulty, the best thing he meant to have kept? In which indeed, before the dreadful *done,* doesn't he ask himself what has become of the thing all for the sweet sake of which it was to proceed to that extremity? Preference and complacency, on these terms, riot in general as they best may; not disputing, however, a grain of which weighty truth, I still make out, between my reconsidered lines, as it were, that I must—my opera-box of a terrace and my great green umbrella indeed aiding—have assisted at the growth and predominance of Fleda Vetch.

For something like Fleda Vetch had surely been latent in one's first apprehension of the theme; it wanted, for treatment, a centre, and, the most obvious centre being "barred," this image, while I still wondered, had, with all the assurance in the world, sprung up in its place. The real centre, as I say, the citadel of the interest, with the fight waged round it, would have been the felt beauty and value of the prize of battle, the Things, always the splendid Things, placed in the middle light, figured and constituted, with each identity made

vivid, each character discriminated, and their common consciousness of their great dramatic part established. The rendered tribute
of these honours, however, no vigilant editor, as I have intimated,
could be conceived as allowing room for; since, by so much as the
general glittering presence should spread, by so much as it should
suggest the gleam of brazen idols and precious metals and inserted
gems in the tempered light of some arching place of worship, by
just so much would the muse of "dialogue," most usurping influence
of all the romancingly invoked, be routed without ceremony, to lay
her grievance at the feet of her gods. The spoils of Poynton were not
directly articulate, and though they might have, and constantly did
have, wondrous things to say, their message fostered about them a
certain hush of cheaper sound—as a consequence of which, in fine,
they would have been costly to keep up. In this manner Fleda Vetch,
maintainable at less expense—though even she, I make out, less expert in spreading chatter thin than the readers of romance mainly
like their heroines today—marked her place in my foreground at one
ingratiating stroke. She planted herself centrally, and the stroke, as I
call it, the demonstration after which she couldn't be gainsaid, was
the simple act of letting it be seen she had character.

For somehow—that was the way interest broke out, once the germ
had been transferred to the sunny south window-sill of one's fond-
er attention—character, the question of what my agitated friends
should individually, and all intimately and at the core, show them-

selves, would unmistakably be the key to my modest drama, and would indeed alone make a drama of any sort possible. Yes, it is a story of cabinets and chairs and tables; they formed the bone of contention, but what would merely "become" of them, magnificently passive, seemed to represent a comparatively vulgar issue. The passions, the faculties, the forces their beauty would, like that of antique Helen of Troy, set in motion, was what, as a painter, one had really wanted of them, was the power in them that one had from the first appreciated. Emphatically, by that truth, there would have to be moral developments—dreadful as such a prospect might loom for a poor interpreter committed to brevity. A character is interesting as it comes out, and by the process and duration of that emergence; just as a procession is effective by the way it unrolls, turning to a mere mob if all of it passes at once. My little procession, I foresaw then from an early stage, would refuse to pass at once; though I could keep it more or less down, of course, by reducing it to three or four persons. Practically, in "The Spoils," the reduction is to four, though indeed—and I clung to that as to my plea for simplicity—the main agents, with the others all dependent, are Mrs. Gereth and Fleda. Fleda's ingratiating stroke, for importance, on the threshold, had been that she would understand; and positively, from that moment, the progress and march of my tale became and remained that of her understanding.

Absolutely, with this, I committed myself to making the affirmation and the penetration of it my action and my "story"; once more, too, with the re-entertained perception that a subject so lighted, a subject residing in somebody's excited and concentrated feeling about something—both the something and the somebody being of course as important as possible—has more beauty to give out than under any other style of pressure. One is confronted obviously thus with the question of the importances; with that in particular, no doubt, of the weight of intelligent consciousness, consciousness of the whole, or of something ominously like it, that one may decently permit a represented figure to appear to throw. Some plea for this cause, that of the intelligence of the moved mannikin, I have already had occasion to make, and can scarce hope too often to evade it. This intelligence, an honourable amount of it, on the part of the person to whom one most invites attention, has but to play with sufficient freedom and ease, or call it with the right grace, to guarantee us that quantum of the impression of beauty which is the most fixed of the possible advantages of our producible effect. It may fail, as a positive presence, on other sides and in other connexions; but more or less of the treasure is stored safe from the moment such a quality of inward life is distilled, or in other words from the moment so fine an inter-pretation and criticism as that of Fleda Vetch's—to cite the present case—is applied without waste to the surrounding tangle.

It is easy to object of course "Why the deuce then Fleda Vetch, why a mere little flurried bundle of petticoats, why not Hamlet or

Milton's Satan at once, if you're going in for a superior display of 'mind'?" To which I fear I can only reply that in pedestrian prose, and in the "short story," one is, for the best reasons, no less on one's guard than on the stretch; and also that I have ever recognised, even in the midst of the curiosity that such displays may quicken, the rule of an exquisite economy. The thing is to lodge somewhere at the heart of one's complexity an irrepressible *appreciation,* but where a light lamp will carry all the flame I incline to look askance at a heavy. From beginning to end, in "The Spoils of Poynton," appreciation, even to that of the very whole, lives in Fleda; which is precisely why, as a consequence rather grandly imposed, every one else shows for comparatively stupid; the tangle, the drama, the tragedy and comedy of those who appreciate consisting so much of their relation with those who don't. From the presented reflexion of this truth my story draws, I think, a certain assured appearance of roundness and felicity. The "things" are radiant, shedding afar, with a merciless monotony, all their light, exerting their ravage without remorse; and Fleda almost demonically both sees and feels, while the others but feel without seeing. Thus we get perhaps a vivid enough little example, in the concrete, of the general truth, for the spectator of life, that the fixed constituents of almost any reproducible action are the fools who minister, at a particular crisis, to the intensity of the free spirit engaged with them. The fools are interesting by contrast, by the salience they acquire, and by a hundred other of their advantages; and the free spirit, always much tormented, and by no means always triumphant, is heroic, ironic, pathetic or whatever, and, as exemplified in the record of Fleda Vetch, for instance, "successful," only through having remained free.

I recognise that the novelist with a weakness for that ground of appeal is foredoomed to a well-nigh extravagant insistence on the free spirit, seeing the possibility of one in every bush; I may perhaps speak of it as noteworthy that this very volume happens to exhibit in two other cases my disposition to let the interest stand or fall by the tried spontaneity and vivacity of the freedom. It is in fact for that respectable reason that I enclose "A London Life" and "The Chaperon" between these covers; my purpose having been here to class my reprintable productions as far as possible according to their kinds. The two tales I have just named are of the same "kind" as "The Spoils," to the extent of their each dealing with a human predicament in the light, for the charm of the thing, of the amount of "appreciation" to be plausibly imputed to the subject of it. They are each—and truly there are more of such to come—"stories about women," very young women, who, affected with a certain high lucidity, thereby become characters; in consequence of which their doings, their sufferings or whatever, take on, I assume, an importance. Laura Wing, in "A London Life," has, like Fleda Vetch, acuteness and intensity, reflexion and passion, has above all a contributive and participant view of her situation; just as Rose Tramore, in "The Chaperon," rejoices, almost to insolence, very much in the same cluster of attributes and advantages. They are thus of a family—which shall have also for us, we seem forewarned, more members, and of each sex.

As to our young woman of "The Spoils," meanwhile, I briefly come back to my claim for a certain definiteness of beauty in the special effect wrought by her aid. My problem had decently to be met—that of establishing for the other persons the vividness of their appearance of comparative stupidity, that of exposing them to the full thick wash of the penumbra surrounding the central light, and yet keeping their motions, within it, distinct, coherent and "amusing." But these are exactly of course the most "amusing" things to do; nothing, for example, being of a higher reward artistically than the shade of success aimed at in such a figure as Mrs. Gereth. A character she too, absolutely, yet the very reverse of a free spirit. I have found myself so pleased with Mrs. Gereth, I confess, on resuming acquaintance with her, that, complete and all in equilibrium as she seems to me to stand and move there, I shrink from breathing upon her any breath of qualification; without which, however, I fail of my point that, thanks to the "value" represented by Fleda, and to the position to which the elder woman is confined by that irradiation, the latter is at the best a "false" character, floundering as she does in the dusk of disproportionate passion. She is *a figure,* oh definitely—which is a very different matter; for you may be a figure with all the blinding, with all the hampering passion in life, and may have the grand air in what shall yet prove to the finer view (which Fleda again, *e.g.,* could at any time strike off) but a perfect rage of awkwardness. Mrs. Gereth was, obviously, with her pride and her pluck, of an admirable fine paste; but she was not intelligent, was only clever, and therefore would have been no use to us at all as centre of our subject—compared with Fleda, who was only intelligent, not distinctively able. The little drama confirms at all events excellently, I think, the contention of the old wisdom that the question of the personal will has more than all else to say to the verisimilitude of these exhibitions. The will that rides the crisis quite most triumphantly is that of the awful Mona Brigstock, who is *all* will, without the smallest leak of force into taste or tenderness or vision, into any sense of shades or relations or proportions. She loses no minute in that perception of incongruities in which half Fleda's passion is wasted and misled, and into which Mrs. Gereth, to her practical loss, that is by the fatal grace of a sense of comedy, occasionally and disinterestedly strays. Every one, every thing, in the story is accordingly sterile *but* the so thriftily constructed Mona, able at any moment to bear the whole of her dead weight at once on any given inch of a resisting surface. Fleda, obliged to neglect inches, sees and feels but in acres and expanses and blue perspectives; Mrs. Gereth too, in comparison, while her imagination broods, drops half the stitches of the web she seeks to weave.

From the preface to *The Spoils of Poynton,* by Henry James. By permission of the publishers: Charles Scribner's Sons, New York City.

WORKING TOOLS

Rudyard Kipling

Let us now consider the Personal Daemon of Aristotle and others, of whom it has been truthfully written, though not published:

> *This is the doom of the Makers—their Daemon lives in their pen.*
> *If he be absent or sleeping, they are even as other men.*
> *But if he be utterly present, and they swerve not from his behest,*
> *The word that he gives shall continue, whether in earnest or jest.*

Most men, and some most unlikely, keep him under an alias which varies with their literary or scientific attainments. Mine came to me early when I sat bewildered among other notions, and said: 'Take this and no other.' I obeyed, and was rewarded. It was a tale in the little Christmas Magazine *Quartette* which we four wrote together, and it was called 'The Phantom Rickshaw.' Some of it was weak, much was bad and out of key; but it was my first serious attempt to think in another man's skin.

After that I learned to lean upon him and recognise the sign of his approach. If ever I held back, Ananias fashion, anything of myself (even though I had to throw it out afterwards) I paid for it by missing what I *then* knew the tale lacked. As an instance, many years later I wrote about a mediaeval artist, a monastery, and the premature discovery of the microscope. ('The Eye of Allah.') Again and again it went dead under my hand, and for the life of me I could not see why. I put it away and waited. Then said my Daemon—and I was meditating something else at the time—'Treat it as an illuminated manuscript.' I had ridden off on hard black-and-white decoration, instead of pumicing the whole thing ivory-smooth, and loading it with thick colour and gilt. Again, in a South African, post-Boer War tale called 'The Captive,' which was built up round the phrase 'a first-class dress parade for Armageddon,' I could not get my lighting into key with the tone of the monologue. The background insisted too much. My Daemon said at last: 'Paint the background first once for all, as hard as a public-house sign, and leave it alone.' This done, the rest fell into place with the American accent and outlook of the teller.

My Daemon was with me in the Jungle Books, *Kim,* and both Puck books, and good care I took to walk delicately, lest he should withdraw. I know that he did not, because when those books were finished they said so themselves with, almost, the water-hammer click of a tap turned off. One of the clauses in our contract was that I should never follow up 'a success,' for by this sin fell Napoleon and a few others. When your Daemon is in charge, do not try to think consciously. Drift, wait, and obey....

In respect to verifying one's references, which is a matter in which one can help one's Daemon, it is curious how loath a man is to take his own medicine. Once, on a Boxing Day, with hard frost coming greasily out of the ground, my friend, Sir John Bland-Sutton, the head of the College of Surgeons, came down to 'Bateman's' very full of a lecture which he was to deliver on `gizzards.' We were settled before the fire after lunch, when he volunteered that So-and-so had said that if you hold a hen to your ear, you can hear the click in its gizzard of the little pebbles that help its digestion. `Interesting,' said I. `He's an authority.' `Oh yes, but'-a long pause-`have you any hens about here, Kipling?' I owned that I had, two hundred yards down a lane, but why not accept So-and-so? `I can't,' said John simply, `till I've tried it.' Remorselessly, he worried me into taking him to the hens, who lived in an open shed in front of the gardener's cottage. As we skated over the glairy ground, I saw an eye at the corner of the drawn-down Boxing-Day blind, and knew that my character for so-briety would be blasted all over the farms before nightfall. We caught an outraged pullet. John soothed her for a while (he said her pulse was a hundred and twenty-six), and held her to his ear. `She clicks all right,' he announced. `Listen.' I did, and there was click enough for a lecture. `Now we can go back to the house,' I pleaded. `Wait a bit. Let's catch that cock. He'll click better.' We caught him after a loud and long chase, and he clicked like a solitaire-board. I went home, my ears alive with parasites, so wrapped up in my own indignation that the fun of it escaped me. It had not been *my* verification, you see.

But John was right. Take nothing for granted if you can check it. Even though that seem waste-work, and has nothing to do with the essentials of things, it encourages the Daemon....

For my ink I demanded the blackest, and had I been in my Father's house, as once I was, would have kept an ink-boy to grind me Indian-ink. All 'blue-blacks' were an abomination to my Daemon, and I never found a bottled vermilion fit to rubricate initials when one hung in the wind waiting.

My writing-blocks were built for me to an unchanged pattern of large, off-white, blue sheets, of which I was most wasteful. All this old-maiderie did not prevent me when abroad from buying and using blocks, and tackle, in any country.

With a lead pencil I ceased to express—probably because I had to use a pencil in reporting. I took very few notes except of names, dates, and addresses. If a thing didn't stay in my memory, I argued it was hardly worth writing out.

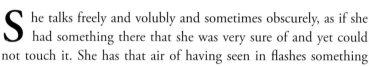

A CONVERSATION
WITH GERTRUDE STEIN

John Hyde Preston

She talks freely and volubly and sometimes obscurely, as if she had something there that she was very sure of and yet could not touch it. She has that air of having seen in flashes something which she does not know the shape of, and can talk about, not out of the flashes but out of the spaces between when she has waited.

I do not mean that there is in her conversation any trace of that curious obscurity which dims so much of her prose, for me at least—and I was frank (without wanting to be) in telling her that I could only guess sometimes at the written words. She seems peacefully resigned to the attacks that have been made upon her all her life and she has that air, so rare in writers, of living outside of both fame and criticism.

II

'You will write,' she said, `if you will write without thinking of the result in terms of a result, but think of the writing in terms of discovery, which is to say that creation must take place between the pen and the paper, not before in a thought or afterwards in a recasting. Yes, before in a thought, but not in careful thinking. It will come if it is there and if you will let it come, and if you have anything you will get a sudden creative recognition. You won't know how it was, even what it is, but it will be creation if it came out of the pen and out of you and not out of an architectural drawing of the thing you are doing. Technique is not so much a thing of form or style as the way that form or style came and how it can come again. Freeze your fountain and you will always have the frozen water shooting into the air and falling and it will be there to see—oh, no doubt about that—but there will be no more coming. I can tell how important it is to have that creative recognition. You cannot go into the womb to form the child; it is there and makes itself and comes forth whole—and there it is and you have made it and have felt it, but it has come itself—and that is creative recognition. Of course you have a little more control over your writing than that; you have to know what you want to get; but when you know that, let it take you and if it seems to take you off the track don't hold back, because that is perhaps where instinctively you want to be and if you hold back and try to be always where you have been before, you will go dry.

'You think you have used up all the air where you are, Preston; you said that you had used it up where you live, but that is not true, for if it were it would mean that you had given up all hope of change. I think writers *should* change their scenes; but the very fact that you do not know where you would go if you could means that you would take nothing truly to the place where you went and so there would be nothing there until you had found it, and when you did find it, it would be something you had brought and thought you had left behind. And that would be creative recognition, too, because it would have all to do with you and nothing really to do with the place.'

But what if, when you tried to write, you felt stopped, suffocated, and no words came and if they came at all they were wooden and without meaning? What if you had the feeling you could never write another word?

'Preston, the way to resume is to resume,' she said laughing. `It is the only way. To resume. If you feel this book deeply it will come as deep as your feeling is when it is running truest and the book will never be truer or deeper than your feeling. But you do not yet know anything about your feeling because, though you may think it is all there, all crystallized, you have not let it run. So how can you know what it will be? What will be best in it is what you really do not know now. If you knew it all it would not be creation but dictation. No book is a book until it is done, and you cannot say that you are writing a book while you are just writing on sheets of paper and all that is in you has not yet come out. And a book—let it go on endlessly—is not the whole man. There is no such thing as a one-book author.

I remember a young man in Paris just after the war—you have never heard of this young man—and we all liked his first book very much and he liked it too, and one day he said to me, "This book will make literary history," and I told him: "It will make some part of literary history, perhaps, but only if you go on making a new part every day and grow with the history you are making until you become a part of it yourself." But this young man never wrote another book and now he sits in Paris and searches sadly for the mention of his name in indexes.

III

Her secretary came in and out of the room, putting things away in a trunk that stood open at the end of the couch (they sail tomorrow noon), exchanging a few words in a voice that was new for its softness; and suddenly out of something that we were saying about America came the discovery that both she and I were from Seattle and that she had known my father when he was a young man and before he went into the Klondike. And then as her secretary spoke a strange deep kinship of land seemed to take possession of the other woman,--who had been born in Pennsylvania and raised in Oakland, California, and had been in far-off Paris for thirty years without sight of her native earth,--for she began to speak with deep-felt fervor of her American experience in the past six months.

'Preston,' she said, `you were saying that you had torn up roots ten years ago and tried to plant them again in New England where there was none of your blood, and that now you have a feeling of being without roots. Something like that happened to *me,* too. I think I must have had a feeling that it had happened or I should not have come back. I went to California. I saw it and felt it and had a tenderness and a horror too. Roots are so small and dry when you have them and they are exposed to you. You have seen them on a plant and sometimes they seem to deny the plant if it is vigorous.' She paused when I lit a cigarette; I could not make out whether she had been alarmed at my smoking so much or whether she was instinctively silent in the face of any physical activity on the part of her listener. 'Well,' she went on, `we're not like that really. Our roots can be anywhere and we can survive, because if you think about it, we take our roots with us. I always knew that a little and now I know it wholly. I know because you can go back to where they are and they can be less real to you than they were three thousand, six thousand miles away. Don't worry about your roots so long as you worry about them. The essential thing is to have the feeling that they exist, that they are somewhere. They will take care of themselves, and they will take care of you too, though you may never know how it has happened. To think only of going back for them is to confess that the plant is dying.'

'Yes,' I said, `but there is something more. There is the hunger for the land, for the speech.'

'I know,' she said almost sadly. `America is wonderful!' Then without any warning she declared: `I feel now that it is my business here. After all, it is my business, this America!' And she laughed with a marvelous heartiness, a real lust. When I asked her if she would come back she looked up slyly and was smiling still and she opened and shut her eyes with the same zestful expression with which a man smacks his lips.

'Well,' I said, 'you have had a long time to look. What is it that happens to American writers?'

'What is it you notice?'

'It is obvious. They look gigantic at first. Then they get to be thirty-five or forty and the juices dry up and there they are. Something goes out of them and they begin to repeat according to formula. Or else they grow silent altogether.'

'The trouble is a simple one,' she said. 'They become writers. They cease being creative men and soon they find that they are novelists or critics or poets or biographers, and they are encouraged to be one of those things because they have been very good in one performance or two or three, but that is silly. When a man says, "I am a novelist," he is simply a literary shoemaker. If Mr. Robert Frost is at all good as a poet, it is because he is a farmer—really in his mind a farmer, I mean. And there is another whom you young men are doing your best—and very really your worst—to forget, and he is the editor of a small-town newspaper and his name is Sherwood Anderson. Now Sherwood'—he was the only man she called by his first name, and then affectionately—'Sherwood is really and truly great because he truly does not care what he is and has not thought what he is except a man, a man who can go away and be small in the world's eyes and yet perhaps be one of the very few Americans who have achieved that perfect freshness of creation and passion, as simple as rain falling on a page, and rain that fell from him and was there miraculously and was all his. You see, he had that *creative recognition,* that wonderful ability to have it all on paper before he saw it and then to be strengthened by what he saw so that he could always go deep for more and not know that he was going. Scott Fitzgerald, you know, had it for a little while, but not any more. He is an American Novelist.'

'What about Hemingway?' I could not resist asking her that question. Her name and the name of Ernest Hemingway are almost inseparable when one thinks of the Paris after the war, of the expatriates who gathered around her there as a sibyl. 'He was good until after *A Farewell to Arms.*'

'No,' she said, 'he was not really good after 1925. In his early short stories he had what I have been trying to describe to you. Then—Hemingway did not lose it; he threw it away. I told him then: "Hemingway, you have a small income; you will not starve; you can work without worry and you can grow and keep this thing and it will grow with you." But he did not wish to grow that way; he wished to grow violently. Now, Preston, here is a curious thing. Hemingway is not an American Novelist. He has not sold himself and he has not settled into any literary mould. Maybe his own mould, but that's not only literary. When I first met Hemingway he had a truly sensitive capacity for emotion, and that was the stuff of the first stories; but he was shy of himself and he began to develop, as a shield, a big Kansas City-boy brutality about it, and so he was "tough" because he was really sensitive and ashamed that he was. Then it happened. I saw it happening and tried to save what was fine there, but it was too late. He went the way so many other Americans have gone before, the way they are still going. He became obsessed by sex and violent death.'

She held up a stubby forefinger. 'Now you will mistake me. Sex and death are the springs of the most valid of human emotions. But they are not all; they are not even all emotion. But for Hemingway everything became multiplied by and subtracted from sex and death. But I knew at the start and I know better now that it wasn't just to find out what these things were; it was the disguise for the thing that was really gentle and fine in him, and then his agonizing shyness escaped into brutality. No, now wait not real brutality, because the truly brutal man wants something more than bullfighting and deep-sea fishing and elephant killing or whatever it is now, and perhaps if Hemingway were truly brutal he could make a real literature out of those things; but he is not, and I doubt if he will ever again write truly about anything. He is skillful, yes, but that is the writer; the other half is the man.'

I asked her: 'Do you really think American writers are obsessed by sex? And if they are, isn't it legitimate?'

'It is legitimate, of course. Literature—creative literature—

unconcerned with sex is inconceivable. But not literary sex, because sex is a part of something of which the other parts are not sex at all. No, Preston, it is really a matter of tone. You can tell, if you can tell anything, by the way a man talks about sex whether he is impotent or not, and if he talks about nothing else you can be quite sure that he is impotent—physically and as an artist too.

'One thing which I have tried to tell Americans,' she went on, 'is that there can be no truly great creation without passion, but I'm not sure that I have been able to tell them at all. If they have not understood it is because they have had to think of sex first, and they can think of sex as passion more easily than they can think of passion as the whole force of man. Always they try to label it, and that is a mistake. What do I mean? I will tell you. I think of Byron. Now Byron had passion. It had nothing to do with his women.

It was a quality of Byron's mind and everything he wrote came out of it, and perhaps that is why his work is so uneven, because a man's passion is uneven if it is real; and sometimes, if he can write it, it is only passion and has no meaning outside of itself. Swinburne wrote all his life about passion, but you can read all of him and you will not know what passions he had. I am not sure that it is necessary to know or that Swinburne would have been better if he had known. A man's passion can be wonderful when it has an object which may be a woman or an idea or wrath at an injustice, but after it happens, as it usually does, that the object is lost or won after a time, the passion does not survive it. It survives only if it was there before, only if the woman or the idea or the wrath was an incident in the passion and not the cause of it—and that is what makes the writer.

'Often the men who really have it are not able to recognize it in themselves because they do not know what it is to feel differently or not to feel at all. And it won't answer to its name. Probably Goethe thought that *Young Werther* was a more passionate book than *Wilhelm Meister,* but in Werther he was only describing passion and in *Wilhelm Meister* he was transferring it. And I don't think he knew what he had done. He did not have to. Emerson might have been surprised if he had been told that he was passionate. But Emerson really had passion; he wrote it; but he could not have written *about it* because he did not know about it. Now Hemingway knows all about it and can sometimes write very surely about it, but he hasn't any at all. Not really any. He merely has passions. And Faulkner and Caldwell and all that I have read in America and before I came. They are good craftsmen and they are honest men, but they do not have it.'

IV

I have never heard talk come more naturally and casually. It had none of the tautness or deadly care that is in the speech of most American intellectuals when they talk from the mind out. If sometime you will listen to workingmen talking when they are concentrated upon the physical job at hand, and one of them will go on without cease while he is sawing and measuring and nailing, not always audible, but keeping on in an easy rhythm and almost without awareness of words—then you will get some idea of her conversation.

'Well, I think Thomas Wolfe has it,' I said. 'I think he really has it—more than any man I know in America.' I had just read *Of Time and the River* and had been deeply moved.

'I read his first book,' she said, misnaming it. 'And I looked for it, but I did not find it. Wolfe is a deluge and you are flooded by him, but if you want to read carefully, Preston, you must learn to know how you are flooded. In a review I read on the train Wolfe was many things and among them he was Niagara. Now that is not so silly as it sounds. Niagara has power and it has form and it is beautiful for thirty seconds, but the water at the bottom that has been Niagara is no better and no different from the water at the top that will be Niagara. Something wonderful and terrible has happened to it, but it is the same water and nothing at all would have happened if it had not been for an aberration in one of nature's forms. The river is the water's true form and it is a very satisfactory form for the water and Niagara is altogether wrong. Wolfe's books are the water at the bottom and they foam magnificently because they have come the wrong way, but they are no better than when they started. Niagara exists because the true form ran out and the water could find no other way. But the creative artist should be more adroit.'

'You mean that you think the novel form has run out?'

'Truly—yes. And when a form is dead it always happens that every-thing that is written in it is really formless. And you know it is dead when it has crystallized and everything that goes into it must be made a certain way. What is bad in Wolfe is made that way and what is good is made very differently—and so if you take what is good, he really has not written a novel at all.'

'Yes—but what difference does it make?' I asked her. 'It was some-thing that was very true for me, and perhaps I didn't care whether it was a novel or not.'

'Preston,' she said, 'you must try to understand me. I was not impatient because it was not a novel but because Wolfe did not see what it might have been—and if he really and truly had the passion you say he has, he would have seen because he would have really and truly felt it, and it would have taken its own form, and with his wonderful energy it would not have defeated him.'

'What has passion got to do with choosing an art form?'

'Everything. There is nothing else that determines form. What Wolfe is writing is his autobiography, but he has chosen to tell it as a story and an autobiography is never a story because life does not take place in events. What he has really done is to release himself, and so he has only told the truth of his release and not the truth of discov-ery. And that is why he means so much to you young men, because it is your release too. And perhaps because it is so long and unselective it is better for you, for if it stays with you, you will give it your own form and, if you have any passion, that too, and then perhaps you will be able to make the discovery he did not make. But you will not read it again because you will not need it again. And if a book has been a very true book for you, you will always need it again.'

Her secretary came into the room, looked at her watch, and said: 'You have twenty-five minutes for your walk. You must be back at ten minutes to one.' I arose, suddenly conscious that, having asked for fifteen minutes out of her last day in America, I had stayed over an hour utterly unaware of time. I made to go.

'No,' she said abruptly, 'there is still more to say. Walk with me because I want to say it.' We went out of the hotel. 'Walk on my left,' she said, 'because my right ear is broken.' She walked very sturdily, almost rapidly, and shouted above the traffic.

'There are two particular things I want to tell you because I have thought about them in America. I have thought about them for many years, but particularly in America I have seen them in a new light. So much has happened since I left. Americans are really beginning to use their heads—more now than at any time since the Civil War. They used them then because they had to and thinking was in the air and they have to use them now or be destroyed. When you write the Civil War you must think of it in terms of then and now and not the time between. Well, Americans have not gone far yet, perhaps, but they have started thinking again and there are *heads* here and something is ahead. It has no real shape, but I feel it and I do not feel it so much abroad and that is why my business is here. You see, there is something for writers that there was not before. You are too close to it and you only vaguely sense it. That is why you let your economic problem bother you. If you see and feel you will know what your work is, and if you do it well the economic problem takes care of itself. Don't think so much about your wife and child being dependent upon your work. Try to think of your work being dependent upon your wife and child, for it will be if it really comes from you, and if it doesn't come from you—the *you* that has the wife and child and this Fifth Avenue and these people—then it is no use anyway and your economic problem will have nothing to do with writing because you will not be a writer at all. I find you young writers worrying about losing your integrity and it is well that you should, but a man who really loses his integrity does not know that it is gone, and nobody can wrest it from you if you really have it. An ideal is good only if it moves you forward and can make you produce, Preston, but it is no good if you prefer to produce nothing rather than write sometimes for money alone, because the ideal defeats itself when the economic problem you have been talking about defeats you.'

We were crossing streets and the crowds were looking curiously at this bronze-faced woman whose picture had been so often in the papers, but she was unaware of them, it seemed to me, but extraordinarily aware of the movement around her and especially of taxicabs.

After all, I reflected, she had lived in Paris.

'The thing for the serious writer to remember,' she said, 'is that he is writing seriously and is not a salesman. If the writer and the salesman are born in the same man it is lucky for both of them, but if they are not, one is sure to kill the other when you force them together. And there is one thing more.'

We turned off Madison Avenue and headed back to the hotel.

'A very important thing—and I know it because I have seen it kill so many writers—is not to make up your mind that you are any one thing. Look at your own case. You have written, first a biography, then a history of the American Revolution, and third a modern novel. But how absurd it would be if you should make up your mind that you are a Biographer, a Historian, or a Novelist!' She pronounced the words in tremendous capitals. 'The truth is probably that all those forms are dead because they have become forms, and you must have felt that or you would not have moved on from one to another. Well, you will go on and you will work in them, and sometime, if your work has any meaning and I am not sure that anything but a lifework has meaning, then you may discover a new form. Somebody has said that I myself am striving for a fourth dimension in literature. I am striving for nothing of the sort and I am not striving at all but only gradually growing and becoming steadily more aware of the ways things can be felt and known in words, and perhaps if I feel them and know them myself in the new ways it is enough, and if I know fully enough there will be a note of sureness and confidence that will make others know too.

'And when one has discovered and evolved a new form, it is not the form but the fact that *you are the form* that is important. That is why Boswell is the greatest biographer that ever lived, because he was no slavish Eckermann with the perfect faithfulness of notes—which are not faithful at all—but because he put into Johnson's mouth words that Johnson probably never uttered, and yet you know when you read it that that is what Johnson would have said under such and such a circumstance—and you know all that because Boswell discovered Johnson's real form which Johnson never knew. The great thing is not ever to think about form but let it come. Does that sound strange from me? They have accused me of thinking of nothing else. Do you see the real joke? It is the critics who have really thought about form always and I have thought about—writing!'

Gertrude Stein laughed enormously and went into the hotel with the crowd.

From "A Conversation," by John Hyde Preston. By permission of the author and the publishers: The Atlantic Monthly, Boston.

HOW FLINT AND FIRE STARTED AND GREW

Dorothy Canfield

I feel very dubious about the wisdom or usefulness of publishing the following statement of how one of my stories came into existence. This is not on account of the obvious danger of seeming to have illusions about the value of my work, as though I imagined one of my stories was inherently worth in itself a careful public analysis of its growth; the chance, remote as it might be, of usefulness to students, would outweigh this personal consideration. What is more important is the danger that some student may take the explanation as a recipe or rule for the construction of other stories, and I totally disbelieve in such rules or recipes.

As a rule, when a story is finished, and certainly always by the time it is published, I have no recollection of the various phases of its development. In the case of "Flint and Fire," an old friend chanced to ask me, shortly after the tale was completed, to write out for his English classes, the stages of the construction of a short story. I set them down, hastily, formlessly, but just as they happened, and this gives me a record which I could not reproduce for any other story I ever wrote. These notes are here published on the chance that such a truthful record of the growth of one short story, may have some general suggestiveness for students.

No two of my stories are ever constructed in the same way, but broadly viewed they all have exactly the same genesis, and I confess I cannot conceive of any creative fiction written from any other beginning...that of a generally intensified emotional sensibility, such as every human being experiences with more or less frequency. Everybody knows such occasional hours or days of freshened emotional responses when events that usually pass almost unnoticed, suddenly move you deeply, when a sunset lifts you to exaltation, when a squeaking door throws you into a fit of exasperation, when a clear look of trust in a child's eyes moves you to tears, or an injustice reported in the newspapers to flaming indignation, a good action to a sunny warm love of human nature, a discovered meanness in yourself or another, to despair.

I have no idea whence this tide comes, or where it goes, but when it begins to rise in my heart, I know that a story is hovering in the offing. It does not always come safely to port. The daily routine of ordinary life kills off many a vagrant emotion. Or if daily humdrum occupation does not stifle it, perhaps this saturated solution of feeling does not happen to crystallize about any concrete fact, episode, word or phrase. In my own case, it is far more likely to seize on some slight trifle, the shade of expression on somebody's face, or the tone of somebody's voice, than to accept a more complete, readymade episode. Especially this emotion refuses to crystallize about, or to have anything to do with those narrations of our actual life, offered by friends who are sure that such-and-such a happening is so strange or interesting that "it ought to go in a story."

The beginning of a story is then for me in more than usual sensitiveness to emotion. If this encounters the right focus (and heaven only knows why it is the "right" one) I get simultaneously a strong thrill of intense feeling, and an intense desire to pass it on to other people. This emotion may be any one of the infinitely varied ones which life affords, laughter, sorrow, indignation, gaiety, admiration, scorn, pleasure. I recognize it for the "right" one when it brings with it an irresistible impulse to try to make other people feel it. And I know that when it comes, the story is begun. At this point, the story begins to be more or less under my conscious control, and it is here that the work of construction begins.

"Flint and Fire" thus hovered vaguely in a shimmer of general emotional tensity, and thus abruptly crystallized itself about a chance phrase and the cadence of the voice which pronounced it. For several days I had been almost painfully alive to the beauty of an especially lovely spring, always so lovely after the long winter in the mountains. One evening, going on a very prosaic errand to a farm-house of our region, I walked along a narrow path through dark pines, beside a brook swollen with melting snow, and found the old man I came to see, sitting silent and alone before his blackened small old house. I did my errand, and then not to offend against our country standards of sociability, sat for half an hour beside him.

The old man had been for some years desperately unhappy about a tragic and permanent element in his life. I had known this, every one knew it. But that evening, played upon as I had been by the stars, the darkness of the pines and the shouting voice of the brook, I suddenly stopped merely knowing it, and felt it. It seemed to me that his misery emanated from him like a soundless wail of anguish. We talked very little, odds and ends of neighborhood gossip, until the old man, shifting his position, drew a long breath and said, "Seems to me I never heard the brook sound so loud as it has this spring." There came instantly to my mind the recollection that his grandfather had drowned himself in that brook, and I sat silent, shaken by that thought and by the sound of his voice. I have no words to attempt to reproduce his voice, or to try to make you feel as I did, hot and cold with the awe of that glimpse into a naked human heart. I felt my own heart contract dreadfully with helpless sympathy...and, I hope this is not as ugly as it sounds, I knew at the same instant that I would try to get that pang of emotion into a story and make other people feel it.

That is all. That particular phase of the construction of the story came and went between two heart-beats.

I came home by the same path through the same pines along the same brook, sinfully blind and deaf to the beauty that had so moved me an hour ago. I was too busy now to notice anything outside the rapid activity going on inside my head. My mind was working with a swiftness and a coolness which I am somewhat ashamed to mention, and my emotions were calmed, relaxed, let down from the tension of the last few days and the last few moments. They had found their way out to an attempt at self-expression and were at rest. I realize that this is not at all estimable. The old man was just as unhappy as he had been when I had felt my heart breaking with sympathy for him, but now he seemed very far away.

I was snatching up one possibility after another, considering it for a moment, casting it away and pouncing on another. First of all, the story must be made as remote as possible from resembling the old man or his trouble, lest he or any one in the world might think he was intended, and be wounded.

What is the opposite pole from an old man's tragedy? A lover's tragedy, of course. Yes, it must be separated lovers, young and passionate and beautiful, because they would fit in with the back-ground of spring, and swollen shouting starlit brooks, and the yearly resurrection which was so closely connected with that ache of emotion that they were a part of it.

Should the separation come from the weakness or faithlessness of one of the lovers? No, ah no, I wanted it without ugliness, pure beautiful sorrow, to fit that dark shadow of the pines...the lovers must be separated by outside forces.

What outside forces? Lack of money? Family opposition? Both, perhaps. I knew plenty of cases of both in the life of our valley.

By this time I had come again to our own house and was swallowed in the usual thousand home-activities. But underneath all that, quite steadily my mind continued to work on the story as a wasp in a barn keeps on silently plastering up the cells of his nest in the midst of the noisy activities of farm life. I said to one of the children, "Yes, dear, wasn't it fun!" and to myself, "To be typical of our tradition-ridden valley-people, the opposition ought to come from the dead hand of the past." I asked a caller, "One lump or two?" and thought as I poured the tea, "And if the character of that opposition could be made to indicate a fierce capacity for passionate feeling in the older generation, that would make it doubly useful in the story, not only as part of the machinery of the plot, but as indicating an inheritance of passionate feeling in the younger generation, with whom the story is concerned." I dozed off at night, and woke to find myself saying, "It could come from the jealousy of two sisters, now old women."

But that meant that under ordinary circumstances the lovers would have been first cousins, and this might cause a subconscious wavering of attention on the part of some readers...just as well to get that stone out of the path! I darned a sock and thought out the relationship in the story, and was rewarded with a revelation of the character of the sick old woman, Niram's step-mother.

Upon this, came one of those veering lists of the ballast aboard which are so disconcerting to the author. The story got out of hand.

The old woman silent, indomitable, fed and deeply satisfied for all of her hard and grinding life by her love for the husband whom she had taken from her sister, she stepped to the front of my stage, and from that moment on, dominated the action. I did not expect this, nor desire it, and I was very much afraid that the result would be a perilously divided interest which would spoil the unity of impression of the story. It now occurs to me that this unexpected shifting of values may have been the emergence of the element of tragic old age which had been the start of the story and which I had conscientiously tried to smother out of sight. At any rate, there she was, more touching, pathetic, striking, to my eyes with her life-time proof of the reality of her passion, than my untried young lovers who up to that time had seemed to me, in the full fatuous flush of invention as I was, as ill-starred, innocent and touching lovers as anybody had ever seen.

Alarmed about this double interest I went on with the weaving back and forth of the elements of the plot which now involved the attempt to arouse in the reader's heart as in mine a sympathy for the bed-ridden old Mrs. Purdon and a comprehension of her sacrifice.

My daily routine continued as usual, gardening, telling stories, music, sewing, dusting, motoring, callers...one of them, a self-consciously sophisticated Europeanized American, not having of course any idea of what was filling my inner life, rubbed me frightfully the wrong way by making a slighting condescending allusion to what he called the mean, emotional poverty of our inarticulate mountain people. I flew into a silent rage at him, though scorning to discuss with him a matter I felt him incapable of understanding, and the character of Cousin Horace went into the story. He was for the first day or two, a very poor cheap element, quite unreal, unrealized, a mere man of straw to be knocked over by the personages of the tale. Then I took myself to task, told myself that I was spoiling a story merely to revenge myself on a man I cared nothing about, and that I must either take Cousin Horace out or make him human. One day, working in the garden, I laughed out suddenly, delighted with the whimsical idea of making him, almost in spite of himself, the *deus ex machina* of my little drama, quite soft and sympathetic under his shell of would-be worldly disillusion, as occasionally happens to elderly bachelors.

At this point the character of 'Niram's long-dead father came to life and tried to push his way into the story, a delightful, gentle, upright man, with charm and a sense of humor, such as none of the rest of my stark characters possessed. I felt that he was necessary to explain the fierceness of the sisters' rivalry for him. I planned one or two ways to get him in, in retrospect—and liked one of the scenes better than anything that finally was left in the story. Finally, very heavy-hearted, I put him out of the story, for the merely material reason that there was no room for him. As usual with my storymaking, this plot was sprouting out in a dozen places, expanding, opening up, till I perceived that I had enough material for a novel. For a day or so I hung undecided. Would it perhaps be better to make it a novel and really tell about those characters all I knew and guessed? But again a consideration that has nothing to do with artistic form, settled the matter. I saw no earthly possibility of getting time enough to write a novel. So I left Mr. Purdon out, and began to think of ways to compress my material, to make one detail do double work so that space might be saved.

One detail of the mechanism remained to be arranged, and this ended by deciding the whole form of the story, and the first-person character of the recital. This was the question of just how it would have been materially possible for the bed-ridden old woman to break down the life-long barrier between her and her sister, and how she could have reached her effectively and forced her hand. I could see no way to manage this except by somehow transporting her bodily to the sister's house, so that she could not be put out on the road without public scandal. This transportation must be managed by some character not in the main action, as none of the persons involved would have been willing to help her to this. It looked like putting in another character, just for that purpose, and of course he could not be put in without taking the time to make him plausible, human, understandable...and I had just left out that charming widower for sheer lack of space. Well, why not make it a first person story, and have the narrator be the one who takes Mrs. Purdon to her sister's? The narrator of the story never needs to be explained, always seems sufficiently living and real by virtue of the supremely human act of so often saying "I."

Now the materials were ready, the characters fully alive in my mind and entirely visualized, even to the smoothly braided hair of Ev'leen Ann, the patch-work quilt of the old woman out-of-doors, and the rustic wedding at the end, all details which had recently chanced to draw my attention; I heard everything through the song of the swollen brook, one of the main characters in the story (although by this time in actual fact, June and lower water had come and the brook slid quiet and gleaming, between placid green banks), and I often found myself smiling foolishly in pleasure over the buggy going down the hill, freighted so richly with hearty human joy.

The story was now ready to write.

I drew a long breath of mingled anticipation and apprehension, somewhat as you do when you stand, breathing quickly, balanced on your skis, at the top of a long white slope you are not sure you are clever enough to manage. Sitting down at my desk one morning, I "pushed off" and with a tingle of not altogether pleasurable excitement and alarm, felt myself "going." I "went" almost as precipitately as skis go down a long white slope, scribbling as rapidly as, my pencil could go, indicating whole words with a dash and a jiggle, filling page after page with scrawls...it seemed to me that I had been at work perhaps half an hour, when someone was calling me impatiently to lunch. I had been writing four hours without stopping. My cheeks were flaming, my feet were cold, my lips parched. It was high time someone called me to lunch.

The next morning, back at the desk, I looked over what I had written, conquered the usual sick qualms of discouragement at finding it so infinitely flat and insipid compared to what I had wished to make it, and with a very clear idea of what remained to be done, plodded ahead doggedly, and finished the first draught before noon. It was almost twice too long.

After this came a period of steady deskwork, every morning, of re-writing, compression, more compression, and the more or less mechanical work of technical revision, what a member of my family calls "cutting out the 'whiches.'" The first thing to do each morning was to read a part of it over aloud, sentence by sentence, to try to catch clumsy, ungraceful phrases, over-weights at one end or the other, "ringing" them as you ring a dubious coin, clipping off too-trailing relative clauses, "'listening" hard. This work depends on what is known in music as "ear," and in my case it cannot be kept up long at a time, because I find my attention flagging. When I begin to suspect that my ear is dulling, I turn to other varieties of revision, of which there are plenty to keep anybody busy; for instance revision to explain facts; in this category is the sentence just after the narrator suspects Ev'leen Ann has gone down to the brook, "my ears ringing with all the frightening tales of the morbid vein of violence which runs through the characters of our reticent people."

It seemed too on re-reading the story for the tenth or eleventh time, that for readers who do not know our valley people, the girl's attempt at suicide might seem improbable. Some reference ought to be brought in, giving the facts that their sorrow and despair is terrible in proportion to the nervous strain of their tradition of repression, and that suicide is by no means unknown. I tried bringing that fact in, as part of the conversation with Cousin Horace, but it never fused with the rest there, "stayed on top of the page" as bad sentences will do, never sank in, and always made the disagreeable impression on me that a false intonation in an actor's voice does. So it came out from there. I tried putting it in Ev'leen Ann's mouth, in a carefully arranged form, but it was so shockingly out of character there, that it was snatched out at once. There I hung over the manuscript with that necessary fact in my hand and no place to lay it down. Finally I perceived a possible opening for it, where it now is in the story, and squeezing it in there discontentedly left it, for I still think it only inoffensively and not well placed.

Then there is the traditional, obvious revision for suggestiveness, such as the recurrent mention of the mountain brook at the beginning of each of the first scenes; revision for ordinary sense, in the first draught I had honeysuckle among the scents on the darkened porch, whereas honeysuckle does not bloom in Vermont till late June; revision for movement to get the narrator rapidly from her bed to the brook; for sound, sense proportion, even grammar...and always

interwoven with these mechanical revisions recurrent intense visualizations of the scenes. This is the mental trick which can be learned,
I think, by practice and effort. Personally, although I never used as
material any events in my own intimate life, I can write nothing if
I cannot achieve these very definite, very complete visualizations of
the scenes; which means that I can write nothing at all about places,
people or phases of life which I, do not intimately know, down to
the last detail. If my life depended on it, it does not seem to me I
could possibly write a story about Siberian hunters or East-side factory hands without having lived long among them. Now the story
was what one calls "finished," and I made a clear copy, picking my
way with difficulty among the alterations, the scratched-out passages, and the cued-in paragraphs, the inserted pages, the rearranged
phrases. As I typed, the interest and pleasure in the story lasted just
through that process. It still seemed pretty good to me, the wedding
still touched me, the whimsical ending still amused me.

But on taking up the legible typed copy and beginning to glance
rapidly over it, I felt fall over me the black shadow of that intolerable
reaction which is enough to make any author abjure his calling for
ever. By the time I had reached the end, the full misery was there,
the heart-sick, helpless consciousness of failure. What! I had had the
presumption to try to translate into words, and make others feel a
thrill of sacred living human feeling, that should not be touched
save by worthy hands. And what had I produced? A trivial, paltry,

complicated tale, with certain cheaply ingenious devices in it. I heard again the incommunicable note of profound emotion in the old man's voice, suffered again with his sufferings; and those little black marks on white paper lay dead, dead in my hands. What horrible people second-rate authors were! They ought to be prohibited by law from sending out their caricatures of life. I would never write again. All that effort, enough to have achieved a master-piece it seemed at the time...and this, *this,* for result!

From the subconscious depths of long experience came up the cynical, slightly contemptuous consolation, "You know this never lasts. You always throw this same fit, and get over it."
So, suffering from really acute humiliation and unhappiness, I went out hastily to weed a flower-bed.

And sure enough, the next morning, after a long night's sleep, I felt quite rested, calm, and blessedly matter-of-fact. "Flint and Fire" seemed already very far away and vague, and the question of whether it was good or bad, not very important or interesting, like the chart of your temperature in a fever now gone by.

From "How 'Flint and Fire' Started and Grew," by Dorothy Canfield Fisher, in *Americans All, edited* by Benjamin A. Heydrick. By permission of the publishers: Harcourt, Brace and Company, Inc., New York City.

LETTER TO WARNER TAYLOR
Llewelyn Powys

My dear Mr. Taylor:

It is difficult to analyze the airy substance we call style. At its best it seems to escape all definitions. It is as evasive as life. It would be as hard to predict the dancing flight of a flock of finches, or the subterranean movements of a single mole, as to explain a great writer's peculiar gift. The reason for this seems to me to lie in the fact that style is the ultimate expression of the author's unique spiritual consciousness. This spiritual consciousness has been arrived at through various influences. Ancestry has bequeathed to it a certain fundamental disposition, environment has thickened this congenital inclination, and the chance temperament of each individual has flashed it into life out of nowhere.

It has been suggested that style consists in saying what has to be said as exactly as possible. This, however, is a different matter altogether. True style has nothing to do with imparting information lucidly. It is not this. It is the scent of the herb, the mist over the blackberry hedge, the soul of the man. It is begotten of the senses, it is the quintesessential feeling, the quintesessential thought, of those fleet immediate messengers finding unity at last in the person of the being they serve. All the nights that a man has experienced, clouding in so mysteriously over the native earth; all the dawns that he has witnessed with wakeful eyes, have engendered it. The taste of wheaten bread, the taste of milk and wine, has caused it to grow. The sound of church bells heard in a wild place far from village or town has impelled words to dance like children in a May-day procession. The contact of sea waves against the skin, or the grateful warmth of fire against human nakedness can, and should, have an influence on every sentence. The smell of snow, the smell of a hay cock in the sun, nay, the smell that rises from the intestines of a rabbit when a man is paunching it with his pocket knife, should prove its periods.

A perfect style is the perfect expression of a man's secret identity. It makes arrogant claims. It demands that the ordinary everyday world should give attention to the wandering goat-cry of a supreme egoism as sensitive as it is tough. It is for this reason that truly great writers are seldom recognized in their lifetime. Commonplace readers invariably appreciate commonplace writers. They prefer books that reflect ideas and methods of thought with which they are already familiar. At all costs the pamphlets they peruse must be partial and platitudinous. They shrink from that terrible spiritual sincerity that burns like fire and prompts a writer to leave his own seal, his own thumb-mark, upon every page he writes.

If I were to be asked by any young person the best way to acquire a style I would tell him to live intensely. The style of a man is the direct result of his passion for life. Learning and scholarship are of small value here. Style is the affirmation of a man's heightened awareness of existence and always grows up from within, from out of the marrow of his bones.

If it were my task to treat of this matter with undergraduates I should draw their attention to certain notable passages of English prose and show them clearly by specific paragraphs, sentences, or even idiosyncratic words, how these men have succeeded in preserving their spirits on parchment for all time. This particular and singular use of the country's language is beyond the scope of the vulgar. It would seem that the innate complexion of a man's mind finds for itself fitting expression. Powerful and original characters write in a powerful and original way, shallow and commonplace characters write in a shallow and commonplace way. Style has to do with the grace, health, and vigour of a man's soul. It is a secret thing dependent upon a natural depth of feeling and no amount of playing the sedulous ape can pass off as authentic what is in truth counterfeit. Just as in the love between a man and a woman true emotion will find convincing expression so it is with writing. Sham feeling makes sham prose and it is easily recognized as such.

My own method is to give no thought whatever to the form of what I am writing. I put down my ideas as they present themselves pell mell to my mind, fanciful, extravagant, sentimental, bawdy, irreverent, irrelevant, they are all equally welcome. In going over my work, however, I am prepared to spend a great deal of care in endeavouring to find the just word or an adequate balance for any particular paragraph. I have noticed that when I am writing at my best I experience a peculiar physical sensation. I first became aware of this peculiarity at school as a boy of twelve when we were given an essay to write on the Pied Piper. I have never been able to think a subject through before writing. I daresay I should do much better if it were my nature to adopt such a method. I consider the greatest difficulty to be overcome by immature, untrained writers is lack of confidence. They are too self-conscious. When once the pen is in the hand it is important to forget about the opinion of others and to write away after your own fashion with careless, proud indifference.

Yours sincerely,

Llewelyn Powys

From "Letter to Warner Taylor," by Llewelyn Powys in *Types and Times in the Essay*, selected and arranged by Warner Taylor. By permission of the publishers: Harper & Brothers, 1932, New York City and London.

REFLECTIONS ON WRITING

Henry Miller

K nut Hamsun once said, in response to a questionnaire, that he wrote to kill time. I think that even if he were sincere in stating it thus he was deluding himself. Writing, like life itself, is a voyage of discovery. The adventure is a metaphysical one: it is a way of approaching life indirectly, of acquiring a total rather than a partial view of the universe. The writer lives between the upper and lower worlds: he takes the path in order eventually to become that path himself.

I began in absolute chaos and darkness, in a bog or swamp of ideas and emotions and experiences. Even now I do not consider myself a writer, in the ordinary sense of the word. I am a man telling the story of his life, a process which appears more and more inexhaustible as I go on. Like the world-evolution, it is endless. It is a turning inside out, a voyaging through X dimensions, with the result that somewhere along the way one discovers that what one has to tell is not nearly so important as the telling itself. It is this quality about all art which gives it a metaphysical hue, which lifts it out of time and space and centers or integrates it to the whole cosmic process. It is this about art which is "therapeutic": significance, purposelessness, infinitude.

From the very beginning almost I was deeply aware that there is no goal. I never hope to embrace the whole, but merely to give in each separate fragment, each work, the feeling of the whole as I go on, because I am digging deeper and deeper into life, digging deeper and deeper into past and future. With the endless burrowing a certitude develops which is greater than faith or belief. I become more and more indifferent to my fate, as writer, and more and more certain of my destiny as man.

I began assiduously examining the style and technique of those whom I once admired and worshipped: Nietzsche, Dostoievski, Hamsun, even Thomas Mann, whom today I discard as being a skillful fabricator, a brickmaker, an inspired jackass or draught-horse. I imitated every style in the hope of finding the clue to the gnawing secret of how to write. Finally I came to a dead end, to a despair and desperation which few men have known, because there was no divorce between myself as writer and myself as man: to fail as a writer meant to fail as a man. And I failed. I realized that I was nothing—less than nothing—a minus quantity. It was at this point, in the midst of the dead Sargasso Sea, so to speak, that I really began to write. I began from scratch, throwing everything overboard, even those whom I most loved. Immediately I heard my own voice I was enchanted: the fact that it was a separate, distinct, unique voice sustained me. It didn't matter to me if what I wrote should be considered bad. Good and bad dropped out of my vocabulary. I jumped with two feet into the realm of aesthetics, the non-moral, non-ethical, non-utilitarian realm of art. My life itself became a work of art. I had found a voice, I was whole again. The experience was very much like what we read of in connection with the lives of Zen initiates. My huge failure was like the recapitulation of the experience of the race: I had to grow foul with knowledge, realize the futility of everything, smash everything, grow desperate, then humble, then sponge myself off the slate, as it were, in order to recover my authenticity. I had to arrive at the brink and then take a leap in the dark.

I talk now about Reality, but I know there is no getting at it, least-wise by writing. I learn less and realize more: I learn in some different, more subterranean way. I acquire more and more the gift of immediacy. I am developing the ability to perceive, apprehend, analyze, synthesize, categorize, inform, articulate—all at once. The structural element of things reveals itself more readily to my eye. I eschew all clear cut interpretations: with increasing simplification the mystery heightens. What I know tends to become more and more unstatable. I live in certitude, a certitude which is not dependent upon proofs or faith. I live completely for myself, without the least egotism or selfishness. I am living out my share of life and thus abetting the scheme of things. I further the development, the enrichment, the evolution and the devolution of the cosmos, every day in every way. I give all I have to give, voluntarily, and take as much as I can possibly ingest. I am a prince and a pirate at the same time. I am the equals sign, the spiritual counterpart of the sign Libra which was wedged into the original Zodiac by separating Virgo from Scorpio. I find that there is plenty of room in the world for everybody—great interspatial depths, great ego universes, great islands of repair, for whoever attains to individuality. On the surface, where the historical battles rage, where everything is interpreted in terms of money and power, there may be crowding, but life only begins when one drops below the surface, when one gives up the struggle, sinks and disappears from sight. Now I can as easily not write as write: there is no longer any compulsion, no longer any therapeutic aspect to it. Whatever I do is done out of sheer joy: I drop my fruits like a ripe tree. What the general reader or the critic makes of it is not my concern. I am not establishing values: I defecate and nourish. There is nothing more to it.

This condition of sublime indifference is a logical development of the egocentric life. I lived out the social problem by dying: the real problem is not one of getting on with one's neighbor or of contributing to the development of one's country, but of discovering one's destiny, of making a life in accord with the deep-centered rhythm of the cosmos. To be able to use the word cosmos boldly, to use the word soul, to deal in things "spiritual"—and to shun definitions, alibis, proofs, duties. Paradise is everywhere and every road, if one continues along it far enough, leads to it. One can only go forward by going backward and then sideways and then up and then down. There is no progress: there is perpetual movement, displacement, which is circular, spiral, endless. Every man has his own destiny: the only imperative is to follow it, to accept it, no matter where it lead him.

I haven't the slightest idea what my future books will be like, even the one immediately to follow. My charts and plans are the slenderest sort of guides: I scrap them at will, I invent, distort, deform, lie, inflate, exaggerate, confound and confuse as the mood seizes me. I obey only my own instincts and intuitions. I know nothing in advance. Often I put down things which I do not understand myself, secure in the knowledge that later they will become clear and meaningful to me. I have faith in the man who is writing, who is myself, the writer. I do not believe in words, no matter if strung together by the most skillful man: I believe in language, which is something beyond words, something which words give only an inadequate illusion of. Words do not exist separately, except in the minds of scholars, etymologists, philologists, etc. Words divorced from language are dead things, and yield no secrets. A man is revealed in his style, the language which he has created for himself. To the man who is pure at heart I believe that everything is as clear as a bell, even the most esoteric scripts. For such a man there is always mystery, but the mystery is not mysterious, it is logical, natural, ordained, and implicitly accepted. Understanding is not a piercing of the mystery, but an acceptance of it, a living blissfully with it, in it, through and by it. I would like my words to flow along in the same way that the world flows along, a serpentine movement through incalculable dimensions, axes, latitudes, climates, conditions. I accept a *priori* my inability to realize such an ideal. It does not bother me in the least. In the ultimate sense, the world itself is pregnant with failure, is the perfect manifestation of imperfection, of the consciousness of failure. In the realization of this, failure is itself eliminated. Like the primal spirit of the universe, like the unshakable Absolute, the One, the All, the creator, i.e., the artist, expresses himself by and through imperfection. It is the stuff of life, the very sign of livingness. One gets nearer to the heart of truth, which I suppose is the ultimate aim of the writer, in the measure that he ceases to struggle, in the measure that he abandons the will. The great writer is the very symbol of life, of the non-perfect. He moves effortlessly, giving the illusion of perfection, from some unknown center which is certainly not the brain center but which is definitely a center, a center connected with the rhythm of the whole universe and consequently as sound, solid, unshakable, as durable, defiant, anarchic, purposeless, as the universe itself. Art teaches, nothing, except the significance of life. The great work must inevitably be obscure, except to the very few, to those who like the author himself are initiated into the mysteries. Communication then is secondary: it is perpetuation which is important. For this only one good reader is necessary.

If I am a revolutionary, as has been said, it is unconsciously. I am not in revolt against the world order. "I revolutionize," as Blaise

Cendrars said of himself. There is a difference. I can as well live on the minus side of the fence as on the plus side. Actually I believe myself to be just above these two signs, providing a ratio between them which expresses itself plastically, non-ethically, in writing. I believe that one has to pass beyond the sphere and influence of art. Art is only a means to life, to the life more abundant. It is not in itself the life more abundant. It merely points the way, something which is overlooked not only by the public, but very often by the artist himself. In becoming an end it defeats itself. Most artists are defeating life by their very attempt to grapple with it. They have split the egg in two. All art, I firmly believe, will one day disappear. But the artist will remain, and life itself will become not "an art," but *art*, i.e., will definitely and for all time usurp the field. In any true sense we are certainly not yet alive. We are no longer animals, but we are certainly not yet *men*. Since the dawn of art every great artist has been dinning that into us, but few are they who have understood it. Once art is really accepted it will cease to be. It is only a substitute, a symbol-language, for something which can be seized directly. But for that to become possible man must become thoroughly religious, not a believer, but a prime mover, a god in fact and deed. He will become that inevitably. And of all the detours along this path art is the most glorious, the most fecund, the most instructive. The artist who becomes thoroughly aware consequently ceases to be one. And the trend is towards awareness, towards that blinding consciousness in which no present form of life can possibly flourish, not even art.

To some this will sound like mystification, but it is an honest statement of my present convictions. It should be borne in mind, of course, that there is an inevitable discrepancy between the truth of the matter and what one thinks, even about himself: but it should also be borne in mind that there exists an equal discrepancy between the judgment of another and this same truth. Between subjective and objective there is no vital difference. Everything is illusive and more or less transparent. All phenomena, including man and his thoughts about himself, are nothing more than a movable, changeable alphabet. There are no solid facts to get hold of. Thus in writing, even if my distortions and deformations be deliberate, they are not necessarily less near to the truth of things. One can be absolutely truthful and sincere even though admittedly the most outrageous liar. Fiction and invention are of the very fabric of life. The truth is no way disturbed by the violent perturbations of the spirit.

Thus, whatever effects I may obtain by technical device are never the mere results of technique, but the very accurate registering by my seismographic needle of the tumultuous, manifold, mysterious and incomprehensible experiences which I have lived through and which, in the process of writing are lived through again, differently, perhaps even more tumultuously, more mysteriously, more incomprehensibly. The so-called core of solid fact, which forms the point of departure as well as repair, is deeply embedded in me: I could not possibly lose it, alter it, disguise it, try as I may. And yet it is altered, just as the face of the world is altered, with each moment that we breathe. To record it then, one must give a double illusion—one of arrestation and one of flow. It is this dual trick, so to speak, which gives the illusion of falsity: it is this lie, this fleeting, metamorphic mask, which is of the very essence of art. One anchors oneself in the flow: one adopts the lying mask in order to reveal the truth.

I have often thought that I should like one day to write a book explaining how I wrote certain passages in my books, or perhaps just one passage. I believe I could write a good-sized book on just one small paragraph selected at random from my work. A book about its inception, its genesis, its metamorphosis, its accouchement, of the time which elapsed between the birth of the idea and its recording, the time it took to write it, the thoughts I had between times while writing it, the day of the week, the state of my health, the condition of my nerves, the interruptions that occurred, those of my own volition and those which were forced upon me, the multifarious varieties of expression which occurred to me in the process of writing, the alterations, the point where I left off and in returning, completely altered the original trend, or the point where I skillfully left off, like a surgeon making the best of a bad job, intending to return and resume some time later, but never doing so, or else returning and continuing the trend unconsciously some few books later when the memory of it had completely vanished. Or I might take one passage against another, passages which the cold eye of the critic seizes on as examples of this or that, and utterly confound them, the analytical-minded critics, by demonstrating how a seemingly effortless piece of writing was achieved under great duress whereas another difficult, labyrinthian passage was written like a breeze, like a geyser erupting. Or I could show how a passage originally shaped itself when in bed, how it became transformed upon arising, and again transformed at the moment of sitting down to record it. Or I could produce my scratch pad to show how the most remote, the most artificial stimulus produced a warm, life-like human flower. I could produce certain words discovered by hazard while riffling the pages of a book, show how they set me off—but who on earth could ever guess how, in what manner, they were to set me off? All that the critics write about a work of art, even at the best, even when most sound, convincing, plausible, even when done with love, which is seldom, is as nothing compared to the actual mechanics, the real genetics of a work of art. I remember my work, not word for word, to be sure, but in some more accurate, trustworthy way; my whole work has come to resemble a terrain of which I have made a thorough, geodetic survey, not from a desk, with pen and ruler, but by touch, by getting down on all fours, on my stomach, and crawling over the ground inch by inch, and this over an endless period of time in all conditions of weather. In short, I am as close to the work now as when I was in the act of executing it—closer perhaps. The conclusion of a book was never anything more than a shift of bodily position. It might have ended in a thousand different ways. No single part of it is finished off: I could resume the narrative at any point, carry on, lay canals, tunnels, bridges, houses, factories, stud it with other inhabitants, other fauna and flora, all equally true to fact. I have no beginning and no ending, actually. Just as life begins at any moment, through an act of realization, so the work. But each beginning, whether of book, page, paragraph, sentence or phrase, marks a vital connection, and it is in the vitality, the durability, the timelessness and changelessness of the thoughts and events that I plunge anew each time. Every line and word is vitally connected with my life, my life only, be it in the form of deed, event, fact, thought, emotion, desire, evasion, frustration, dream, revery, vagary, even the unfinished nothings which float listlessly in the brain like the snapped filaments of a spider's web. There is nothing really vague or tenuous—even the nothingnesses are sharp, tough, definite, durable. Like the spider I return again and again to the task, conscious that the web I am spinning is made of my own substance, that it will never fail me, never run dry.

In the beginning I had dreams of rivaling Dostoievski. I hoped to give to the world huge, labyrinthian soul struggles which would devastate the world. But before very far along I realized that we had evolved to a point far beyond that of Dostoievski—beyond in the sense of degeneration. With us the soul problem has disappeared, or rather presents itself in some strangely distorted chemical guise. We are dealing with crystalline elements of the dispersed and shattered soul. The modern painters express this state or condition perhaps even more forcibly than the writer: Picasso is the perfect example of what I mean. It was quite impossible for me, therefore, to think of writing novels; equally unthinkable to follow the various blind alleys represented by the various literary movements in England, France and America. I felt compelled, in all honesty, to take the disparate and dispersed elements of our life—the soul life, not the cultural life—and manipulate them through my own personal mode, using my own shattered and dispersed ego as heartlessly and recklessly as I would the flotsam and jetsam of the surrounding phenomenal world. I have never felt any antagonism for or anxiety over the anarchy represented by the prevailing forms of art; on the contrary, I have always welcomed the dissolving influences. In an age marked by dissolution, liquidation seems to me a virtue, nay a moral imperative. Not only have I never felt the least desire to conserve, bolster up or buttress anything, but I might say that I have always looked upon decay as being just as wonderful and rich an expression of life as growth.

I think I should also confess that I was driven to write because it proved to be the only outlet open to me, the only task worthy of my powers. I had honestly tried all the other roads to freedom. I was a self-willed failure in the so-called world of reality, not a failure because of lack of ability. Writing was not an "escape," a means of evading the every day reality: on the contrary, it meant a still deeper plunge into the brackish pool—a plunge to the source where the waters were constantly being renewed, where there was perpetual movement and stir. Looking back upon my career, I see myself as a person capable of undertaking almost any task, any vocation. It was the monotony and sterility of the other outlets which drove me to desperation. I demanded a realm in which I should be both master and slave at the same time: the world of art is the only such realm. I entered it without any apparent talent, a thorough novice, incapable, awkward, tongue-tied, almost paralyzed by fear and apprehensiveness. I had to lay one brick on another, set millions of words to paper before writing one real, authentic word dragged up from my own guts. The facility of speech which I possessed was a handicap; I had all the vices of the educated man. I had to learn to think, feel and see in a totally new fashion, in an uneducated way, in my own way, which is the hardest thing in the world. I had to throw myself into the current, knowing that I would probably sink. The great majority of artists are throwing themselves in with life-preservers around their necks, and more often than not it is the life-preserver which sinks them. Nobody can drown in the ocean of reality who voluntarily gives himself up to the experience. Whatever there be of progress in life comes not through adaptation but through daring, through obeying the blind urge. "No daring is fatal," said René Crevel, a phrase which I shall never forget. The whole logic of the universe is contained in daring, i.e., in creating from the flimsiest, slenderest support. In the beginning this daring is mistaken for will, but with time the will drops away and the automatic process takes its place, which again has to be broken or dropped and a new certitude established which has nothing to do with knowledge, skill, technique or faith. By daring one arrives at the mysterious X position of the artist, and it is this anchorage which no one can describe in words but yet subsists and exudes from every line that is written.

From "Reflections on Writing," by Henry Miller in *The Wisdom of the Heart*. By permission of the author and the publishers: New Directions, 1941, Norfolk, Connecticut.

A Story Of A Novel

Thomas Wolfe

I had been to Europe five times now; each time I had come with delight, with maddening eagerness to return, and each time how, where, and in what way I did not know, I had felt the bitter ache of homelessness, a desperate longing for America, an overwhelming desire to return.

During that summer in Paris, I think I felt this great homesickness more than ever before, and I really believe that from this emotion, this constant and almost intolerable effort of memory and desire, the material and the structure of the books I now began to write were derived.

The quality of my memory is characterized, I believe, in a more than ordinary degree by the intensity of its sense impressions, its power to evoke and bring back the odors, sounds, colors, shapes, and feel of things with concrete vividness. Now my memory was at work night and day, in a way that I could at first neither check nor control and that swarmed unbidden in a stream of blazing pageantry across my mind, with the million forms and substances of the life that I had left, which was my own, America. I would be sitting, for example, on the terrace of a café watching the flash and play of life before me on the Avenue de l'Opéra and suddenly I would remember the iron railing that goes along the boardwalk at Atlantic City. I could see it instantly just the way it was, the heavy iron pipe; its raw, galvanized look; the way the joints were fitted together. It was all so vivid and concrete that I could feel my hand upon it and know the exact dimensions, its size and weight and shape. And suddenly I would realize that I had never seen any railing that looked like this in Europe. And this utterly familiar, common thing would suddenly be revealed to me with all the wonder with which we discover a thing which we have seen all our life and yet have never known before. Or again, it would be a bridge, the look of an old iron bridge across an American river, the sound the train makes as it goes across it; the spoke-and-hollow rumble of the ties below; the look of the muddy banks; the slow, thick, yellow wash of an American river; an old flat-bottomed boat half filled with water stogged in the muddy bank....

I would sit there, looking out upon the Avenue de l'Opéra and my life would ache with the whole memory of it; the desire to see it again; somehow to find a word for it; a language that would tell its shape, its color, the way we have all known and felt and seen it. And when I understood this thing, I saw that I must find for myself the tongue to utter what I knew but could not say. And from the moment of that discovery, the line and purpose of my life was shaped. The end toward which every energy of my life and talent would be henceforth directed was in such a way as this defined. It was as if I had discovered a whole new universe of chemical elements and had begun to see certain relations between some of them but had by no means begun to organize the whole series into a harmonious and coherent union. From this time on, I think my efforts might be described as the effort to complete that organization, to discover that articulation for which I strove, to bring about that final coherent union. I know that I have failed thus far in doing so, but I believe I understand pretty thoroughly just where the nature of my failure lies, and of course my deepest and most earnest hope is that the time will come when I shall not fail.

At any rate, from this time on the general progress of the three books which I was to write in the next four and a half years could be fairly described in somewhat this way. It was a progress that began in a whirling vortex and a creative chaos and that proceeded slowly at the expense of infinite confusion, toil, and error toward clarification and the articulation of an ordered and formal structure. An extraordinary image remains to me from that year, the year I spent abroad when the material of these books first began to take on an articulate form. It seemed that I had inside me, swelling and gathering all the time, a huge black cloud, and that this cloud was loaded with electricity, pregnant, crested, with a kind of hurricane violence that could not be held in check much longer; that the moment was approaching fast when it must break. Well, all I can say is that the storm did break. It broke that summer while I was in Switzerland. It came in torrents, and it is not over yet.

I cannot really say the book was written. It was something that took hold of me and possessed me, and before I was done with it— that is, before I finally emerged with the first completed part—it seemed to me that it had done for me. It was exactly as if this great black storm cloud I have spoken of had opened up and, mid flashes of lightning, was pouring from its depth a torrential and ungovernable flood. Upon that flood everything was swept and borne along as by a great river. And I was borne along with it.

There was nothing at first which could be called a novel. I wrote about night and darkness in America, and the faces of the sleepers in ten thousand little towns; and of the tides of sleep and how the rivers flowed forever in the darkness. I wrote about the hissing glut of tides upon ten thousand miles of coast; of how the moonlight blazed down on the wilderness and filled the cat's cold eye with blazing yellow. I wrote about death and sleep, and of that enfabled rock of life we call the city. I wrote about October, of great trains that thundered through the night, of ships and stations in the morning; of men in harbors and the traffic of the ships.

I spent the winter of that year in England from October until March, and here perhaps because of the homely familiarity of the English life, the sense of order and repose which such a life can give one, my work moved forward still another step from this flood tide chaos of creation. For the first time the work began to take on the lineaments of design. These lineaments were still confused and bro-ken, sometimes utterly lost, but now I really did get the sense at last that I was working on a great block of marble, shaping a figure which no one but its maker could as yet define, but which was emerging more and more into the sinewy lines of composition.

From the beginning—and this was one fact that in all my times of hopelessness returned to fortify my faith in my conviction—the idea, the central legend that I wished my book to express had not changed. And this central idea was this: the deepest search in life, it seemed to me, the thing that in one way or another was central to all living was man's search to find a father, not merely the father of his flesh, not merely the lost father of his youth, but the image of a strength and wisdom external to his need and superior to his hunger, to which the belief and power of his own life could be united.

Yet I was terribly far away from the actual accomplishment of a book—how far away I could not at that time foresee. But four more years would have to pass before the first of a series of books on which I was now embarked would be ready for the press, and if I could have known that in those next four years there would be packed a hundred lives of birth and death, despair, defeat, and triumph and the sheer exhaustion of a brute fatigue, I do not know whether or not I could have found the power within myself to continue. But I was still sustained by the exuberant optimism of youth. My tem-perament, which is pessimistic about many things, has always been a curiously sanguine one concerning time, and although more than a year had now gone by and I had done no more than write great chants on death and sleep, prepare countless notes and trace here and there the first dim outlines of a formal pattern, I was confident that by the spring or the fall of the next year my book would somehow miraculously be ready.

So far as I can describe with any accuracy, the progress of that winter's work in England was not along the lines of planned design, but along this line that I have mentioned—writing some of the sections which I knew would have to be in the book. Meanwhile what was really going on in my whole creative consciousness, during all this time, although I did not realize it at the moment, was this: What I was really doing, what I had been doing all the time since my discovery of my America in Paris the summer before, was to explore day by day and month by month with a fanatical intensity, the whole material domain of my resources as a man and as a writer. This exploration went on for a period which I can estimate conservatively as two years and a half. It is still going on, although not with the same all-absorbing concentration, because the work it led to, the work that after infinite waste and labor it helped me wonderfully to define, that work has reached such a state of final definition that the immediate task of finishing it is the one that now occupies the energy and interest of my life.

In a way, during that period of my life, I think I was like the

Ancient Mariner who told the Wedding Guest that his frame was wrenched by the woeful agony which forced him to begin his tale before it left him free. In my own experience, my wedding guests were the great ledgers in which I wrote, and the tale which I told to them would have seemed, I am afraid, completely incoherent, as meaningless as Chinese characters, had any reader seen them. I could by no means hope to give a comprehensive idea of the whole extent of this labor because three years of work and perhaps a million and a half words went into these books. It included everything from gigantic and staggering lists of the towns, cities, counties, states, and countries I had been in, to minutely thorough, desperately evocative descriptions of the undercarriage, the springs, wheels, flanges, axle rods, color, weight, and quality of the day coach of an American railway train. There were lists of the rooms and houses in which I had lived or in which I had slept for at least a night, together with the most accurate and evocative descriptions of those rooms that I could write—their size, their shape, the color and design of the wallpaper, the way a towel hung down, the way a chair creaked, a streak of water rust upon the ceiling. There were countless charts, catalogues, descriptions that I can only classify here under the general heading of Amount and Number. What were the total combined populations of all the countries in Europe and America? In how many of those countries had I had some personal and vital experience? In the course of my twenty-nine or thirty years of living, how many people had I seen? How many had I passed by on the streets? How many had I seen on trains and subways, in theatres, at baseball or football games? With how many had I actually had some vital and illuminating experience, whether of joy, pain, anger, pity, love, or simple casual companionship, however brief?

In addition, one might come upon other sections under some such cryptic heading as "Where now?" Under such a heading as this, there would be brief notations of those thousands of things which all of us have seen for just a flash, a moment in our lives, which seem to be of no consequence whatever at the moment that we see them, and which live in our minds and hearts forever, which are somehow pregnant with all the joy and sorrow of the human destiny, and which we know, somehow, are therefore more important than many things of more apparent consequence. "Where now?" Some quiet steps that came and passed along a leafy night-time street in summer in a little town down South long years ago; a woman's voice, her sudden burst of low and tender laughter; then the voices and the footsteps going, silence, the leafy rustle of the trees....Where now—in these great ledger books, month after month, I wrote such things as this, not only the concrete, material record of man's ordered memory, but all the things he scarcely dares to think he has remembered; all the flicks and darts and haunting lights that flash across the mind of man that will return unbidden at an unexpected moment: a voice once heard; a face that vanished; the way the sunlight came and went; the rustling of a leaf upon a bough; a stone, a leaf, a door.

It may be objected, it has been objected already by certain critics, that in such research as I have here attempted to describe there is a quality of intemperate excess, an almost insane hunger to devour the entire body of human experience, to attempt to include more, experience more, than the measure of one life can hold, or than the limits of a single work of art can well define. I readily admit the validity of this criticism. I think I realize as well as any one the fatal dangers that are consequent to such a ravenous desire, the damage it may wreak upon one's life and on one's work. But having had this thing within me, it was in no way possible for me to reason it out of me, no matter how cogently my reason worked against it. The only way I could meet it was to meet it squarely, not with reason but with life.

It was part of my life; for many years it was my life; and the only way I could get it out of me was to live it out of me. And that is what I did. I have not wholly succeeded in that purpose yet, but I have succeeded better than I at one time dared to hope. And now I really believe that so far as the artist is concerned, the unlimited extent of human experience is not so important for him as the depth and intensity with which he experiences things. I also know now that it is a great deal more important to have known one hundred living men and women in New York, to have understood their lives, to have got, somehow, at the root and source from which their natures came than to have seen or passed or talked with 7,000,000 people upon the city streets. And what finally I should most like to say about this research which I have attempted to describe is this: That foolish and mistaken as much of it may seem, the total quality, end, and impact of that whole experience was not useless or excessive. And from my own point of view, at least, it is in its whole implication the one thing I may have to tell about my experience as a writer which may be of some concrete value to other people. I consider this experience on the whole the most valuable and practical in my whole writing life thus far. With all the waste and error and confusion it led me into, it brought me closer to a concrete definition of my resources, a true estimate of my talents at this period of my life, and, most of all, toward a rudimentary, a just-beginning, but a living apprehension of the articulation I am looking for, the language I have got to have if, as an artist, my life is to proceed and grow, than any other thing that has ever happened to me.

I know the door is not yet open. I know the tongue, the speech, the language that I seek is not yet found, but I believe with all my heart that I have found the way, have made a channel, am started on my first beginning. And I believe with all my heart, also, that each man for himself and in his own way, each man who ever hopes to make a living thing out of the substances of his one life, must find that way, that language, and that door—must find it for himself as I have tried to do.

When I returned to America in the spring of 1931, although I had three or four hundred thousand words of material, I had nothing that could be published as a novel....

The spring passed into the summer; the summer, into autumn. I was working hard, day after day, and still nothing that had the unity and design of a single work appeared. October came and with it a second full year since the publication of my first book. And now, for the first time, I was irrevocably committed so far as the publication of my book was concerned. I began to feel the sensation of pressure, and of naked desperation, which was to become almost maddeningly intolerable in the next three years. For the first time I began to realize that my project was much larger than I thought it would be. I had still believed at the time of my return from Europe that I was writing a single book, which would be comprised within the limits of about 200,000 words. Now as scene followed scene, as character after character came into being, as my understanding of my material became more comprehensive, I discovered that it would be impossible to write the book I had planned within the limits I had thought would be sufficient.

All of this time I was being baffled by a certain time element in the book, by a time relation which could not be escaped, and for which I was now desperately seeking some structural channel. There were three time elements inherent in the material. The first and most obvious was an element of actual present time, an element which carried the narrative forward, which represented characters and events as living in the present and moving forward into an immediate future. The second time element was of past time, one which represented these same characters as acting and as being acted upon by all the accumulated impact of man's experience so that each moment of their lives was conditioned not only by what they experienced in that moment, but by all that they had experienced up to that moment. In addition to these two time elements, there was a third which I conceived as being time immutable, the time of rivers, mountains, oceans, and the earth; a kind of eternal and unchanging universe of time against which would be projected the transience of man's life, the bitter briefness of his day. It was the tremendous problem of these three time elements that almost defeated me and that cost me countless hours of anguish in the years that were to follow.

As I began to realize the true nature of the task I had set for myself, the image of the river began to haunt my mind. I actually felt that I had a great river thrusting for release inside of me and that I had to find a channel into which its flood-like power could pour. I knew I had to find it or I would be destroyed in the flood of my own creation, and I am sure that every artist who ever lived has had the same experience.

Meanwhile, I was being baffled by a fixed and impossible idea whose error at the time I did not fully apprehend. I was convinced at that time that this whole gigantic plan had to be realized within the limits of a single book which would be called "The October Fair." It was not until more than a year had passed, when I realized finally that what I had to deal with was material which covered almost 150 years in history, demanded the action of more than 2000 characters, and would in its final design include almost every racial type and social class of American life, that I realized that even the pages of a book of 200,000 words were wholly inadequate for the purpose.

How did I finally arrive at this conclusion? I think it is not too much to say that I simply wrote myself into it. During all that year, I was writing furiously, feeling now the full pressure of inexorable time, the need to finish something. I wrote like mad; I finished scene after scene, chapter after chapter. The characters began to come to life, to grow and multiply until they were numbered by the hundreds, but so huge was the extent of my design, as I now desperately realized, that I can liken these chapters only to a row of lights which one sometimes sees at night from the windows of a speeding train, strung out across the dark and lonely countryside.

I would work furiously day after day until my creative energies were utterly exhausted, and although at the end of such a period I would have written perhaps as much as 200,000 words, enough in itself to make a very long book, I would realize with a feeling of horrible despair that what I had completed was only one small section of a single book.

During this time I reached that state of naked need and utter isolation which every artist has got to meet and conquer if he is to survive at all. Before this I had been sustained by that delightful illusion of success which we all have when we dream about the books we are going to write instead of actually doing them. Now I was face to face with it, and suddenly I realized that I had committed my life and my integrity so irrevocably to this struggle that I must conquer now or be destroyed. I was alone with my own work, and now I knew that I had to be alone with it, that no one could help me with it now no matter how any one might wish to help. For the first time I realized another naked fact which every artist must know, and that is that in a man's work there are contained not only the seeds of life, but the seeds of death, and that that power of creation which sustains us will also destroy us like a leprosy if we let it rot stillborn in our vitals. I had to get it out of me somehow. I saw that now. And now for the first time a terrible doubt began to creep into my mind that I might not live long enough to get it out of me, that I had created a labor so large and so impossible that the energy of a dozen lifetimes would not suffice for its accomplishment.

During this time, however, I was sustained by one piece of inestimable good fortune. I had for a friend a man of immense and patient wisdom and a gentle but unyielding fortitude. I think that if I was not destroyed at this time by the sense of hopelessness which these gigantic labors had awakened in me, it was largely because of the courage and patience of this man. I did not give in because he would not let me give in, and I think it is also true that at this particular time he had the advantage of being in the position of a skilled observer at a battle. I was myself engaged in that battle, covered by its dust and sweat and exhausted by its struggle, and I understood far less clearly than my friend the nature and the progress of the struggle in which I was engaged. At this time there was little that this man could do except observe, and in one way or another keep me at my task, and in many quiet and marvelous ways he succeeded in doing this.

I was now at the place where I must produce, and even the greatest editor can do little for a writer until he has brought from the secret darkness of his own spirit into the common light of day the completed concrete accomplishment of his imagining. My friend, the editor, has likened his own function at this painful time to that of a man who is trying to hang on to the fin of a plunging whale, but hang on he did, and it is to his tenacity that I owe my final release.

Meanwhile, my creative power was functioning at the highest intensity it had ever known. I wrote at times without belief that I would ever finish, with nothing in me but black despair, and yet I wrote and wrote and could not give up writing. And it seemed that despair itself was the very goad that urged me on, that made me write even when I had no belief that I would ever finish. It seemed to me that my life in Brooklyn, although I had been there only two and a half years, went back through centuries of time, through ocean depths of black and bottomless experience which no ordinary scale of hours would ever measure. People have sometimes asked me what happened to my life during these years. They have asked me how I ever found time to know anything that was going on in the world about me when my life was so completely absorbed by this world of writing. Well, it may seem to be an extraordinary fact, but the truth is that never in my whole life have I lived so fully, have I shared so richly in the common life of man as I did during these three years when I was struggling with the giant problem of my own work.

For one thing, my whole sensory and creative equipment, my powers of feeling and reflection—even the sense of hearing, and above all, my powers of memory, had reached the greatest degree of sharpness that they had ever known. At the end of the day of savage labor, my mind was still blazing with its effort, could by no opiate of reading, poetry, music, alcohol, or any other pleasure, be put at rest. I was unable to sleep, unable to subdue the tumult of these creative energies, and as a result of this condition, for three years I prowled the streets, explored the swarming web of the million-footed city and came to know it as I had never done before. It was a black time in the history of the nation, a black time in my own life and, I suppose, it is but natural that my own memory of it now should be a pretty grim and painful one.

Everywhere around me, during these years, I saw the evidence of an incalculable ruin and suffering....

And from it all, there has come as the final deposit, a burning memory, a certain evidence of the fortitude of man, his ability to suffer and somehow to survive. And it is for this reason now that I think I shall always remember this black period with a kind of joy that I could not at that time have believed possible, for it was during this time that I lived my life through to a first completion, and through the suffering and labor of my own life came to share those qualities in the lives of people all around me. And that is another thing which the making of a book has done for me. It has given my life that kind of growth which I think the fulfillment of each work does give the artist's life, and insofar as I have known these things, I think that they have added to my stature.

The early winter of 1933 arrived and with it, it seemed to me, the final doom of an abysmal failure. I still wrote and wrote, but blindly, hopelessly, like an old horse who trots around in the unending circle of a treadmill and knows no other end nor purpose for his life than this. If I slept at night, it was to sleep an unceasing nightmare of blazing visions that swept across my fevered and unresting mind. And when I woke, it was to wake exhausted, not knowing anything but work, lashing myself on into a hopeless labor, and so furiously at it through the day; and then night again, a frenzied prowling of a thousand streets, and so to bed and sleepless sleep again, the nightmare pageantry to which my consciousness lay chained a spectator....

Such was the state my life had come to in the early winter of 1933, and even at that moment, although I could not see it, the end of my huge labor was in sight. In the middle of December of that year the editor, of whom I have spoken, and who, during all this tormented period, had kept a quiet watch upon me, called me to his home and calmly informed me that my book was finished. I could only look at him with stunned surprise, and finally I only could tell him out of the depth of my own hopelessness, that he was mistaken, that the book was not finished, that it could never be completed, that I could write no more. He answered with the same quiet finality that the book was finished whether I knew it or not, and then he told me to go to my room and spend the next week in collecting in its proper order the manuscript which had accumulated during the last two years.

I followed his instructions, still without hope and without belief. I worked for six days sitting in the middle of the floor surrounded by mountainous stacks of typed manuscript on every side. At the end of a week I had the first part of it together, and just two days before Christmas, 1933, I delivered to him the manuscript of "The October Fair," and a few days later, the manuscript of "The Hills Beyond Pentland." The manuscript of "The Fair" was, at that time, something over 1,000,000 words in length. He had seen most of it in its dismembered fragments during the three preceding years, but now, for the first time, he was seeing it in its sequential order, and once again his intuition was right; he had told me the truth when he said that I had finished the book.

It was not finished in any way that was publishable or readable. It was really not a book so much as it was the skeleton of a book, but for the first time in four years the skeleton was all there. An enormous labor of revision, weaving together, shaping, and, above all, cutting remained, but I had the book now so that nothing, not even the despair of my own spirit, could take it from me. He told me so, and suddenly I saw that he was right.

I was like a man who is drowning and who suddenly, at the last gasp of his dying effort, feels earth beneath his feet again. My spirit was borne upward by the greatest triumph it had ever known, and although my mind was tired, my body exhausted, from that moment on I felt equal to anything on earth.

It was evident that many problems were before us, but now we had the thing, and we welcomed the labor before us with happy confidence. In the first place there was the problem of the book's gigantic length. Even in this skeletonized form the manuscript of "The October Fair" was about twelve times the length of the average novel or twice the length of *War and Peace.* It was manifest, therefore, that it would not only be utterly impossible to publish such a manuscript in a single volume, but that even if it were published in several volumes, the tremendous length of such a manuscript would practically annihilate its chances of ever finding a public which would read it.

This problem now faced us, and the editor grappled with it immediately. As his examination of the manuscript of "The October Fair" proceeded, he found that the book did describe two complete and separate cycles. The first of these was a movement which described the period of wandering and hunger in a man's youth. The second cycle described the period of greater certitude, and was dominated by the unity of a single passion. It was obvious, therefore, that what we had in the two cyclic movements of this book was really the material of two completely different chronicles, and although the second of the two was by far the more finished, the first cycle, of course, was the one which logically we ought to complete and publish first, and we decided on this course.

We took the first part first. I immediately prepared a minutely thorough synopsis which described not only the course of the book from first to last, but which also included an analysis of those chapters which had been completed in their entirety, of those which were completed only in part, and of those which had not been written at all, and with this synopsis before us, we set to work immediately to prepare the book for press. This work occupied me throughout the whole of the year 1934. The book was completed at the beginning of 1935, and was published in March of that year under the title of *Of Time and the River.*

In the first place, the manuscript, even in its unfinished form, called for the most radical cutting, and because of the way in which the book had been written, as well as the fatigue which I now felt, I was not well prepared to do by myself the task that lay ahead of us.

Cutting had always been the most difficult and distasteful part of writing to me; my tendency had always been to write rather than to cut. Moreover, whatever critical faculty I may have had concerning my own work had been seriously impaired, for the time being at least, by the frenzied labor of the past four years. When a man's work has poured from him for almost five years like burning lava from a volcano; when all of it, however superfluous, has been given fire and passion by the white heat of his own creative energy, it is very difficult suddenly to become coldly surgical, ruthlessly detached....

My spirit quivered at the bloody execution. My soul recoiled before the carnage of so many lovely things cut out upon which my heart was set. But it had to be done, and we did it....

Meanwhile I was proceeding at full speed with the work of completing my design, finishing the unfinished parts and filling in the transition links which were essential.

This in itself was an enormous job and kept me writing all day long as hard as I could go for a full year. Here again the nature of my chief fault was manifest. I wrote too much again. I not only wrote what was essential, but time and time again my enthusiasm for a good scene, one of those enchanting vistas which can open up so magically to a man in the full flow of his creation, would overpower me, and I would write thousands of words upon a scene which contributed nothing of vital importance to a book whose greatest need already was ruthless condensation.

During the course of this year, I must have written well over a half million words of additional manuscript, of which, of course, only a small part was finally used.

The nature of my method, the desire fully to explore my material, had led me into another error. The whole effect of those five years of incessant writing had been to make me feel not only that everything had to be used, but that everything had to be told, that nothing could be implied. Therefore, at the end, there were at least a dozen additional chapters which I felt had to be completed to give the book its final value. A thousand times I debated this question desperately with my editor. I told him that these chapters had to go in simply because I felt the book would not be complete without them, and with every argument he had, he tried to show me that I was wrong. I see now that on the whole he was right about it, but at the time I was so inextricably involved in my work, that I did not have the detachment necessary for a true appraisal.

The end came suddenly—the end of those five years of torment and incessant productivity. In October I took a trip to Chicago, a two weeks' vacation, my first in over a year. When I returned I found that my editor had quietly and decisively sent the manuscript to the press, the printers were already at work on it, the proof was beginning to come in. I had not foreseen it; I was desperate, bewildered. "You can't do it," I told him, "the book is not yet finished. I must have six months more on it."

To this he answered that the book was not only finished, but that if I took six months more on it, I would then demand another six months and six months more beyond that, and that I might very well become so obsessed with this one work that I would never get it published. He went on to say, and I think with complete justice, that such a course was wrong for me. I was not, he said, a Flaubert kind of writer. I was not a perfectionist. I had twenty, thirty, almost any number of books in me, and the important thing was to get them produced and not to spend the rest of my life in perfecting one book. He agreed that with six months' additional work upon the book, I might achieve a certain finish and completeness, but he did not think that the benefit would be nearly as great as I thought it would be, and his own deep conviction was that the book should be published at once without further delay, that I should get it out of me, forget about it, turn my life to the final completion of the work which was already prepared and ready, waiting for me. He told me, furthermore, exactly what the nature of the criticism would be, the criticism of its length, its adjectives, its overabundance, but he told me not to despair.

He told me finally that I would go on and do better work, that I would learn to work without so much confusion, waste, and useless torment, that my future books would more and more achieve the unity, sureness, and finality that every artist wants his work to have, but that I had to learn in the way I had learned, groping, struggling, finding my own way for myself, that this was the only way to learn....

The life of the artist at any epoch of man's history has not been an easy one. And here in America, it has often seemed to me, it may well be the hardest life that man has ever known. I am not speaking of some frustration in our native life, some barrenness of spirit, some arid Philistinism which contends against the artist's life and which prevents his growth. I do not speak of these things because I do not put the same belief in them that I once did. I am speaking as I have tried to speak from first to last in the concrete terms of the artist's actual experience, of the nature of the physical task before him. It seems to me that the task is one whose physical proportions are vaster and more difficult here than in any other nation on the earth. It is not merely that in the cultures of Europe and of the Orient the American artist can find no antecedent scheme, no structural plan, no body of tradition that can give his own work the validity and truth that it must have. It is not merely that he must make somehow a new tradition for himself, derived from his own life and from the enormous space and energy of American life, the structure of his own design; it is not merely that he is confronted by these problems; it is even more than this, that the labor of a complete and whole articulation, the discovery of an entire universe and of a complete language, is the task that lies before him...

NOTES ON WRITING

Katherine Anne Porter

B erlin, December, 1931. From a letter to G.
...I can't tell you what gives true intensity, but I know it when I find it, even in my own work—there perhaps first of all. It is not a matter of how you feel, at any one moment, certainly not at the moment of writing. A calculated coldness is the best mood for that, most often. Feeling is more than mood, it is a whole way of being, it is the nature you are born with, you cannot invent it. The question is, how to convey a sense of whatever is *there,* as feeling, within you, to the reader; and that is a problem of technical expertness. I can't tell you how to go about getting this technique either, for that also is an internal matter, if it is to have any value beyond a kind of juggling or tight rope walking. You'll know it when you have it, and you will finally be able to depend upon it somewhat. But for myself, unless my material, my feelings and my problem in each new piece of work are not well ahead of my technical skill at that moment, I should distrust the whole thing. When virtuosity gets the upper hand of your theme, or is better than your idea, it is time to quit. Be bold, and try not to fall in love with your faults. Don't be so afraid of giving yourself away either, for if you write, you must. And if you

can't face that, better not write.

Paris, Fall 1936

Perhaps in time I shall learn to live more deeply and consistently in that undistracted center of being where the will does not intrude, and the sense of time passing is lost, or has no power over the imagination. Of the three dimensions of time, only the past is "real" in the absolute sense that it has occurred, the future is only a concept, and the present is that fateful split second in which all action takes place. One of the most disturbing habits of the human mind is its willful and destructive forgetting of whatever in its past does not flatter or confirm its present point of view. I must very often refer far back in time to seek the meaning or explanation of today's smallest event, and I have long since lost the power to be astonished at what I find there. This constant exercise of memory seems to be the chief occupation of my mind, and all my experience seems to be simply memory, with continuity, marginal notes, constant revision and comparison of one thing with another. Now and again thousands of memories converge, harmonize, arrange themselves around a central idea in a coherent form, and I write a story. I keep notes and journals only because I write a great deal, and the habit of writing helps me to arrange, annotate, stow away conveniently the references I may need later. Yet when I begin a story, I can never work in any of those promising paragraphs, those apt phrases, those small turns of anecdote I had believed would be so valuable. I must know a story "by heart" and I must write from memory. Certain writing friends whose judgments I admire, have told me I lack detail, exact observation of the physical world, my people hardly ever have features, or not enough—that they live in empty houses, etcetera. At one time, I was so impressed by this criticism, I used to sit on a camp stool before a landscape and note down literally every object, every color, form, stick and stone before my eyes. But when I remembered that landscape, it was quite simply not in those terms that I remembered it, and it was no good pretending I did, and no good attempting to describe it because it got in the way of what I was really trying to tell. I was brought up with horses, I have harnessed, saddled, driven and ridden many a horse, but to this day I do not know the names for the different parts of a harness. I have often thought I would learn them and write them down in a note book. But to what end? I have two large cabinets full of notes already.

From "Notes on Writing, from the Journal of Katherine Anne Porter," by Katherine Anne Porter in *New Directions* 1940, edited by James Laughlin. By permission of the author and the publishers: New Directions, 1940, Norfolk, Connecticut.

COMPOSITION OF THUS SPAKE ZARATHUSTRA

Friedrich Nietzsche

I would now like to tell you the history of my *Zarathustra*. Its fundamental conception, the idea of Eternal Recurrence, the highest formula of affirmation that can ever be attained, belongs to August, 1881. I made a hasty note of it on a sheet of paper, with the postscript: "Six thousand feet beyond man and time." That day I was walking through the woods beside Lake Silvaplana; I halted not far from Surlei, beside a huge, towering, pyramidal rock. It was there that the idea came to me. If I count back two months previous to this day, I can discover a warning sign in the form of an abrupt and profoundly decisive change in my tastes—more especially in music. Perhaps the whole of *Zarathustra* may be classified as music—I am sure that one of the conditions of its production was a renaissance in me of the art of hearing. In Recoaro, a little mountain watering-place near Vicenza, where I spent the spring of 1881, I, together with my friend and maestro, Peter Gast (another who had been reborn), discovered that the phoenix bird of music hovered over us, decked in more beautiful and brilliant plumage than it had ever before exhibited. If, therefore, I reckon from that day to the sudden birth of the book, amid the most unlikely circumstances, in February,

1883, its last part, from which I quoted a few lines in my preface, was finished exactly during the hallowed hour of Richard Wagner's death in Venice,--it would appear that the period of gestation was eighteen months. This period of exactly eighteen months might suggest, at least to Buddhists, that I am in reality a female elephant. The interval was devoted to the *Gaya Scienza,* which has a hundred indications of the approach of something unparalleled; its conclusion shows the beginning of *Zarathustra,* since it presents *Zarathustra's* fundamental thought in the last aphorism but one of the fourth book. To this interval also belongs that *Hymn to Life* (for a mixed choir and orchestra), the score of which was published in Leipzig two years ago by E. W. Fritsch. Perhaps it is no small indication of my spiritual state during this year, when the essentially yea-saying pathos, which I call the tragic pathos, filled my soul to the brim.

...During the following winter, I was living not far from Genoa on that pleasant peaceful Gulf of Rapallo, which cuts inland between Chiavari and Cape Porto Fino. I was not in the best of health; the winter was cold and exceptionally rainy; and my small *albergo* was so close to shore that the noise of a rough sea rendered sleep impossible. These circumstances were the very reverse of favorable; and yet, despite them, and as if in proof of my theory that everything decisive arises as the result of opposition, it was during this very winter and amid these unfavorable circumstances that my *Zarathustra* was born. In the morning I used to start out in a southerly direction on the glorious road to Zoagli, which rises up through a forest of pines and gives one a view far out to sea. In the afternoon, whenever my health permitted, I would walk around the whole bay from Santa Margherita to beyond Porto Fino. This spot and the country around it is the more firmly enshrined in my affections because it was so dearly loved by the Emperor Frederick III. In the fall of 1886 I happened to be there again when he was revisiting this small forgotten world of happiness for the last time. It was on these two roads that all Zarathustra, and particularly Zarathustra himself as a type, came to me—perhaps I should rather say—*invaded me....*

Can any one at the end of this nineteenth century possibly have any distinct notion of what poets of a more vigorous period meant by inspiration? If not, I should like to describe it. Provided one has the slightest remnant of superstition left, one can hardly reject completely the idea that one is the mere incarnation, or mouthpiece, or medium of some almighty power. The notion of revelation describes the condition quite simply; by which I mean that something profoundly convulsive and disturbing suddenly becomes visible and audible with indescribable definiteness and exactness. One hears—one does not seek; one takes—one does not ask who gives : a thought flashes out like lighting, inevitably without hesitation—I have never had any choice about it. There is an ecstasy whose terrific tension is sometimes released by a flood of tears, during which one's progress varies from in voluntary impetuosity to involuntary slowness. There is the feeling that one is utterly out of hand, with the most distinct consciousness of an infinitude of shuddering thrills that pass through one from head to foot; —there is a profound happiness in which the most painful and gloomy feelings are not discordant in effect, but are required as necessary colors in this overflow of light. There is an instinct for rhythmic relations which embraces an entire world of forms (length, the need for a widely extended rhythm, is almost a measure of the force of inspiration, a sort of counterpart to its pressure and tension). Everything occurs quite without volition, as if in an eruption of freedom, independence, power and divinity. The spontaneity of the images and similes is most remarkable; one loses all perception of what is imagery and simile; everything. offers itself as the most immediate, exact, and simple means of expression. If I may recall a phrase of Zarathustra's, it actually seems as if the things themselves came to one, and offered themselves as similes. ("Here do all things come caressingly to thy discourse and flatter thee, for they would fain ride upon thy back. On every simile thou ridest here to every truth. Here fly open before thee all the speech and word shrines of existence, here all existence would become speech, here all Becoming would learn of thee how to speak.") This is *my* experience of inspiration. I have no doubt that I should have to go back millenniums to find another who could say to me: "It is mine also!"

For a few weeks afterwards I lay ill in Genoa. Then followed a depressing spring in Rome, where I escaped with my life. It was not a pleasant experience. This city, which I did not choose myself and which is of all places the most unsuited to the author of *Zarathustra,* weighed heavily upon my spirit.... About this time I was continually obsessed by a melody of ineffable sadness, whose refrain I recognized in the words, "dead through immortality." ...In the summer, on my return to the sacred spot where the first thought of *Zarathustra* had flashed like lightning across my mind, I conceived the second part. Ten days sufficed. Neither for the second, the first, nor the third part, have I required a day longer. The following winter, beneath the halcyon sky of Nice, which then for the first time filled me with its brilliant light, I found the third *Zarathustra*—and so completed the work. The whole composition had taken scarcely a year. Many hidden corners and heights in the country round Nice are hallowed for me by unforgettable moments. That decisive section, "Old and New Tables," was composed during the arduous ascent from the station to Eza, that wonderful Moorish eyrie. When my creative energy flowed most freely, my muscular activity was always greatest. The body is inspired: let us leave the "soul" out of consideration. I might often have been seen dancing; I used to walk through the hills for seven or eight hours on end without a hint of fatigue. I slept well, laughed a good deal—I was perfectly vigorous and patient.

Translated by Clifton P. Fadiman

From *Ecce Homo,* by Friedrich Nietzsche, translated by Clifton P. Fadiman. By permission of the publishers: Random House, Inc., New York City.

SUBCONSCIOUS INTELLIGENCE
UNDERLYING DREAMS

Morton Prince

In dreams, then, or, as we should strictly limit ourselves for the present to saying, in certain dreams, there are, as Freud first showed, two processes; one is the conscious dream, the other is a subconscious process which is the actuated residuum of a previous experience and determines the dream. It would be going beyond the scope of our subject to enter into a full exposition of this interpretation at this time and I must refer you for a discussion of the dream problem to works devoted to the subject.

We have not, of course, touched the further problem of the How: how a subconscious intelligence induces a conscious dream which is not an emergence of the elements of that intelligence into self-consciousness, but a symbolization of them. This is a problem which still awaits solution.

From certain data at hand it seems likely that so far as concerns the hallucinatory perceptual elements of a dream they can be accounted for as the emergence of the secondary images pertaining to the subconscious "ideas."

The following observation is an example of subconscious versification and also of constructive imagination. It also, I think, gives an insight into the character and content of the underlying process which constructs a dream. I give the observation in the subject's own words:

"I woke suddenly some time between three and four in the morning. I was perfectly wide awake and conscious of my surroundings but for a short time—perhaps two or three minutes—I could not move, and I saw this vision which I recognized as such.

"The end of my room seemed to have disappeared, and I looked out into boundless space. It looked misty but bright, as if the sun was shining behind a light fog. There were shifting wisps of fog blowing lightly about, and these wisps seemed to gather into the forms of a man and a woman. The figures were perfectly clear and life-like—I recognized them both. The man was dressed in dark everyday clothes, the woman in rather flowing black; her face was partly hidden on his breast; one arm was laid around his neck; both his arms were around her, and he was looking down at her, smiling very tenderly. They seemed to be surrounded by a sort of rosy atmosphere; a large, very bright star was above their heads—not in the heavens, but just over them; tall rose bushes heavy with red roses in full bloom grew up about them, and the falling petals were heaped up around their feet. Then the man bent his head and kissed her.

"The vision was extraordinarily clear and I thought I would write it down at once. I turned on the light by my bedside, took pencil and paper lying there and wrote, as I supposed, *practically what I have written here.* I then got up, was up some minutes, went back to bed, and after a while to sleep. The clock struck four soon after getting back into bed. I do not think I experienced any emotion at the moment of seeing the vision, but after writing it down I did.

"The next morning I picked up the paper to read over what I had written and was amazed at the language and the rhythm. This is what I had written:

" *'Last night I waked from sleep quite suddenly,*
    And though my brain was clear my limbs were tranced.
Beyond the walls of my familiar room
    I gazed outward into luminous space.
Before my staring eyes two forms took shape,
    Vague, shadowy, slowly gathering from the mists,
Until I saw before me, you—my Love!
    And folded to your breast in close embrace
Was she, that other, whom I may not name.
    A rosy light bathed you in waves of love;
Above your heads there shone a glowing star;
    Red roses shed their leaves about your feet.
And as I gazed with eyes that could not weep
    You bent your head and laid your lips on hers.
And my rent soul'...[Apparently unfinished.]

"The thoughts were the same as my conscious thoughts had been—the vision was well described—but the language was entirely different from anything I had thought, and the writing expressed the emotion which I had not consciously experienced in seeing the vision, but which (I have since learned) I had felt during the dream, and which I did consciously feel *after* writing. When I wrote I meant simply to state the facts of the vision."

The subject was unable to give any explanation of the vision or of the composition of the verse. She rarely remembers her dreams and had no memory of any dream the night of this vision. By hypnotic procedure, however, I was able to recover memories of a dream which occurred just before she woke up. It appeared that in the dream she was wandering in a great open space and saw this "picture in a thin mist. The mist seemed to blow apart" and disclosed the "picture" which was identical with the vision. At the climax of the dream picture the dreamer experienced an intense emotion well described in the verse by the unfinished phrase, "My rent soul..." The dreamer "shrieked, and fell on the ground on her face, and grew cold from head to foot and waked up."

The vision after waking, then, was a repetition of a preceding dream vision and we may safely assume that it was fabricated by the same underlying process which fabricated the *dream,* this process repeating itself after waking.

So far the phenomenon was one which is fairly common. Now

when we come to examine the automatically written script we find it has a number of significant characteristics. (1) It describes a conscious episode; (2) As a literary effort for one who is not a poetical writer it is fairly well written and probably quite as good verse as the subject can consciously write; (3) It expresses the mental attitude, sentiments and emotions experienced in the dream but not at the time of the vision. *These had also been antecedent experiences;* (4) Both the central ideas of the verse and the vision symbolically represented certain antecedent presentiments of the future; (5) The script gives of the vision an interpretation which was not consciously in mind at the moment of writing.

Now, inasmuch as these sentiments and interpretations were not in the conscious mind at the moment of writing, the script *suggests* that the process that wrote it was not simply a subconscious memory of the vision but the same process which fabricated the dream. Indeed, the phenomenon is open to the suspicion that this same process expresses the same ideas in verbal symbolism as a substitution for the hallucinatory symbolism. To determine this point, an effort was made to recover by technical methods memories of this process; that is to determine what wrote the verse and by what sort of a process. The following was brought out:

1. The script was written automatically. The subject thought she was writing certain words and expressing certain thoughts and did not perceive that she was writing different words. "Something

seemed to prevent her seeing the words she wrote." There were two trains of "thought."

2. The "thoughts" of the verse were in her "subconscious mind." These "thoughts" (also described as "words") were not logically arranged or as written in the verse, but "sort of tumbled together-mixed up a little." "They were not like the thoughts one thinks in *composing* a verse." There did not seem to be any attempt at selection from the thoughts or words. No evidence could be elicited to show that the composing was done here.

3. Concurrently with these subconscious, mixed-up thoughts coconscious "images" of the words of the verse came just at the moment of writing them down. The images were bright, printed words. Sometimes one or two words would come at a time and sometimes a whole line.

In other words all happened *as if* there was a deeper underlying process which did the composing and from this process certain thoughts without logical order emerged to form a subconscious stream and after the composing was done the words of the verse emerged as coconscious images as they were to be written. This underlying process, then, "automatically" did the writing and the composing. Hence it seemed to the subject even when remembering in hypnosis the subconscious thoughts and images that both were done unconsciously.

As to whether this underlying process was the same as that which fabricated the dream and the hallucination, the evidence, albeit circumstantial, would seem to render this almost certain. In the first place the verse was only a poetical arrangement of the subconscious thoughts disclosed; the vision was an obvious symbolic expression or visual representation of the same thoughts (that is, of course, of those concerned with the subject matter of the vision). The only difference would seem to be in the form of the expression-verbal and visual imagery respectively. In the second place the vision was an exact repetition of the dream vision. It is not at all rare to find certain phenomena of dreams (visual, motor, sensory, etc.) repeating themselves after waking. This can only be explained by the subconscious repetition of the dream process. Consequently we are compelled to infer the same subconscious process underlying the dream-vision. More than this, it was possible to trace these thoughts back to antecedent experiences of the dreamer, so that in the last analysis the dream-vision, waking-vision, and poetical expression of the vision could be related with almost certainty to the same antecedent experiences as the causal factors.

Certain conclusions then seem compulsory: underlying the dream, vision, and script was a subconscious process in which the fundamental factors were the same. As this process showed itself capable of poetical composition, constructive imagination, volition, memory, and affectivity it was *a subconscious intelligence.*

From "Subconscious Intelligence Underlying Dreams," by Morton Prince in *The Unconscious.* By permission of Morton P. Prince and the publishers: The Macmillan Company, 1915, New York City.

PSYCHOLOGY
AND LITERATURE

Carl Gustav Jung

I t is obvious enough that psychology, being the study of psychic processes, can be brought to bear upon the study of literature, for the human psyche is the womb of all the sciences and arts. We may expect psychological research, on the one hand, to explain the formation of a work of art, and on the other to reveal the factors that make a person artistically creative. The psychologist is thus faced with two separate and distinct tasks, and must approach them in radically different ways.

In the case of the work of art we have to deal with a product of complicated psychic activities—but a product that is apparently intentional and consciously shaped. In the case of the artist we must deal with the psychic apparatus itself. In the first instance we must attempt the psychological analysis of a definitely circumscribed and concrete artistic achievement, while in the second we must analyse the living and creative human being as a unique personality. Although these two undertakings are closely related and even interdependent, neither of them can yield the explanations that are sought by the other. It is of course possible to draw inferences about the artist from the work of art, and *vice versa,* but these inferences are never conclusive. At best they are probable surmises or lucky guesses. A knowledge of Goethe's particular relation to his mother throws some light upon Faust's exclamation: "The mothers—mothers—how very strange it sounds!" But it does not enable us to see how the attachment to his mother could produce the Faust drama itself, however unmistakably we sense in the man Goethe a deep connection between the two. Nor are we more successful in reasoning in the reverse direction. There is nothing in *The Nibelungenring* that would enable us to recognize or definitely infer the fact that Wagner occasionally liked to wear womanish clothes, though hidden connections exist between the heroic masculine world of the Nibelungs and a certain pathological effeminacy in the man Wagner.

The present state of development of psychology does not allow us to establish those rigorous causal connections which we expect of a science. It is only in the realm of the psycho-physiological instincts and reflexes that we can confidently operate with the idea of causality. From the point where psychic life begins—that is, at a, level of greater complexity—the psychologist must content himself with more or less widely ranging descriptions of happenings and with the vivid portrayal of the warp and weft of the mind in all its amazing intricacy. In doing this, he must refrain from designating any one psychic process, taken by itself, as "necessary." Were this not the state of affairs, and could the psychologist be relied upon to uncover the causal connections within a work of art and in the process of artistic creation, he would leave the study of art no ground to stand on and would reduce it to a special branch of his own science. The psychologist, to be sure, may never abandon his claim to investigate and establish causal relations in complicated psychic events. To do so would be to deny psychology the right to exist. Yet he can never make good this claim in the fullest sense, because the creative aspect of life which finds its clearest expression in art baffles all attempts at rational formulation. Any reaction to stimulus may be causally explained; but the creative act, which is the absolute antithesis of mere reaction, will for ever elude the human understanding. It can only be described in its manifestations; it can be obscurely sensed, but never wholly grasped. Psychology and the study of art will always have to turn to one another for help, and the one will not invalidate the other. It is an important principle of psychology that psychic events are derivable. It is a principle in the study of art that a psychic product is something in and for itself-whether the work of art or the artist himself is in question. Both principles are valid in spite of their relativity.

The Work of Art

There is a fundamental difference of approach between the psychologist's examination of a literary work, and that of the literary critic. What is of decisive importance and value for the latter may be quite irrelevant for the former. Literary products of highly dubious merit are often of the greatest interest to the psychologist. For instance, the so-called "psychological novel" is by no means as rewarding for the psychologist as the literary-minded suppose. Considered as a whole such a novel explains itself. It has done its own work of psychological interpretation, and the psychologist can at most criticize or enlarge upon this. The important question as to how a particular author came to write a particular novel is of course left unanswered, but I wish to reserve this general problem for the second part of my essay.

The novels which are most fruitful for the psychologist are those in which the author has not already given a psychological interpretation of his characters, and which therefore leave room for analysis and explanation, or even invite it by their mode of presentation. Good examples of this kind of writing are the novels of Benoit, and English fiction in the manner of Rider Haggard, including the vein exploited by Conan Doyle which yields that most cherished article of mass-production, the detective story. Melville's *Moby Dick,* which I consider the greatest American novel, also comes within this class of writings. An exciting narrative that is apparently quite devoid of psychological exposition is just what interests the psychologist most of all. Such a tale is built upon a groundwork of implicit psychological assumptions, and, in the measure that the author is unconscious of them, they reveal themselves, pure and unalloyed, to the critical discernment. In the psychological novel, on the other hand, the author himself attempts to reshape his material so as to raise it from the level of crude contingency to that of psychological exposition and illumination—a procedure which all too often clouds the psychological significance of the work or hides it from view. It is precisely to novels of this sort that the layman goes for "psychology"; while it is novels of the other kind that challenge the psychologist, for he alone can give them deeper meaning.

I have been speaking in terms of the novel, but I am dealing with a psychological fact which is not restricted to this particular form of literary art. We meet with it in the works of the poets as well, and are confronted with it when we compare the first and second parts of the *Faust* drama. The lovetragedy of Gretchen explains itself; there is nothing that the psychologist can add to it that the poet has not already said in better words. The second part, on the other hand, calls for explanation. The prodigious richness of the imaginative material has so overtaxed the poet's formative powers that nothing is self-explanatory and every verse adds to the reader's need of an interpretation. The two parts of *Faust* illustrate by way of extremes this psychological distinction between works of literature.

In order to emphasize the distinction, I will call the one mode of artistic creation *psychological,* and the other *visionary.* The psychological mode deals with materials drawn from the realm of human consciousness-for instance, with the lessons of life, with emotional shocks, the experience of passion and the crises of human destiny in general—all of which go to make up the conscious life of man, and his feeling life in particular. This material is psychically assimilated by the poet, raised from the commonplace to the level of poetic experience, and given an expression which forces the reader to greater clarity and depth of human insight by bringing fully into his consciousness what he ordinarily evades and overlooks or senses only with a feeling of dull discomfort. The poet's work is an interpretation and illumination of the contents of consciousness, of the ineluctable experiences of human life with its eternally recurrent sorrow and joy. He leaves nothing over for the psychologist, unless, indeed, we expect the latter to expound the reasons for which Faust falls in love with Gretchen, or which drive Gretchen to murder her child! Such themes go to make up the lot of humankind; they repeat themselves millions of times and are responsible for the monotony of the police-court and of the penal code. No obscurity whatever surrounds them, for they fully explain themselves.

Countless literary works belong to this class: the many novels dealing with love, the environment, the family, crime and society, as well as didactic poetry, the larger number of lyrics, and the drama, both tragic and comic. Whatever its particular form may be, the psychological work of art always takes its materials from the vast realm of conscious human experience from the vivid foreground of life, we might say. I have called this mode of artistic creation psychological because in its activity it nowhere transcends the bounds of psychological intelligibility. Everything that it embraces—the experience as well as its artistic expression—belongs to the realm of the understandable. Even the basic experiences themselves, though non-rational, have nothing strange about them; on the contrary, they are that which has been known from the beginning of time—passion and its fated outcome, man's subjection to the turns of destiny, eternal nature with its beauty and its horror.

The profound difference between the first and second parts of *Faust* marks the difference between the psychological and the visionary modes of artistic creation. The latter reverses all the conditions of the former. The experience that furnishes the material for artistic expression is no longer familiar. It is a strange something that derives its existence from the hinterland of man's mind—that suggests the abyss of time separating us from pre-human ages, or evokes a super-human world of contrasting light and darkness. It is a primordial experience which surpasses man's understanding, and to which he is therefore in danger of succumbing. The value and the force of the experience are given by its enormity. It arises from timeless depths; it is foreign and cold, many-sided, demonic and grotesque. A grimly ridiculous sample of the eternal chaos—*a crimen laesae majestatis humanae,* to use Nietzsche's words—it bursts asunder our human standards of value and of aesthetic form. The disturbing vision of monstrous and meaningless happenings that in every way exceed the grasp of human feeling and comprehension makes quite other demands upon the powers of the artist than do the experiences of the foreground of life. These never rend the curtain that veils the cosmos; they never transcend the bounds of the humanly possible, and for this reason are readily shaped to the demands of art, no matter how great a shock to the individual they may be. But the primordial experiences rend from top to bottom the curtain upon which is painted the picture of an ordered world, and allow a glimpse into the unfathomed abyss of what has not yet become. Is it a vision of other worlds, or of the obscuration of the spirit, or of the beginning of things before the age of man, or of the unborn generations of the future? We cannot say that it is any or none of these.

> *Shaping—re-shaping—*
> *The eternal spirit's eternal pastime.*

We find such vision in *The Shepherd of Hermas,* in Dante, in the second part of *Faust,* in Nietzsche's Dionysian exuberance, in Wagner's *Nibelungenring,* in Spitteler's *Olympischer Fruhling,* in the poetry of William Blake, in the *Ipnerotomachia* of the monk Francesco Colonna, and in Jacob Boehme's philosophic and poetic stammerings. In a more restricted and specific way, the primordial experience furnishes material for Rider Haggard in the fiction-cycle that turns upon *She,* and it does the same for Benoit, chiefly in *L'Atlantide,* for Kubin in Die andere Seite, for Meyrink in Das grune Gesich—a book whose importance we should not undervalue—for Goetz in

Das Reich ohne Raum, and for Barlach in *Der tote Tag.* This list might be greatly extended.

In dealing with the psychological mode of artistic creation, we never need ask ourselves what the material consists of or what it means. But this question forces itself upon us as soon as we come to the visionary mode of creation. We are astonished, taken aback, confused, put on our guard or even disgusted—and we demand commentaries and explanations. We are reminded in nothing of everyday, human life, but rather of dreams, nighttime fears and the dark recesses of the mind that we sometimes sense with misgiving. The reading public for the most part repudiates this kind of writing—unless, indeed, it is coarsely sensational—and even the literary critic feels embarrassed by it. It is true that Dante and Wagner have smoothed the approach to it. The visionary experience is cloaked, in Dante's case, by the introduction of historical facts, and, in that of Wagner, by mythological events—so that history and mythology are sometimes taken to be the materials with which these poets worked. But with neither of them does the moving force and the deeper significance lie there. For both it is contained in the visionary experience. Rider Haggard, pardonably enough, is generally held to be a mere inventor of fiction. Yet even with him the story is primarily a means of giving expression to significant material. However much the tale may seem to overgrow the content, the latter outweighs the former in importance.

The obscurity as to the sources of the material in visionary creation is very strange, and the exact opposite of what we find in the psychological mode of creation. We are even led to suspect that this obscurity is not unintentional. We are naturally inclined to suppose—and Freudian psychology encourages us to do so—that some highly personal experience underlies this grotesque darkness. We hope thus to explain these strange glimpses of chaos and to understand why it sometimes seems as though the poet had intentionally concealed his basic experience from us. It is only a step from this way of looking at the matter to the statement that we are here dealing with a pathological and neurotic art—a step which is justified in so far as the material of the visionary creator shows certain traits that we find in the fantasies of the insane. The converse also is true; we often discover in the mental output of psychotic persons a wealth of meaning that we should expect rather from the works of a genius. The psychologist who follows Freud will of course be inclined to take the writings in question as a problem in pathology. On the assumption that an intimate, personal experience underlies what I call the "primordial vision"—an experience, that is to say, which cannot be accepted by the conscious outlook—he will try to account for the curious images of the vision by calling them cover-figures and by supposing that they represent an attempted concealment of the basic experience. This, according to his view, might be an experience in love which is morally or aesthetically incompatible with the personality as a whole or at least with certain fictions of the conscious mind. In order that the poet, through his ego, might repress this experience and make it unrecognizable (unconscious), the whole arsenal of a pathological fantasy was brought into action. Moreover, this attempt to replace reality by fiction, being unsatisfactory, must be repeated in a long series of creative embodiments. This would explain the proliferation of imaginative forms, all monstrous, demonic, grotesque and perverse. On the one hand they are substitutes for the unacceptable experience, and on the other they help to conceal it.

Although a discussion of the poet's personality and psychic disposition belongs strictly to the second part of my essay, I cannot avoid taking up in the present connection the Freudian view of the visionary work of art. For one thing, it has aroused considerable attention. And then it is the only well-known attempt that has been made to give a "scientific" explanation of the sources of the visionary material or to formulate a theory of the psychic processes that underlie this curious mode of artistic creation. I assume that my own view of the question is not well known or generally understood. With this preliminary remark, I will now try to present it briefly.

If we insist on deriving the vision from a personal experience, we must treat the former as something secondary—as a mere substitute for reality. The result is that we strip the vision of its primordial quality and take it as nothing but a symptom. The pregnant chaos then shrinks to the proportions of a psychic disturbance. With this account of the matter we feel reassured and turn again to our picture of a well-ordered cosmos. Since we are practical and reasonable, we do not expect the cosmos to be perfect; we accept these unavoidable imperfections which we call abnormalities and diseases, and we take it for granted that human nature is not exempt from them. The frightening revelation of abysses that defy the human understanding is dismissed as illusion, and the poet is regarded as a victim and perpetrator of deception. Even to the poet, his primordial experience was "human—all too human," to such a degree that he could not face its meaning but had to conceal it from himself.

We shall do well, I think, to make fully explicit all the implications of that way of accounting for artistic creation which consists in reducing it to personal factors. We should see clearly where it leads. The truth is that it takes us away from the psychological study of the work of art, and confronts us with the psychic disposition of the poet himself. That the latter presents an important problem is not to be denied, but the work of art is something in its own right, and may not be conjured away. The question of the significance to the poet of his own creative work—of his regarding it as a trifle, as a screen, as a source of suffering or as an achievement—does not concern us at the moment, our task being to interpret the work of art psychologically. For this undertaking it is essential that we give serious consideration to the basic experience that underlies it—namely, to the vision. We must take it at least as seriously as we do the experiences that underlie the psychological mode of artistic creation, and no one doubts that they are both real and serious. It looks, indeed, as if the visionary experience were something quite apart from the ordinary lot of man, and for this reason we have difficulty in believing that it is real. It has about it an unfortunate suggestion of obscure metaphysics and of occultism, so that we feel called upon to intervene in the name of a well-intentioned reasonableness. Our conclusion is that it would be better not to take such things too seriously, lest the world revert again to a benighted superstition. We may, of course, have a predilection for the occult; but ordinarily we dismiss the visionary experience as the outcome of a rich fantasy or of a poetic mood—that is to say, as a kind of poetic licence psychologically understood. Certain of the poets encourage this interpretation in order to put a wholesome distance between themselves and their work. Spitteler, for example, stoutly maintained that it was one and the same whether the poet sang of an Olympian spring or to the theme: "May is here!" The truth is that poets are human beings, and that what a poet has to say about his work is often far from being the most illuminating word on the subject. What is required of us, then, is nothing less than to defend the importance of the visionary experience against the poet himself.

It cannot be denied that we catch the reverberations of an initial love-experience in *The Shepherd of Hermas,* in the *Divine Comedy* and in the *Faust* drama—an experience which is completed and fulfilled by the vision. There is no ground for the assumption that the second part of *Faust* repudiates or conceals the normal, human experience of the first part, nor are we justified in supposing that Goethe was normal at the time when he wrote *Part I,* but in a neurotic state of mind when he composed *Part II. Hermas,* Dante and Goethe can be taken as three steps in a sequence covering nearly two thousand years of human development, and in each of them we find the personal love-episode not only connected with the weightier visionary experience, but frankly subordinated to it. On the strength of this evidence which is furnished by the work of art itself and which throws out of court the question of the poet's particular psychic disposition, we must admit that the vision represents a deeper and more impressive experience than human passion. In works of art of this nature—and we must never confuse them with the artist as a person—we cannot doubt that the vision is a genuine, primordial experience, regardless of what reason-mongers may say. The vision is not something derived or secondary, and it is not a symptom of something else. It is true symbolic expression-that is, the expression of something existent in its own right, but imperfectly known; The love-episode is a real experience really suffered, and the same statement applies to the vision. We need not try to determine whether the content of the vision is of a physical, psychic or metaphysical nature. In itself it has psychic reality, and this is no less real than physical reality. Human passion falls within the sphere of conscious experience, while the subject of the vision lies beyond it. Through our feelings we experience the known, but our intuitions point to things that are unknown and hidden—that by their very nature are secret. If ever they become conscious, they are intentionally kept back and concealed, for which reason they have been regarded from earliest times as mysterious, uncanny and deceptive. They are hidden from the scrutiny of man, and he also hides himself from them out of *deisidaemonia.* He protects himself with the shield of science and the armour of reason. His enlightenment is born of fear; in the day-time he believes in an ordered cosmos, and he tries to maintain this faith against the fear of chaos that besets him by night. What if there were some living force whose sphere of action lies beyond our world of every day? Are there human needs that are dangerous and unavoidable? Is there something more purposeful than electrons? Do we delude ourselves in thinking that we possess and command our own souls? And is that which science calls the "psyche" not merely a question-mark arbitrarily confined within the skull, but rather a door that opens upon the human world from a world beyond, now and again allowing strange and unseizable potencies to act upon man and to remove him, as if upon the wings of the night, from the level of common humanity to that of a more than personal vocation? When we consider the visionary mode of artistic creation, it even seems as if the love-episode had served as a mere release—as if the personal experience were nothing but the prelude to the all-important "divine comedy."

It is not alone the creator of this kind of art who is in touch with the night-side of life, but the seers, prophets, leaders and enlighteners also. However dark this nocturnal world may be, it is not wholly unfamiliar. Man has known of it from time immemorial—here, there, and everywhere; for primitive man today it is an unquestionable part of his picture of the cosmos. It is only we who have repudiated it because of our fear of superstition and metaphysics, and because we strive to construct a conscious world that is safe and manageable in that natural law holds in it the place of statute law in a commonwealth. Yet, even in our midst, the poet now and then catches sight of the figures that people the night-world-the spirits, demons and gods. He knows that a purposiveness out-reaching human ends is the life-giving secret for man; he has a presentiment of incomprehensible happenings in the pleroma. In short, he sees something of that psychic world that strikes terror into the savage and the barbarian.

From the very first beginnings of human society onward man's efforts to give his vague intimations a binding form have left their traces. Even in the Rhodesian cliff-drawings of the Old Stone Age there appears, side by side with the most amazingly lifelike representations of animals, an abstract pattern—a double cross contained in a circle. This design has turned up in every cultural region, more or less, and we find it today not only in Christian churches, but in Tibetan monasteries as well. It is the so-called sunwheel, and as it dates from a time when no one had thought of wheels as a mechanical device, it cannot have had its source in any experience of the external world.

It is rather a symbol that stands for a psychic happening; it covers an experience of the inner world, and is no doubt as lifelike a representation as the famous rhinoceros with the tick-birds on its back. There has never been a primitive culture that did not possess a system of secret teaching, and in many cultures this system is highly developed. The men's councils and the totem-clans preserve this teaching about hidden things that lie apart from man's daytime existence—things which, from primeval times, have always constituted his most vital experiences. Knowledge about them is handed on to younger men in the rites of initiation. The mysteries of the Graeco-Roman world performed the same office, and the rich mythology of antiquity is a relic of such experiences in the earliest stages of human development.

It is therefore to be expected of the poet that he will resort to mythology in order to give his experience its most fitting expression. It would be a serious mistake to suppose that he works with materials received at secondhand. The primordial experience is the source of his creativeness; it cannot be fathomed, and therefore requires mythological imagery to give it form. In itself it offers no words or images, for it is a vision seen "as in a glass, darkly." It is merely a deep presentiment that strives to find expression. It is like a whirlwind that seizes everything within reach and, by carrying it aloft, assumes a visible shape. Since the particular expression can never exhaust the possibilities of the vision, but falls far short of it in richness of content, the poet must have at his disposal a huge store of materials if he is to communicate even a few of his intimations. What is more, he must resort to an imagery that is difficult to handle and full of contradictions in order to express the weird paradoxicality of his vision. Dante's presentiments are clothed in images that run the gamut of Heaven and Hell; Goethe must bring in the Blocksberg and the infernal regions of Greek antiquity; Wagner needs the whole body of Nordic myth; Nietzsche returns to the hieratic style and recreates the legendary seer of prehistoric times; Blake invents for himself indescribable figures, and Spitteler borrows old names for new creatures of the imagination. And no intermediate step is missing in the whole range from the ineffably sublime to the perversely grotesque.

Psychology can do nothing towards the elucidation of this colourful imagery except bring together materials for comparison and offer a terminology for its discussion. According to this terminology, that which appears in the vision is the collective unconscious. We mean by collective unconscious, a certain psychic disposition shaped by the forces of heredity; from it consciousness has developed. In the physical structure of the body we find traces of earlier stages of evolution, and we may expect the human psyche also to conform in its make-up to the law of phylogeny. It is a fact that in eclipses of consciousness—in dreams, narcotic states and cases of insanity—there come to the surface psychic products or contents that show all the traits of primitive levels of psychic development. The images themselves are sometimes of such a primitive character that we might suppose them derived from ancient, esoteric teaching. Mythological themes clothed in modern dress also frequently appear. What is of particular importance for the study of literature in these manifestations of the collective unconscious is that they are compensatory to the conscious attitude. This is to say that they can bring a one-sided, abnormal, or dangerous state of consciousness into equilibrium in an apparently purposive way. In dreams we can see this process very clearly in its positive aspect. In cases of insanity the compensatory process is often perfectly obvious, but takes a negative form. There are persons, for instance, who have anxiously shut themselves off from all the world only to discover one day that their most intimate secrets are known and talked about by everyone.

If we consider Goethe's *Faust,* and leave aside the possibility that it is compensatory to his own conscious attitude, the question that we must answer is this: In what relation does it stand to the conscious outlook of his time? Great poetry draws its strength from the life of mankind, and we completely miss its meaning if we try to derive it from personal factors. Whenever the collective unconscious becomes a living experience and is brought to bear upon the conscious outlook of an age, this event is a creative act which is of importance to everyone living in that age. A work of art is produced that contains what may truthfully be called a message to generations of men. So *Faust* touches something in the soul of every German. So also Dante's fame is immortal, while *The Shepherd of Hermas* just failed of inclusion in the New Testament canon. Every period has its bias, its particular prejudice and its psychic ailment. An epoch is like an individual; it has its own limitations of conscious outlook, and therefore requires a compensatory adjustment. This is effected by the collective unconscious in that a poet, a seer or a leader allows himself to be guided by the unexpressed desire of his times and shows the way, by word or deed, to the attainment of that which everyone blindly craves and expects—whether this attainment results in good or evil, the healing of an epoch or its destruction.

It is always dangerous to speak of one's own times, because what is at stake in the present is too vast for comprehension. A few hints must therefore suffice. Francesco Colonna's book is cast in the form of a dream, and is the apotheosis of natural love taken as a human relation; without countenancing a wild indulgence of the senses, he leaves completely aside the Christian sacrament of marriage. The book was written in 1453. Rider Haggard, whose life coincides with the flowering-time of the Victorian era, takes up this subject and deals with it in his own way; he does not cast it in the form of a dream, but allows us to feel the tension of moral conflict. Goethe weaves the theme of Gretchen-Helen-Mater Gloriosa like a red thread into the colourful tapestry of Faust. Nietzsche proclaims the death of God, and Spitteler transforms the waxing and waning of the gods into a myth of the seasons. Whatever his importance, each of these poets speaks with the voice of thousands and ten thousands, foretelling changes in the conscious outlook of his time.

The Poet

Creativeness, like the freedom of the will, contains a secret. The psychologist can describe both these manifestations as processes, but he can find no solution of the philosophical problems they offer. Creative man is a riddle that we may try to answer in various ways, but always in vain, a truth that has not prevented modern psychology from turning now and again to the question of the artist and his art. Freud thought that he had found a key in his procedure of deriving the work of art from the personal experiences of the artist. It is true that certain possibilities lay in this direction, for it was conceivable that a work of art, no less than a neurosis, might be traced back to those knots in psychic life that we call the complexes. It was Freud's great discovery that neuroses have a causal origin in the psychic realm—that they take their rise from emotional states and from real or imagined childhood experiences. Certain of his followers, like Rank and Stekel, have taken up related lines of enquiry and have achieved important results. It is undeniable that the poet's psychic disposition permeates his work root and branch. Nor is there anything new in the statement that personal factors largely influence the poet's choice and use of his materials. Credit, however, must certainly be given to the Freudian school for showing how far-reaching this influence is and in what curious ways it comes to expression.

Freud takes the neurosis as a substitute for a direct means of gratification. He therefore regards it as something inappropriate—a mistake, a dodge, an excuse, a voluntary blindness. To him it is essentially a shortcoming that should never have been. Since a neurosis, to all appearances, is nothing but a disturbance that is all the more irritating because it is without sense or meaning, few people will venture to say a good word for it. And a work of art is brought into questionable proximity with the neurosis when it is taken as something which can be analysed in terms of the poet's repressions. In a sense it finds itself in good company, for religion and philosophy are regarded in the same light by Freudian psychology. No objection can be raised if it is admitted that this approach amounts to nothing more than the elucidation of those personal determinants without which a work of art is unthinkable. But should the claim be made that such an analysis accounts for the work of art itself, then a categorical denial is called for. The personal idiosyncrasies that creep into a work of art are not essential; in fact, the more we have to cope with these peculiarities, the less is it a question of art. What is essential in a work of art is that it should rise far above the realm of personal life and speak from the spirit and heart of the poet as man to the spirit and heart of mankind. The personal aspect is a limitation—and even a sin—in the realm of art. When a form of "art" is primarily personal it deserves to be treated as if it were a neurosis. There may be some validity in the idea held by the Freudian school that artists without exception are narcissistic—by which is meant that they are undeveloped persons with infantile and auto-erotic traits. The statement is only valid, however, for the artist as a person, and has nothing to do with the man as an artist. In his capacity of artist he is neither auto-erotic, nor hetero-erotic, nor erotic in any sense. He is objective and impersonal—even inhuman—for as an artist he is his work, and not a human being.

Every creative person is a duality or a synthesis of contradictory aptitudes. On the one side he is a human being with a personal life, while on the other side he is an impersonal, creative process. Since as a human being he may be sound or morbid, we must look at his psychic make-up to find the determinants of his personality. But we can only understand him in his capacity of artist by looking at his creative achievement. We should make a sad mistake if we tried to explain the mode of life of an English gentleman, a Prussian officer, or a cardinal in terms of personal factors. The gentleman, the officer and the cleric function as such in an impersonal role, and their psychic make-up is qualified by a peculiar objectivity. We must grant that the artist does not function in an official capacity—the very opposite is nearer the truth. He nevertheless resembles the types I have named in one respect, for the specifically artistic disposition involves an overweight of collective psychic life as against the personal. Art is a kind of innate drive that seizes a human being and makes him its instrument. The artist is not a person endowed with free will who seeks his own ends, but one who allows art to realize its purposes through him. As a human being he may have moods and a will and personal aims, but as an artist he is "man" in a higher sense—he is "collective man"—one who carries and shapes the unconscious, psychic life of mankind. To perform this difficult office it is sometimes necessary for him to sacrifice happiness and everything that makes life worth living for the ordinary human being.

All this being so, it is not strange that the artist is an especially interesting case for the psychologist who uses an analytical method. The artist's life cannot be otherwise than full of conflicts, for two forces are at war within him—on the one hand the common human longing for happiness, satisfaction and security in life, and on the other a ruthless passion for creation which may go so far as to override every personal desire. The lives of artists are as a rule so highly unsatisfactory—not to say tragic—because of their inferiority on the human and personal side, and not because of a sinister dispensation. There are hardly any exceptions to the rule that a person must pay dearly for the divine gift of the creative fire. It is as though each of us were endowed at birth with a certain capital *of* energy. The strongest force in our make-up will seize and all but monopolize this energy, leaving so little over that nothing of value can come of it. In this way the creative force can drain the human impulses to such a degree that the personal ego must develop all sorts of bad qualities—ruthlessness, selfishness and vanity (so-called "auto-erotism")—and even every kind of vice, in order to maintain the spark of life and to keep itself from being wholly bereft. The autoerotism of artists resembles that of illegitimate or neglected children who from their tenderest years must protect themselves from the destructive influence of people who have no love to give them—who develop bad qualities for that very purpose and later maintain an invincible egocentrism by remaining all their lives infantile and helpless or by actively offending against the moral code or the law. How can we doubt that it is his art that explains the artist, and not the insufficiencies and conflicts of his personal life? These are nothing but the regrettable results of the fact that he is an artist—that is to say, a man who from his very birth has been called to a greater task than the ordinary mortal. A special ability means a heavy expenditure of energy in a particular direction, with a consequent drain from some other side of life.

It makes no difference whether the poet knows that his work is begotten, grows and matures with him, or whether he supposes that by taking thought he produces it out of the void. His opinion of the matter does not change the fact that his own work outgrows him as a child its mother. The creative process has feminine quality, and the creative work arises from unconscious depths—we might say, from the realm of the mothers. Whenever the creative force predominates, human life is ruled and moulded by the unconscious as against the active will, and the conscious ego is swept along on a subterranean current, being nothing more than a helpless observer of events. The work in process becomes the poet's fate and determines his psychic development. It is not Goethe who creates *Faust,* but *Faust* which creates Goethe. And what is *Faust* but a symbol? By this I do not mean an allegory that points to something all too familiar, but an expression that stands for something not clearly known and yet profoundly alive. Here it is something that lives in the soul of every German, and that Goethe has helped to bring to birth. Could we conceive of anyone but a German writing *Faust or Also sprach Zarathustra?* Both play upon something that reverberates in the German soul—a "primordial image," as Jacob Burckhardt once called it—the figure of a physician or teacher of mankind. The archetypal image of the wise man, the saviour or redeemer, lies buried and dormant in man's unconscious since the dawn of culture; it is awakened whenever the times are out of joint and a human society is committed to a serious error. When people go astray they feel the need of a guide or teacher or even of the physician. These primordial images are numerous, but do not appear in the dreams of individuals or in works of art until they are called into being by the waywardness of the general outlook. When conscious life is characterized by one-sidedness and by a false attitude, then they are activated—one might say, "instinctively"—and come to light in the dreams of individuals and the visions of artists and seers, thus restoring the psychic equilibrium of the epoch.

In this way the work of the poet comes to meet the spiritual need of the society in which he lives, and for this reason his work means more to him than his personal fate, whether he is aware of this or not. Being essentially the instrument for his work, he is subordinate to it, and we have no reason for expecting him to interpret it for us. He has done the best that in him lies in giving it form, and he must leave the interpretation to others and to the future. A great work of art is like a dream; for all its apparent obviousness it does not explain itself and is never unequivocal. A dream never says: "You ought," or: "This is the truth." It presents an image in much the same way as nature allows a plant to grow, and we must draw our own conclusions. If a person has a nightmare, it means either that he is too much given to fear, or else that he is too exempt from it; and if he dreams of the old wise man it may mean that he is too pedagogical, as also that he stands in need of a teacher. In a subtle way both meanings come to the same thing, as we perceive when we are able to let the work of art act upon us as it acted upon the artist. To grasp its meaning, we must allow it to shape us as it once shaped him. Then we understand the nature of his experience. We see that he has drawn upon the healing and redeeming forces of the collective psyche that underlies consciousness with its isolation and its painful errors; that he has penetrated to that matrix of life in which all men are embedded, which imparts a common rhythm to all human existence, and allows the individual to communicate his feeling and his striving to mankind as a whole.

The secret of artistic creation and of the effectiveness of art is to be found in a return to the state of *participation mystique*—to that level of experience at which it is man who lives, and not the individual, and at which the weal or woe of the single human being does not count, but only human existence. This is why every great work of art is objective and impersonal, but none the less profoundly moves us each and all. And this is also why the personal life of the poet cannot be held essential to his art—but at most a help or a hindrance to his creative task. He may go the way of a Philistine, a good citizen, a neurotic, a fool or a criminal. His personal career may be inevitable and interesting, but it does not explain the poet.

Translated by W. S. Dell and Cary F. Baynes

From *Modern Man in Search of a Soul,* by Carl Gustav Jung. By permission of the publishers: Routledge and Kegan Paul Ltd., London, and Harcourt, Brace and Company, Inc., New York City.

CONVERSATION WITH GEORGE ELIOT

Herbert Spencer

Social Statics having, I presume, been referred to, she said that, considering how much thinking I must have done, she was surprised to see no lines on my forehead. "I suppose it is because I am never puzzled," I said. This called forth the exclamation—"O! that's the most arrogant thing I ever heard uttered." To which I rejoined—"Not at all, when you know what I mean." And I then proceeded to explain that my mode of thinking did not involve that concentrated effort which is commonly accompanied by wrinkling of the brows.

It has never been my way to set before myself a problem and puzzle out an answer. The conclusions at which I have from time to time arrived, have not been arrived at as solutions of questions raised; but have been arrived at unawares—each as the ultimate outcome of a body of thoughts which slowly grew from a germ. Some direct observation, or some fact met with in reading, would dwell with me: apparently because I had a sense of its significance. It was not that there arose a distinct consciousness of its general meaning; but rather that there was a kind of instinctive interest in those facts which have general meanings. For example, the detailed structure of this or that species of mammal, though I might willingly read about it, would leave little impression; but when I met with the statement that, almost without exception, mammals, even as unlike as the whale and the giraffe, have seven cervical vertebrae, this would strike me and be remembered as suggestive. Apt as I thus was to lay hold of cardinal truths, it would happen occasionally that one, most likely brought to mind by an illustration, and gaining from the illustration fresh distinctiveness, would be contemplated by me for a while, and its bearings observed. A week afterwards, possibly, the matter would be remembered; and with further thought about it, might occur a recognition of some wider application than I had before perceived: new instances being aggregated with those already noted. Again after an interval, perhaps of a month perhaps of half a year, something would remind me of that which I had before remarked; and mentally running over the facts might be followed by some further extension of the idea. When accumulation of instances had given body to a generalization, reflexion would reduce the vague conception at first framed to a more definite conception; and perhaps difficulties or anomalies passed over for a while, but eventually forcing themselves on attention, might cause a needful qualification and a truer shaping of the thought. Eventually the growing generalization, thus far inductive, might take a deductive form: being all at once recognized as a necessary consequence of some physical principle— some established law. And thus, little by little, in unobtrusive ways, without conscious intention or appreciable effort, there would grow up a coherent and organized theory. Habitually the process was one of slow unforced development, often extending over years; and it was, I believe, because the thinking done went on in this gradual, almost spontaneous, way, without strain, that there was an absence of those lines of thought which Miss Evans remarked—an absence almost as complete thirty years later, notwithstanding the amount of thinking done in the interval.

I name her remark, and give this explanation, partly to introduce the opinion that a solution reached in the way described is more likely to be true than one reached in pursuance of a determined effort to find a solution. The determined effort causes perversion of thought. When endeavouring to recollect some name or thing which has been forgotten, it frequently happens that the name or thing sought will not arise in consciousness; but when attention is relaxed, the missing name or thing often suggests itself. While thought continues to be forced down certain wrong turnings which had originally been taken, the search is vain; but with the cessation of strain the true association of ideas has an opportunity of asserting itself. And, similarly, it may be that while an effort to arrive forthwith at some answer to a problem, acts as a distorting factor in consciousness and causes error, a quiet contemplation of the problem from time to time, allows those proclivities of thought which have probably been caused unawares by experiences, to make themselves felt, and to guide the mind to the right conclusion.

From *An Autobiography,* by Herbert Spencer. By permission of the publishers: D. Appleton-Century Company, Inc., New York City.

THE BIOLOGICAL BASIS
OF IMAGINATION
R. W. Gerard

A satisfactory interpretation of imaginative phenomena in terms of neural mechanisms may be presented by some fortunate author at a future time. But even now there is still much of substance to be said. Knowledge normally grows by such progressive steps as clarifying and isolating a problem, identifying the variables relevant to it, and following their correlations. Only later, often much later, does the nature of the basic entities begin to become manifest and does it become possible to grapple with them.

In the field of heredity, for example, Mendel isolated the problem in terms of simple characters and followed their behavior during inheritance. These results suggested separable inherited units, which remained as hypothetical for half a century as were the atoms of Democritus for nearly two millennia. Then chromosomes were seen; in another half-century the genes became visible; and studies are now proceeding in terms of the chemical properties of specific substances. In dealing with imagination it will be profitable similarly to examine its common meaning, to consider how psychological study has defined and measured relevant mental abilities, to note the relation of local brain damage to these abilities, and to develop the relation of these psychological phenomena to neural mechanisms.

What is Imagination?

Imagination is more than bringing images into consciousness; that is imagery or at most hallucination. Imagination, creative imagination, is an action of the mind that produces a new idea or insight. "Out of chaos the imagination frames a thing of beauty" (Lowes's *The Road to Xanadu*) or of truth. The thing comes unheralded, as a flash, full-formed. We have all had this experience, and famous or important cases abound.

Kekule solved the chemical problem of the benzene molecule, a ring rather than a chain of carbon atoms, when in a fatigue- (or alcohol-) engendered daydream he saw a snake swallow its tail. Michelson's "intuition" gave him the equation for some complicated tidal phenomena, and when an expert mathematician reported a different result from his calculations, Michelson sent him away to find, as he did, an error.

Otto Loewi, recently awarded the Nobel prize for proving that active chemicals are involved in the action of nerves, once told me the story of his discovery. His experiments on the control of a beating frog heart were giving puzzling results. He worried over these, slept fitfully and, lying wakeful one night, saw a wild possibility and the experiment which would test it. He scribbled some notes and slept peacefully till morning. The next day was agony—he could not read the scrawl nor recall the solution, though remembering that he had had it. That night was even worse until at three in the morning lightning flashed again. He took no chances this time but went to the laboratory at once and started his experiment...

Imagination, not reason, creates the novel. It is to social inheritance what mutation is to biological inheritance; it accounts for the arrival of the fittest. Reason or logic, applied when judgment indicates that the new is promising, acts like natural selection to pan the gold grains from the sand and insure the survival of the fittest. Imagination supplies the premises and asks the questions from which reason grinds out the conclusions as a calculating machine supplies answers. Wood's story of how a plausible answer to a perplexing problem came to him while dozing, only to be later exploded by his experiments, is illustrative. Dryden, presenting The Rival Ladies, to the Earl of Orrery, said:

"This worthless Present was design'd you, long before it was a Play; when it was only a confus'd Mass of Thoughts, tumbling over one another in the Dark: When the Fancy was yet in its first Work, moving the Sleeping Images of things towards the Light, there to be distinguish'd, and then either chosen or rejected by the Judgment." And Coleridge's artistry has compacted the matter into the phrase, "the streamy nature of association, which thinking curbs and rudders."...

Simple imagination is observable in a pure and untrammeled state in dreams, in the hallucinations of drugs and other agents, in those hypnagogic states which interpose between wake and sleep or in the slightly fettered daydreaming while awake, in the free fancies of the child and the less free fancies of the amateur. For ideas, like mutations, are mostly bad by the criteria of judgment, and experience or expertness suppresses them—unless imaginings get out of hand and displace reality, as in the insanities. But the imaginative hopper is fed from and feeds back to the conscious and critical level. There the heat of mental work transforms the soft ingots of fancy into the hard steel of finished creations. Baudelaire refers to "the labor by which a revery becomes a work of art," and Mary Boole has likened the alternate conscious and unconscious digestion of a problem to the rumination of a cow—as indeed our language does in using "rumination" for a loose form of mental activity...

Clearly, then, pursuit of imagination leads us into the unconscious and its mechanisms. Nor is this any longer a completely uncharted wilderness, for psychoanalysis especially has even now developed a usable body of knowledge to guide the explorer. It has recognized and isolated such unconscious mechanisms as condensation, displacement, projection, and identification—as well as repression, sublimation, substitution, rejection, denial, introjection, suppression, and conversion, to extend the list—which often enable the student not only to see further into the how of imagining but even to account for what is imagined. This is true for the normal and perhaps more strikingly for the disturbed; the previously meaningless chatter of the schizophrenic patient, for example, is quite intelligible in terms of known dynamics. Condensation and identification, respectively, are dearly revealed in the following statements by Coleridge concerning himself: "Ideas and images exist in the twilight realms of consciousness, that shadowy half-being, that state of nascent existence in the twilight of imagination and just on the vestibule of consciousness, a confluence of our recollections, through which we establish a centre, as it were, a sort of nucleus in [this] reservoir of the soul." And: "From my very childhood, I have been accustomed to abstract, and as it were, unrealize whatever of more than common interest my eyes dwelt on, and then by a sort of transfusion and transmission of my consciousness to identify myself with the object." And Lowes, in a painstaking study of the materials Coleridge had immersed himself in during the years prior to his writing "The Ancient Mariner," was able to trace to these sources every word and phrase of the poem's most vivid stanzas. As Lowes says:

"Facts which sank at intervals out of conscious recollection drew together beneath the surface through almost chemical affinities of common elements... And there in Coleridge's unconscious mind, while his consciousness was busy with the toothache, or Hartley's infant ills, or pleasant strollings with the Wordsworths between Nether Stowey and Alfoxden, or what is dreamt in this or that philosophy-there in the dark moved the phantasms of the fishes and animalculae and serpentine forms of his vicarious voyagings, thrusting out tentacles of association; and interweaving beyond disengagement." This is not, of course, to detract a grain from Coleridge's achievement; it is only a recognition and demonstration of the sensory components on which imagination operates. For the components had to be integrated, the poem given form. Again to quote Lowes:

"Behind `The Rime of the Ancient Mariner' lie crowding masses of impressions, incredible in their richness and variety. But the poem is not the sum of the impressions, as a heap of diamond dust is the sum of its shining particles; nor is the poet merely a sensitized medium for their reception and transmission. Beneath the poem lie also innumerable blendings and fusings of impressions, brought about below the level of conscious mental processes. But the poem is not the confluence of unconsciously merging images, as a pool of water forms from the coalescence of scattered drops; nor is the poet a somnambulist in a subliminal world. Neither the conscious impressions nor their unconscious interpenetrations constitute the poem. They are inseparable from it, but it is an entity which they do not create. On the contrary, every impression, every new creature rising from the potent waters of the [unconscious] Well, is what it now is through its participation in a whole, foreseen as a *whole* in each integral part—a whole which is the working out of a controlling imaginative design. The incommunicable, unique essence of the poem is its *form.*"

And Hartmann says:

"Thus works ordinary talent; it produces artistically by means of rational selection and combination, guided by its esthetic judgment. At this point stand the ordinary dilettante and the majority of professional artists. They one and all cannot comprehend that these means, supported by technical routine, may perhaps accomplish something excellent, but can never attain to anything great.... Combination procures the unity of the whole by laborious adaptation and experimentation in detail, and therefore, in spite of all its labour, never accomplishes its purpose, but always allows, in its bungling work, the conglomerate of the details to be visible. Genius, in virtue of the conception from the Unconscious, has, in the necessary appropriateness and mutual relations of the several parts, a unity so perfect that it can only be compared to the unity of natural organisms, which likewise springs out of the Unconscious." Form, structure, relationship, organism (or org in my usage), part-whole systems, gestalt, or closure is basic for the product of imagination and for its process. To see star groups, constellations, instead of unrelated stars—the literal meaning of "consider"—is the gist of closure, of a confluence of elements. Since imagination only regroups sensory material, there is truly nothing new under the sun. Perception is really a harder problem, for red rays and green rays, even falling on separate eyes, do give the "new" sensation of yellow; but imagination cannot conjure a hue·for ultraviolet. A mermaid, griffin, or centaur, as Lucretius recognized, are only recombinations of familiar elements. Yet when we recall that a single inning of a chess game may offer some four hundred choices, that all literature is built from the same words and these of the same letters, as all material is of the same elements and their handful of subatomic particles, novelty in combination does not seem too barren. A new and fertile pattern of thought may come from a conceptual reslicing of the universe into fresh classes and the making of new combinations of them. A good insight is likely to recognize the universal in the particular and in the strange—perhaps overexemplified in this statement by Coleridge:

"My illustrations swallow up my thesis. I feel too intensely the omnipresence of all in each, platonically speaking; or, psychologically, my brain-fibers, or the spiritual light which abides in the brain-marrow, as visible light appears to do in sundry rotten mackerel and other smashy matters, is of too general an affinity with all things, and though it perceives the difference of things, yet is eternally pursuing the likenesses, or, rather, that which is common [between them]."

A good insight generalizes progressively, as is so well illustrated by the growth of mathematics and the formulation of ever more inclusive and freer equations (e.g., the Pythagorian theorem) which can then he applied to an increasing range of particular cases. George Boole, for example, introduced modern logic by recognizing class as basic to, and more general than, number. Finally, a good insight sees (or foresees) in a welter of impressions that which is relevant to the goal earlier indicated by reason; it winnows the important facts from the unimportant. But now we are reaching the domain of more formal psychological studies.

The Psychology of Imagination

The gestalt school of psychologists, especially, has emphasized the importance of closure or structuring—of "considering"—in insight. Insight is an imaginative way of learning or problem solving, in contrast to the blind and buffeted way of trial and error, often called "at-sight" for contrast. (A neurotic behavior development, inappropriate to the actual situation and, in a sense, no longer goal-directed, might similarly be called "out-sight.") Beyond sensation and even simple perception, involving the correlation of current sense data and of past experience, closure is a basic property of mind. It is, in Goldstein's formulation, the ability to separate a figure from its ground, to formulate a gestalt, or form, to identify an entity. (It operates in seeing three separated dots as the corners of a triangle.) From this flows the setting up of classes and the recognition of spatial—or temporal—relations. Thus Conrad notes the ability to combine parts or elements into a whole, to integrate systems; and also the converse ability to identify parts or elements in the whole, to fragment or differentiate systems. And Wertheimer further recognizes the ability to shift from one whole to another one, to restructure a system.

These activities may seem tautological restatements and are certainly closely related intuitively; yet, as we shall see, they enjoy considerable independence and can be separately measured. Most immediately exemplifying imagination would seem to be the last, flexibility of structure; for Wertheimer correctly says, "Creative thinking is the process of destroying one gestalt in favor of a better one." It is the highest imaginative achievement to be able to restructure in useful ways the basic propositions or axioms on which our great logical thought edifices have been erected. And, as an indirect sign that even such intangible mind work may still be sharply tied to the properties of the brain, there is the observation (Brickner) that stimulation of just one particular small region of the exposed human brain is able to arrest movement in thought. A conscious patient counts smoothly except while the electric current is acting, when the same number is simply repeated. Thus (with the period of stimulation italicized) the subject says,

"1,2,3,*4,4,4,4,4,4,*5, 6,7,..."

Some examples of imagination at the comfortable and familiar level of parlor problems will serve best, perhaps, to illustrate the points made above.

The victim is asked to draw four straight lines which shall pass through all nine dots arranged in a square of three rows of three dots. The presentation sets the gestalt of the square, but within that pattern a solution is impossible. When the imagination overcomes this restriction, however, and extends lines beyond the self-imposed margin of the figure, the answer is given almost by inspection. Entirely comparable is the problem of constructing from six matches tossed on a table four equilateral triangles, each having its sides the length of a match. So long as the solver limits himself to the suggested plane of the table he struggles in vain; as soon as he adds a third dimension in his consideration the tetrahedron almost leaps at him.

In contrast to the above instances, many problems require essentially no imagination but either memory or reason. The great bulk of questions aired in quiz programs are ones of simple memory. A problem that can be solved without imagination is that of exchanging dimes and pennies. Three of each are lined up, with one central space vacant between the dimes and the pennies. Any coin can slide forward into a space or can jump over a single coin of the opposite kind into a space. The necessary moves can be found by brute trial and error or, more simply, by a little reasoning; but the initial gestalt is retained throughout.

Numerous examples of insight could be given at the infrahuman level: Kohler's chimpanzees which "closed" two elements and brought a box and a stick to reach a banana; Yerkes' ape which, having accidentally whirled into the correct solution of a choice-of-gates problem, regularly thereafter whirled before trying the gate of his choice; Maier's rats which were able to combine "knowledge-of-general-maze pattern" and "block-between-me-and-food" and choose the shortest available path; and the innumerable animals that, during conditioning, seem suddenly to make the induction of "bigger-than" or "nearer-than" or "same-as" and thereafter give errorless performances. But a further pursuit of imagination in man will be more interesting.

If imagination is a definable property of the mind it should also be measurable; and as the definition progresses from the vague impressions of ordinary human dealings to that offered by standardized situations, so the measure moves from the subjective judgment of a person, as having a good or poor imagination, to a fairly quantitative statement about performance. Thurstone, especially, has pressed forward the analysis of mental abilities. By extensive testing with a rich variety of problems he has shown at least seven such abilities which are independent of each other. Thus, individual A may outperform individual B by ten- or a hundredfold on tests which utilize ability 1, while B may similarly outperform A on tests involving ability 2. A similar analysis has revealed some ten perceptual abilities, and others surely remain to be uncovered. Some abilities, such as those of word fluency or verbal understanding, depend for their exercise on learned language, and so performance improves over much of the life-span. But others, such as space visualization, show little improvement in their use after the age of six to eight years; in fact, performance may actually decline. The case for inborn capacities, of particular degrees for each capacity in each person, is thus strong.

Is imagination some one or several of these separable abilities or some common "power factor" underlying them? The answer is not yet available, but it is within easy grasp when persons of outstanding talents of various sorts are measured by such standardized tests. Meanwhile, some interesting guesses may be made. At least four of Thurstone's factors might be involved in imagination, and one of these seems almost to define it. The I, or induction, factor is the ability to see logical patterns or relations (and so would be less related to imagination than to reason). A convenient test for it is to have the subject supply the next item of a series. A very elementary series is: OXXOXXOX?. A more severe demand is made by: 1,7,3,6,5,5,7,4,9,?. The K factor, measured by the Rohrschach "inkblot" test, is almost at the other end of the mental spectrum and, far from impinging on logic, plumbs the unconscious. It is of the free completion type; the subject is given an amorphous stimulus and allowed to react with no restraints—as when a person gazes into the flames playing over a fire or at clouds drifting in the sky and "sees" castles or bears or witches acting out untold stories. It is suggestive that a group of successful executives performed (in richness, variety, etc., of responses to the ink blots) significantly above the average on this test.

Two other factors rather specifically deal with closure. The A factor is the ability to make a closure or complete a gestalt and is measured, for example, by having the subject identify partially erased pictures or words. The E factor is the ability to replace one closure by another and is tested by the Gottschalt figures, or by "hidden faces" in a picture of different manifest content. The two abilities, especially E, are rather precisely those considered earlier in defining the act of creative imagination. It is impressive that two independent factors can in fact be isolated for such intuitively equivalent actions as making or remarking a closure! When such primary abilities have been measured in our Einsteins, Edisons, Toscaninis, Van Goghs, Masefields, and Lincolns we shall be far along the way. From descriptions of Coleridge, for example, there is little doubt that he would have performed very well indeed on tests for K, S (space), W (word facility), M (memory), and I and A.

"Zoology" of Imagination

The inheritance of imagination will be ever more easily studied as identification becomes more precise. Even now the comparison of the mental abilities in twins and siblings is in progress. Pending such finer analysis, I may mention evidence that a strong hereditary element is present for "averaged" intelligence and for particular talents. Newman and Holzinger, for example, have found an average difference in I.Q. of 5.9 for identical twins raised together and that this value increases only to 7.7 for those raised apart. In contrast, fraternal twins raised together differ by 8.4, and sibs by 14.5 if raised together, 15.5 if raised apart. Orphan pairs differ by 17.7, whether apart or together.

A study of outstanding contemporary virtuosi and singers by

Scheinfeld shows that two-thirds of the parents of these artists possessed high musical talent. Conversely, in families with both parents talented, two-thirds of the children also were gifted, whereas in those in which neither parent showed talent (but of course one child was outstanding) only one-fourth of the offspring were gifted. He suggests that the minimal genetic interpretation of these facts is that musical talent demands the presence of at least two dominant genes. The importance of the hereditary factor is further attested by the age at which these outstanding musicians had clearly manifested unmistakable talent—an age under six years!

Interesting data in the field of science come from the starring results in *American Men of Science.* Mathematicians achieve their star at the average age of twenty-nine, with physicists close behind; botanists and geologists wait until they are fifty-two for the same kudos. All will probably agree that sheer imagination and intellectual power, as compared with experience and learning, are relatively more important in the former fields than in the latter. That the growth of mental *capacity* is more a matter of biological maturation than of life experience is suggested by all these findings, as well as by the high performance of children on some of Thurstone's factor tests. Similar conclusions in other fields of neural performance are justified by Coghill's evidence that salamanders kept anaesthetized during the developmental days when their fellow embryos struggle about "learning" to swim, swim well at once on ending their trance state; and by the fact that a normal human baby begins to smile at two months after birth, a seven-month premature, four months after birth.

A final comment in this area, on the evolution of mental abilities. Several men have attempted to construct a scale of comparative intelligence of animals in terms of such learning criteria as the maximum time over which a trace-conditioned reflex could be established, but without convincing success. That man's abilities differ in degree more than in kind from those of his slower-witted biological relatives is nonetheless probable. Apes show learning by insight as well as by trial and error and have even been taught to work for money as industriously as do their gifted cousins. Wolfe has trained chimpanzees to put counters into the slot of a vending machine to obtain food, different amounts for different colors. Having learned the purchasing value of these colored bits, the animals will do "chores" to obtain them and will work harder for the more valuable ones.

Since the gross and microscopic structure and the chemical and electrical functioning of the brain are measurably comparable in all vertebrates, reasonably alike in all mammals, and strikingly similar in the higher primates, where enormously detailed parallels have been demonstrated, a likeness in mental capacities is not surprising. The gray cortex of the cerebrum has swelled out from the primitive nerve cell groups to which came messages from nose, ear, and eye. These "distance receptors," sensitive to changes in the world at a distance from their possessor and so posing problems to the animal for a priori solution, somehow whipped into existence a brain capable of solving them. It is the same cerebrum in man and monkey; but man has a deal more of it, which permits rich additional permutations. And now that the brain is introduced into the picture, we must consider knowledge in the more medical areas.

The Brain and Imagination

Pathology. It remains sadly true that most of our present understanding of mind would remain as valid and useful if, for all we knew, the cranium were stuffed with cotton wadding. In time, the detailed correlation of psychic phenomena and neural processes will surely come; but today we are hardly beyond the stage of unequivocal evidence that the correlation does exist. The neuro-anatomist and physiologist are still crudely deciphering the architecture and operation of the organ of mind; the psychologist and psychiatrist are concerned with nuances in the overtones it plays. Yet the gap is narrowing, and a primitive bridge is offered by the grosser disturbances of brain and mind. Perhaps most dramatic are the aphasias, a group of disturbances in the ability to handle "meaning," associated with more or less sharply delimited regions of brain damage. Since disease or accident rarely destroys an exact division of the cerebrum and since different divisions have unique functions, the symptoms are commonly mixed and vary from case to case; but such a diagrammatic instance as the following has been reported.

An educated man, proficient in several languages, suffered a "stroke" which left him aphasic. At one stage in his slow improvement he could converse freely and intelligently but could not read. His vision was not disturbed; he could copy a paragraph correctly, but it carried no meaning to him. He was able, in fact, to take dictation in one language, translate in his mind, and write the correct passage in another tongue. But having written it, he could not read his own writing; it was Chinese to him! One is reminded of the small boy who, called on to read aloud in class, was asked the meaning of what he had read and gave the startled and startling reply, "I don't know. I wasn't listening." Another type of case, with disturbance more on the motor than the sensory side, could not give the word for seven but could say it by counting aloud from one. Another, wanting to say "ruler" could not do so until he had made a sketch of one. Yet another could not say words but demonstrated, by holding up fingers for syllables, that he "knew" them. For example, "What is a baby cat?" No sound of kitten, but two fingers raised in response. Even when words remain, they are often inexact or roundabout, and the subject seems to be indulging in fancy speech or "overwriting," as shown by the following quotations from a patient during and subsequent to an aphasic episode: "I trust I am now learning to do my very best to secure the ideas to put myself carefully to operate the item to me which was seeming away when needed so much by me." And, later, describing his aphasic condition, "Personally I got dumb and could not remember things." (These cases are quoted from Weisenburg and McBride's *Aphasia.)*

As these instances show, there is commonly a disturbance in the use of language, but this is too limited a view of the defect. Language is man's main symbolic system, and aphasia has been considered as a disturbance in symbolism (Head) or in propositional expression (Jackson). But formal symbols are still but one avenue to meaning, and the others may also be disturbed in aphasia. A patient may fail to recognize familiar tunes, or may be unable to identify by touch a common object placed in his hand, such as a key or knife or pencil, although he recognizes well enough that some object is there and may name it at once on sight. Similarly on the motor side, a man could not at will move his tongue over his lip on instructions, which he understood, but could do so to remove a crumb placed there. Comparable defects in meaningfulness have been produced in monkeys by appropriate brain operations on the parietal lobes (Kluever and Bucy). Such an animal still sees and feels objects as well as ever, but it no longer recognizes them. It will pick up, bring to its mouth, and drop again, in interminable random activity, such normally intensely discriminated objects as a banana, a stone, and a live snake. This behavior is in sharp contrast to that of a monkey whose visual sensory cortex (occipital) has been removed. Then, while light sensitivity is fully retained, as shown by eye reflexes, all visual perception is gone; the animal is effectively blind.

Thus meaning, in its widest sense, is imperiled by such brain insults, and the gestalt psychologists have not failed to point out that the very ability to create closures is damaged in aphasics. But, in man, language (with mathematics as one form of language) remains an especial index to the workings of mind; and Pick, combining philological study with his clinical observations, has formulated a series of stages in language use, which may be interrupted anywhere by the aphasic slash. On the sensory or receptive side there is, first, the perception of speech as distinct from mere sound. There follows the recognition of words as separate entities and then of the "musical" parts of speech, cadence, and intonation. Only then comes an awareness of meaning, followed by full understanding of sentences with their proper word relations and emphases. Turning now to the motor or expressive sides, the sequence is intuitive thought (also called verbalizing or inner speech), which becomes structured thought, and is then cast into the schema of a sentence, only after which are the actual words chosen and the result articulated. Aphasia may thus prevent sensation from emerging into meaning, meaning from eventuating in behavior, or meaning itself from coming clear. The last would be a disturbance in closure or structuring. This represents, perhaps, the basic disintegration of imagination. Imagination may be the word for that all-important no man's land between the end of the receptive process and the start of the expressive one.

The future is parturient with the answers. For the advance of neurosurgery is offering to study clean-cut cases of brain defects (or stimulation); patients with local brain amputations or incisions for tumors or infections or even, rather less soundly, for mental disturbances. And the advance of psychological measuring is supplying better precision tools with which to make the study. Thus, at the receptive levels, superficial damage to a region (r7) of the visual cortex destroys color sensations but preserves pattern; more profound damage destroys pattern recognition as well while leaving (as in the monkey) light sensitivity. Comparably, direct stimulation of area 17 in a conscious patient produces an awareness of lights; when the next area, i8, is stimulated, the lights move about; and, if the next brain region is excited, complete pictures flash into consciousness—as of a man somersaulting toward the observer.

And at the integrative or imaginative levels of meaningfulness, we need only the results of applying the tests for primary abilities, especially for Thurstone's A, E, I, and K factors, to patients with specific brain operations to make a great step forward. Even now, Halsted has found a striking defect, in patients whose frontal lobes have been partly removed, in the ability to make categories. A normal adult, given a miscellaneous collection of familiar objects and asked to group them in as many ways as possible, can set up dozens of categories for grouping—by color, shape, material, use, and so on and on. The operated patient can make few, if any, groups. Now making groups or classes is a form of closure, and here again we see imagination crumbling along with the brain that spawns it. But we must look more closely at the structure of the brain and the problem of localization.

Anatomy. The introspective psychologists have distinguished between crude sensation, organized perception, and full-formed imagery on the sensory side; reason, will, and action on the motor side. The boundaries are not sharp, to be sure, yet one can almost follow the one into the other on moving with nerve messages along the nervous system. From the single receptor, or sense organ—tactile corpuscle of the skin, eye, ear, etc.-comes but one modality of sensation—touch, light, sound. This has the attribute of intensity, given by the frequency or closeness with which impulses follow each other in each nerve fiber and, less, by the number of fibers activated. When the message reaches appropriate regions of the nervous system, the sensation also has its particular quality of touch, or pitch, and this much of pattern that a "local sign" is attached, so that the region of the body (touch) or receptor (eye) from which the messages come remains identifiable. As nerve fibers from receptors gather into nerve bundles (along with motor fibers for much of the way, but separating at the ends, especially where they join the central nervous system), sensory messages are grouped together either by modality, in special cases like those of seeing in the optic nerve and those of hearing in the auditory nerve, or more generally by region, as all the skin and other sensations from one finger in a particular nerve or nerve branch.

Yet as soon as these latter nerves enter the nervous system, mainly along the spinal cord, the relay fibers are shuffled about so that they also become grouped by modality. Thus, if a nerve to the leg is cut, some portion of the leg skin (and muscle) will have lost all sensation of touch, pressure, temperature, pain, position, vibration, etc. But if one of the relay bundles in the spinal cord is damaged, the entire limb will lose only the sense of touch or of pain or of position, as examples, depending on which part of the cross section of the cord is injured, while retaining the other senses unimpaired. When these second relay fibers pass on their messages to the third member of the team, in the thalamus at the base of the great cerebral hemispheres, there is another reshuffling so that region again enters strongly into the arrangement. And from here the nerve wires fan out to reach the cerebral cortex, each to its own particular spot.

Optic fibers run to the occipital lobe and are there ordered so that each region of the retina is represented at a roughly comparable position on the cortex. Fibers from the skin carry all the cutaneous sense messages, remixed as to modality, to the parietal lobe just behind the great Rolandic fissure, where the various body regions are neatly arranged in order; from the foot at the vertex of the brain to the head well down the lateral surface—as if a tiny and rather grotesque manikin of the body lay upside down (and right side left) on this region of the brain. Sound, smell, balance, hearing are similarly "placed" in given parts of the cerebral cortex, and, on the motor side, the body muscles are represented just in front of the cutaneous area, across the Rolandic fissure, and are ordered as a manikin in like fashion. Muscle sense, which tells us limb position, for example, overlaps the cutaneous and motor areas, again in the same order from foot to head. The spatial arrangement of entering nerve fibers in the auditory cortex is in terms of pitch, rather than of position and, just discovered, there is a double location for hearing—two distinct brain areas in each hemisphere.

These cortical areas to which sensory nerve messages are projected from the thalamus, or from which motor messages project through the thalamus, are called the projection areas. They occupy but a small portion of the cerebral cortex, being surrounded by various association areas; and indeed both the microscopic characteristics and arrangements of the nerve cells and the functional influences that have been traced between them show that some half a hundred individual and distinctive areas are present in the cortex of man. Some of the association areas, in close relation to projection areas, are primary and concerned directly with an elaboration of the particular projected messages. More of them, the secondary association areas, are concerned with the most general interrelation and reworking of the elaborated sensory clues, present and past. Thus, referring again to the aphasias, destruction of the visual projection area (17) causes blindness; of the visual primary association area (18), a pure sensory aphasia (agnosia) for seen objects or symbols—inability to give meaning to written words; of secondary association areas, a greater or lesser loss in meaningfulness in general, an integrative aphasia (aconia). A pure motor aphasia (apraxia), like the pure sensory one, would involve a primary association area related to the motor area for, say, speech. Stimulation, conversely, gives lights (17), moving lights (18), and moving pictures, respectively, as described earlier.

Now what of sensation, perception, and the like, and especially imagination, in relation to this sketched-in organization of the nervous system? Clearly, a knowledge of structure and localization of function is not enough; for a single nerve impulse running in a single nerve fiber in one or another part of the brain is much the same thing, and a billion of them simply added together are only a billion of the same things. But nerve impulses are not simply added. Messages set up from a single hair on a cat's paw—by touching it with a hair on the observer's hand so lightly that the observer feels nothing—run up a sensory nerve fiber to the spinal cord and there "explode" into many impulses running up to the brain in many fibers, which further interact along the way. A person listening to a watch tick hears it as louder while a light is being looked at; and experiments on cats show a similar enhancement of messages in the auditory sensory paths when the nearby optic paths are simultaneously active. The point is that as sensory messages ascend toward and into the cerebrum they are not merely relayed and regrouped, they are also reorganized and reworked; in fact, we shall see they even reverberate.

What may be the conscious concomitants of these various stages of neural work is not known; but all the evidence suggests that they would rise in richness along with the intricacy of activity patterns in the nervous system. If awareness is the internal view of events or systems which are material to the external view, as many hold, then some proto-consciousness (probably not self-consciousness, or an awareness of being conscious) must exist in the simplest blob of living protoplasm or, for that matter, even in all substance. But, just as behavioral capacity leaps upward when a nervous system is present and again as each major improvement in it evolves, especially as the great cerebral cortex comes to flower, so subjective awareness does likewise. Some consciousness of sensation may exist in the spinal cord, as does some ability to recombine and learn, but this would be difficult to prove and is surely of negligible degree compared to what is experienced by man's brain. Nevertheless, the sensory messages from receptor through sensory nerve and spinal bundles probably represent pretty pure and raw (but unsensed) "sensation"—as suggested by some of the facts on the results of damage. And if they reach projection areas without much interaction with other activity patterns they will result in simple consciously recognized sensation. There is even some evidence that the most primitive undiscriminated "feelings," such vague discomfort as accompanies mild bowel cramps, may depend on older subcortical brain regions, such as part of the thalamus. If, however, they interact with other current sensory messages, and with the memory traces of past ones, then they are probably more of the character of perceptions, after moving on from the thalamus and into the projection areas. By the time the primary association areas are engaged, with their added complexity, imagery is probably also present.

A comparable but reverse sequence exists on the motor side, with drive or willing or maybe intuitive speech at the start and particular muscle contractions at the end; with the same possibilities of interruption along the way, grading from the aphasias to the out-and-out paralyses. Volition may be disengaged from motor expression in less drastic ways than by anatomical damage: a person recovering from the stupor due to inhaling concentrated carbon dioxide "wills" to move his hand in response to a request, but nothing happens for a minute or more when, to his surprise, the hand moves "of itself" (McCulloch). The leaden limbs of a nightmare, when the dreamer cannot run for his very life, may be a comparable neural block; at least in deep sleep the toe reflex from scratching the sole (Babinski) behaves just as it does when the motor pathways of the nervous system have been injured.

Between perception and imagery on the one hand and volition on the other lie the great mental territories of imagination and reason. It might be useful to consider imagination as the culmination of sensory events, reason as the origin of the motor ones. Or perhaps reason, with its attendant logic, verbalization, decision, and willing, is more properly the start of motor events, and imagination is the more pervasive and encompassing mind work which is the keystone of the sensory-motor arch. Men with moderately severe brain injuries may perform well on the usual intelligence tests, while falling down on those which sample imagination. Indeed, imagination may include a "power" factor of intelligence underlying the others, as Spearman believed, and depending on the mass functioning of the whole brain, as Lashley's work on animals suggests.

Certainly, as earlier outlined, imagination depends on sensory information. Man cannot see the world other than as it unfolds itself within the sensory projection areas of his brain. These determine his basic orientation to externality. In the very spatial arrangement of the areas of vision, skin, and muscle sense is embedded an unformulated geometry. The basic units of physical science are distilled from these areas: space (centimeters) from vision, touch, muscle sense, and vestibular system (the balance organs located within the ear) ; substance (mass, grams) from smell, taste, touch, muscle sense, and, secondarily, vision—a congenitally blind person, on achieving vision, feels objects "hitting" his eyes until he learns to project his experience into the third dimension, as we all project the sense of touch to the end of a stick with which we explore the bottom of a pond—and perhaps, even, the notion of force comes from touch and muscle sense, of matter more from taste and smell; and time (seconds) most directly from hearing. At least, as evidence for this last, is the powerful reaction to heard rhythm, tapping to a tune, and the fact that a sound track of words or music run backwards is completely meaningless, whereas a reversed light track, though often ludicrous or impossible, is perfectly meaningful. Moreover, one's subjective judgment of time certainly depends on a brain clock, which runs fast in fever according to a precise mathematical function of the brain temperature (Hoagland). (In another, more fanciful, sense one might think of time running through the cortex from behind forward. Sensations, from already past events, enter behind the Rolandic fissure; motor impulses, which will set off future actions, leave from in front of it.)

From space, mass, and time comes, in turn, the notion of entity—the basic gestalt of all and the first flutter of imagination. In this sense, that entity is given by the sensory organization of the nervous system, Kronecker's famous mathematical dictum takes on a profounder meaning: "God made the integers, man did all the rest." And, in supplying the substratum for thought, vision in man is surely of overwhelming importance. Our thought words are almost all of visual reference, although we do "apprehend" a meaning and refer to a "tangible suggestion" or a "weighty problem," and we may say of something, "it looks heavy or hard," but never that "it feels red."

The distinguished art critic Ivens has made the provocative suggestion that Greek art and architecture and mathematics are distinctly inferior to those of more modern times (a critical judgment which he supports in considerable detail) because the classic Greeks were essentially hand-minded (touch and muscle sense), and modern man, eye-minded. The former, he urges, gave the finite, discrete, and particulate; the latter, the infinite and graded. Aside from such historical evidence as the continuity implied in Zeno's paradoxes, this view seems unsound on a biological basis. Greek brains were built like ours, of the same human race; and an earlier race, Neanderthal man, had, if anything, a more emphasized vision than our own—at least the occipital lobe of his brain, with its visual areas, was mightily developed. True, individuals vary in the degree to which their imagery is visual, auditory, tactile, and the like (it might even be possible to measure this in terms of the relative strengths of the occipital (a) and the parietal (3) rhythms in their electrical brain waves); but this variation almost surely follows the chromosomes, alike in old or new Greeks.

No, the more static constructs of the classical period are to be understood rather as an earlier phase of imaginative creativity. In all human thought, the constant is adumbrated before the variable (mathematics), statics before dynamics (physics), structure before function, and classification before relationship or evolution (biology). It is not surprising that this is so, for thus does the brain create imaginings: remember that stimulation of the visual projection area generates static lights; of the first association area, dynamic ones; and of the second association area, moving pictures!

Physiology. What, then, of the mechanisms of brain functioning, of the generation of thought? Granting, again, that the exact relation between neural processes and conscious events remains unknown, it is still possible to recognize some striking parallels. Are closure and patterning basic to imagination? They are simply shot through the entire felt-work of the nervous system! Not only in the large-scale organization we have already noted but in the small-scale one no less. True, particular nerve fiber bundles connect each of the separate areas of the cortex with all; many directly, the others by relays. True, some of the bundles carry messages which excite the nerve cells they reach, so that when cells in area X fire messages to area Y the cells in Y become active. But it is also true that comparable nerve bundles connect cortical areas with thalamus, with spinal cord, with all parts of the nervous system; so that a nerve impulse entering the central mass along any fiber path could, in principle, find its way by one route or another to every part of the nervous system. (And in fact, too, under some conditions; as when strychnine has rendered the whole neural apparatus more sensitive, and a slight irritation anywhere can set off a general convulsive reflex contraction of all the muscles of the body.) And it is further true that the nerve impulses running from area X may not excite but inhibit or suppress the cells in area Y so that these stop their current action and cannot be re-excited for a time. Thus, stimulating the arm region of the motor area

(4) will cause arm movements; but stimulating a region (4-S) only a few millimeters forward will stop arm movements and even prevent further stimulation of area 4 from starting them. Surprisingly, although 4 and 4-S lie next to each other on the cerebral cortex, this suppressor action depends on a distant locus of interaction; and part of the interplay is via a complex relay path, from 4-S to deep cells in the cerebrum (basal nucleus) and from there to the thalamus and from there back up to 4.

Each nerve cell is so richly supplied by nerve fibers reaching it from all sorts of local and distant neural regions, reaching it and making functional connection (synapse) with it, that it is rather like an egg packed in sticky excelsior. Messages bombard it along these many paths, some pushing it to action and some to quietude, some perhaps powerful enough to tip the balance individually but most surely requiring the help of their like fellows. Further, the nerve cell is being influenced by the blood passing it, by the oxygen and sugar it receives, the salts that bathe it, the electric currents from its neighbors, the temperature at which it finds itself, by drugs which reach it. And from this welter of influences—its state of health, the condition of the environment in which it is living, and, particularly, the clamor of allied and opposed messages reaching it—from all this comes a single result: the cell fires messages along its own fiber to still other cells, or it does not fire. There is, to be sure, some gradation in number and frequency of impulses sent or in duration of inactivity and depth of inactivability, but essentially the balance is between action or no action. Just so the judge, depending on the state of his stomach, or the temperature of the courtroom, or the bombardment of arguments on each side of the case, renders a single decision for or against. (Freedom of the individual to make the decision is equally easy or hard to discover in the nerve cell and in the judge.) It is the collective and patterned actions of the several billion nerve cells of our brains that determine our behavior and accompany our thoughts. We must explore further this neural patterning.

A few years back, the only well-recognized pattern was the reflex arc. A message entered along a sensory nerve, continued through the nervous system along direct or relayed connections, and finally emerged in a motor nerve. Except as messages were in transit, the nervous system was presumably quiet. Today we know, largely from the electrical pulses of the "brain waves," that nerve cells are continuously active in wake or sleep, and many beat on like the heart. In part, this beat depends on the chemical and physical state of the cell and its surrounding fluid; in part, on the nerve messages playing upon it. Suppose cell A sends its fiber to connect, among others, with cell B, B with C, C with D, and D with A. If A were once activated by a message from X it would excite B, and so through C and D be reexcited itself. Another branch from D might excite Y. Then, once started, such a circuit might continue active, with excitation going round and round like a pin wheel and throwing off regular sparks of activity on each cycle. Of course this picture is too simple—the circuit would not be set off so singly, it would vary in its path and speed of spinning, it would have to stop by cell fatigue or other impulse interference, it would involve many more cells and connections, were it to accord with the actual behavior of the brain. But what is important is that just such circuit patterns, with all the needed complexities, have been shown to exist and function in this manner (Lorente de No). Closure in mental processes, did we say? Here is closure woven into the very fabric of the nervous system!

These closed circuits are mostly over minute distances, in single centers of the nervous system, but comparable ones exist on a gross scale. In many cases, also, a nerve cell cannot be made to fire by impulses reaching it along a single fiber but requires a nudge from two or several arriving at the same time (the main effect of a single impulse is expended in a few ten-thousandths of a second) and even from different regions. Again, what a beautiful basis for making new gestalts or recombinations of sensory material! As one example, recall that light can make sounds seem louder; as another, how association areas rework and embroider the activity of projection areas. A further instance shows that messages from the frontal lobe of the brain, as well as from the optic nerve and thalamus, must reach the visual centers for them to become fully active; for after injury to the front of the cerebrum the field of vision is narrowed, even though the retina and its immediate brain connections to the optic brain areas remain intact (Halsted).

Several important interactions occur between the cerebrum and thalamus, besides those already mentioned. Through the latter pass all sensory messages on their way to the projection areas and to full consciousness; and in another part of the thalamus are coordinated the bodily responses and perhaps the subjective aspects of emotion and other primitive feeling. When the cerebrum of an animal is removed, affective behavior is grotesquely exaggerated; so nerve paths from the cerebrum hold the thalamus in check. Other fibers from the cortex can activate the thalamus, and, indeed, even as sensory messages relay up through this part of the brain, other messages coming down to it from the cortex can block or enhance their passage (Dusser de Barenne). Perhaps what we call attention is in action through these paths which functionally open or close the gates of the thalamus and allow now one, now another, group of sensory messages access to the cortex and full consciousness while relegating the others to the fringe of awareness or even to the unconscious. (This is not to say that all cortical activity is conscious or self-conscious, for such is not the case. James's figure of consciousness, as a single lighted candle carried from place to place in the cavernous darkness of a great building, is still a good one.) And, a final example, certain paths from the thalamus radiate out to much of the cerebral cortex and, when stimulated, set the whole cortical sheet into vigorous electrical beating (Morison and Dempsey). Perhaps this mechanism is responsible for the overactive mind work that follows an emotional shock. Perhaps just this occurred in Goethe's brain when news of his friend's suicide "crystallized" the plan of "Werther" as, "the whole shot together from all directions and became a solid mass." And surely here again is a neural basis for closure.

Besides such provocative nerve messages, able to influence the action of millions of nerve cells, other integrating mechanisms exist in the brain. Waves of action can be made to travel slowly over the cerebrum, for example, even when all anatomical connecting paths have been severed. Electric currents are probably involved here, and, indeed, these are a major factor in that environment which influences the discharge of the single nerve cell and the coordination of the many. Electrical fields have been richly demonstrated in brains; have been shown to vary their pattern with state of activity, chemical environment, drug action, and the like (Gerard) ; and have even been successfully invoked to explain in detail a variety of optical illusions in man (Kohler). By such various mechanisms, then, great masses of nerve cells—the brain as a great unity—act together; and not merely do two or a billion units sum their separate contributions, but each is part of a dynamic fluctuating activity pattern of the whole. This is the orchestra which plays thoughts of truth and beauty, which creates creative imagination.

Plenty of problems remain; some demand attention. Most urgent to our present theme is how novel neural patterns originate, since they must accompany novel thoughts or learning in general. Much attention has been given to the phenomena of learning: by "at sight," the slow cumulation of a new "correct" response in the course of conditioning experience, the conditioned reflex, and by insight, the sudden grasp of a solution and abrupt performance of the correct response, the gestalt or closure or imaginative act. They seem very different, and, as Terman put it, conditioning serves admirably to explain stupid behavior; gestalts, intelligent behavior. The mechanisms may indeed be quite different, but it is possible, perhaps probable, that they are basically quite similar. In both cases, new functional connections must be established in the brain; and this process may be more gradual and cumulative in the case of insights than appears. For here, also, much brain work precedes the imaginative flash—the theory of gravitation may result only when the metaphorical apple falls on the prepared mind—and only when the process has progressed to some threshold level does it overflow into a conscious (self-conscious) insight.

So long as our picture of the nervous system was that of the telephone exchange, with reflex plugs all set and each sense organ subscriber connected with, and able to call to action, its allotted muscles, the appearance of new responses seemed to demand the presence in the brain of rather mysterious telephone operators to shift the plugs. Now, with our discovery of a far more fluid nervous system, one unceasingly active and with neural and electrical messages rippling the whole into" dynamic patterns, which flow from one contour to another as present influences play upon the condition left by past ones-with such a picture the arrival of new neural relationships is no great problem. Schemata have been offered—in terms of nerve impulse balance, electrical fields, fiber growth—which at least indicate reasonable avenues for further exploration. More difficult still is the question of whether the new closures come to occupy particular neural regions, whether experience is parceled out in brain cubbyholes from which memory can withdraw and examine one package or another.

The answer seems to be mainly No, but with considerable reserve. A conditioned reflex established exclusively via one eye or executed by one hand can be at once elicited through the other eye or with the other hand; a learned response to a particular figure will be given unhesitatingly when the figure is changed in size, color, intensity, position, and even, within narrower limits, contour. Yet in each of the shifts indicated, different particular nerve fibers and connections are involved, at least in part. Further, Lashley has shown that the learning ability of rats parallels the total brain mass and is decreased as the brain is whittled away by operations. But the loss is not greater when any one region is destroyed as compared to another nor even when extensive thin cuts are made rather than removing a compact lump. Yet even here there begins to appear some suggestion of localization, for, though removal of the visual cortex does not prevent a rat from learning a light-discrimination problem, it does wash out a previously learned problem of this sort. And recent work on animals like the dog, with more elaborated brains, suggests some striking localizations.

Thus Culler established a conditioned leg flexion by sounding a given tone when an electric shock was administered to the paw. The tone alone then led to flexion, unless this conditioned response was elicited for a number of times without being "reinforced" with the shock, in which case the response was temporarily "extinguished." This is all routine; what is startling is his report that he found a region of the cortex only two millimeters in size and lying in association areas well away from cutaneous, hearing, or motor areas, which, on direct stimulation, caused leg flexion in animals with an active conditioned reflex but which was inactive in animals in whom the reflex was extinguished or had never been established. Another report, by Martino, is perhaps even more dramatic. He performed his conditioning so that the right eyelid blinked when red light was shown, the left eyelid with violet light. He then put strychnine locally on the optic cortex of either the right hemisphere (connected to the left field of vision) or the left one. With the left side rendered overactive by the drug, red (but not violet) light led to eye spasms and convulsions; with the right side drugged, only violet light produced the response.

If such indications hold up, a rapid advance in understanding in this field is imminent. Perhaps learning is initially a function of the whole brain and as ephemeral as a pattern of activity. But even activity leaves some more permanent change in the active part—think of the hypertrophy of an exercised muscle. And brain regions which are most active in particular patterns—think of the nodes and internodes of crossed wave trains—might well acquire, with repetition of these patterns, alterations which are both more local and more enduring than the initiating disturbance. With such regions located it will become practicable to look for the kind of change which endures; change in chemical composition or metabolism, electrical potential or resistance, cell structure or connection, or whatever it turns out to be when found. The figure of a river and its bed, used so vividly by Child in picturing the general relation of structure and function, is apposite here. The river carves its bed and the bed controls its waters; only by their continual interplay can a particular system develop. The spring floods are mass responses of the whole to environmental conditions and are transitory dynamic patterns, yet they leave local and lasting changes. Where the waters pile up most and the currents are swiftest—where the activity disturbance is most extreme in a particular total situation, as the potential fields in the occipital lobe on visual stimulation—there are produced the washed-out banks or the undercut cliffs which determine the river's flow for decades to come—the concrete regional changes wherewith the past directs the future, the basis of memory.

A final problem before coming to the implications of our analysis:

What is the neural basis for the striking quantitative differences between man and man in intelligence or in the several abilities which constitute intelligence or its component, imagination? Surely brain size as such is not the answer, as many studies have demonstrated. Perhaps absolute or relative size of the association areas would show better correlation with intelligence; or perhaps the richness of fiber connections and the architectural intricacy—as the more elaborate circuits make the better radios, large or small. And the factor of activity level is almost surely involved; not only the size and number of nerve cells but their rates of beat, maintained potentials, irritabilities; their functional vigor. This, in turn, depends on their composition (make what you will of the fact that the brains of women contain a higher percentage of lipins-fats-than those of men) and on their metabolism; and this, on the blood supply and the amount of oxygen and sugar it brings, on the salt and acid and other components of the tissue fluids, on particular stimulants or depressants, as the thyroid hormone or anesthetic drugs, and the like. The influence of caffeine, alcohol, strychnine, cocaine, morphine, hashish, absinthe, and mescaline on brain metabolism and activity are being steadily worked out; their dramatic effects on the mind, especially on hallucinations and imaginings, are commonly enough known and are also being further studied (Kluever). As the sets of facts are brought together new understanding will arise. Possibly from this direction we shall get a clue as to the finer differential between brains: what gives one man a vivid imagination but a poor memory, another an encyclopedic memory but dull imagination. And when that answer is at hand science will indeed have established the biological basis of imagination.

Implications

Without awaiting these riper fruits of research, some immediate morals are worth plucking. The ideas tossed into consciousness by imagination are, we have seen, overwhelmingly bad—untrue or unbeautiful—and must be curbed and ruddered by reason. Here, surely, lies a difference between the more imaginative initiator and the more rational critic. Formal education is directed to our conscious reason, which can at least be supplied with content and practice; if the more intuitive and unconscious imagination can be cultivated we have yet to learn the secret. There is the danger of reason stifling imagination, that "enterprises of great pith and moment" will be "sicklied o'er with the pale cast of thought." From the young, the naive, the dreaming, the drug users, comes a great spate of fresh imaginings, overwhelmingly dross but with those rare grains of great insight yet more common than from the old, the critical, the staid, or the sophisticated. To teach rigor while preserving imagination is an unsolved challenge to education.

Again, each important advance in form, in structured truth or beauty, is the result of a new closure, of a fresh set of axioms; a better set, resulting from the greater knowledge and understanding built with the aid of those dying. The forming mind of the young can use the new as comfortably as the old, but the formed mind of the teacher cannot readily run along the new-gauge tracks. The concepts of infinity, relativity, indeterminism in the physical realm, as evolution in the biological, were difficult for the established generation, simple for the oncoming one. Yet unless we forever question the basic imaginative constructs of our predecessors we condemn ourselves to working at progressively more detailed and trivial levels, to filling in further digits past the decimal point. Recall Trotter's provocative statement

"When, therefore, we find ourselves entertaining an opinion about the basis of which there is a quality of feeling which tells us that to inquire into it would be absurd, obviously unnecessary, unprofitable, undesirable, bad form, or wicked, we may know that that opinion is a non-rational one, and probably, therefore, founded upon inadequate evidence. Opinions, on the other hand, which are acquired as the result of experience alone do not possess this quality of primary certitude. They are true in the sense of being verifiable, but they are unaccompanied by that profound feeling of truth which belief possesses, and, therefore, we have no sense of reluctance in admitting inquiry into them."

In ethical and religious attitudes, even more, the axioms are set at childhood; the re-education of a generation of "Hitler Youth" gives little promise of success. Why, even in aesthetics we learn our particular values; the dissonances of a mere generation ago are consonances to ears of today. To preserve open-mindedness while teaching current systems is another unsolved problem of education.

A final word on creative imagination. Besides the intellectual factors, certain emotional ones are demanded. The unconscious work goes on only over problems that are important to the waking mind, only when the mind's possessor worries about them, only when he cares, passionately. As Pavlov wrote shortly before his death at 87, advising young men on the requisites for effective pursuit of science: "Third, Passion. Remember that science demands from a man all his life. If you had two lives that would not be enough for you. Be passionate in your work and your searchings." This is related to the conscious work recognized by Poincaré as preceding the unconscious work of imagination; another emotional factor is involved with the second period of conscious work which follows: courage. It takes courage to face the unfamiliar, to espouse the different; courage to fight one's own prejudices only less than those of others. Was it not a little child who first dared call the emperor naked? It took great fortitude for Kepler to adhere to his new notion of infinity (as the second focus of a parabola), for, as he said, "The idea seems absurd, but I can find no flaw in it"; just as it did for Galileo to murmur among his inquisitors, "Yet the world does move." Most of us will never achieve great imaginative insights; we might at least attempt to be tolerant of those offered us by others.

Somehow, "this power of human thinking...seems in times of emergency or conflict to leap ahead to new truth" (Dummer). Sometime, when research in this "constructive power of the unconscious" has increased our understanding of insight, man will more effectively guide his onward movement.

From "The Biological Basis of Imagination," by R. W. Gerard, in *The Scientific Monthly*, June, 1946. By permission of the author and the publishers of *The Scientific Monthly:* The American Association for the Advancement of Science.

We hope you enjoyed this book.
If you'd like additional information, please contact:

Transformational Book Circle
12711 Ventura Blvd., Suite, 330
Studio City, CA 91604
866-288-4469 (customer service)
866-300-4386 (orders)
www.transformationalbookcircle.com
info@transformationalbookcircle.com